WITHDRAWN

THE NEW POLICE SCIENCE

Critical Perspectives on Crime and Law

Edited by Markus D. Dubber

EDITED BY MARKUS D. DUBBER
AND MARIANA VALVERDE

The New Police Science

The Police Power in Domestic and International Governance

STANFORD UNIVERSITY PRESS

STANFORD, CALIFORNIA 2006

Stanford University Press
Stanford, California

Printed in the United States of America on acid-free,
archival-quality paper

Library of Congress Cataloging-in-Publication Data

The new police science : the police power in
domestic and international governance / Edited by
Markus D. Dubber and Mariana Valverde.
    p. cm.—(Critical perspectives on crime and law)
  Includes bibliographical references and index.
  ISBN-13: 978-0-8047-5392-0 (cloth : alk. paper)
  ISBN-10: 0-8047-5392-X (cloth : alk. paper)
  1. Police power—Philosophy. 2. Police—
  Philosophy. 3. International police—
  Philosophy. I. Dubber, Markus
  Dirk. II. Valverde, Mariana, date–
K3220.N49 2007
342'.0418—dc22   2006022052

Typeset by G&S Book Services in 10/14 Janson

Contents

Contributors

Mitchell Dean is Dean, Division of Society, Culture, Media and Philosophy at Macquarie University.

Markus D. Dubber is Professor of Law and Director of the Buffalo Criminal Law Center at SUNY Buffalo School of Law.

Lindsay Farmer is Professor of Law at the University of Glasgow School of Law.

John Hagan is John D. MacArthur Professor of Sociology and Law at Northwestern University and Senior Research Fellow at the American Bar Foundation, Chicago.

Alan Hunt is Chancellor's Professor in the Departments of Law and Sociology/Anthropology at Carleton University.

Ron Levi is Assistant Professor at the Centre of Criminology, University of Toronto.

Mark Neocleous is Professor of the Critique of Political Economy at Brunel University.

Pasquale Pasquino is Directeur de Recherche, Centre national de la recherche scientifique (CNRS), Paris, and Professor in Politics at New York University.

Christopher Tomlins is Senior Research Fellow at the American Bar Foundation, Chicago.

Mariana Valverde is Professor at the Centre of Criminology, University of Toronto.

Acknowledgments

We happily acknowledge the support of the Baldy Center for Law and Social Policy at SUNY Buffalo Law School for its generous financial support of this project. The June 2004 workshop that played a key role in shaping this book was cohosted by the Baldy Center, the Canada–United States Legal Studies Centre at SUNY Buffalo, and the Buffalo Criminal Law Center. Among the many people who provided crucial assistance and encouragement along the way, Sara Faherty, Anne Gaulin, Ellen Kausner, Jean-Francois Lozier, Laura Mangan, Lynn Mather, Joe Schneider, and Chris Tomlins deserve special mention. Amanda Moran of Stanford University Press masterfully guided the manuscript through the publication process.

Markus D. Dubber
Mariana Valverde

THE NEW POLICE SCIENCE

Perspectives on the Power and Science of Police

MARKUS D. DUBBER AND MARIANA VALVERDE

Police Science and Literatures on "Police"

In U.S. law, the term "police" appears as a strange creature, endowed with the curious ability to refer to totally different things in different contexts—thus authorizing quite heterogeneous governing activities. In the field of property law, the "police power" authorizes such burdens on private capital as municipal expropriations of land and buildings and restrictions on the siting of private businesses through zoning requirements. Criminal lawyers, on their part, think of officers enforcing the criminal law when they hear the word "police." Constitutional lawyers encounter both of these types of police—when examining police powers of search and seizure, for example, and when considering the restrictions on commercial speech authorized by recent court decisions upholding municipalities' use of the police power in zoning ordinances. But neither of these uses of "police" is thought of as central to constitutional law.

Elsewhere in the scholarly world, intellectual historians of early-modern Europe are very familiar with yet another instance of "police": *Polizeiwis-senschaft*, that is, the "police science" that, centuries before uniformed police forces existed, explored the fields that later became public administration and municipal law. This intellectual history, little known in the English-speaking world (despite the efforts of Freund 1904; Small 1909; and Raeff 1983), was made known to a broad international audience of social and po-litical theorists by Foucault and some of his collaborators in a tremendously influential volume published in 1991 (Burchell, Gordon, and Miller 1991), a volume that sparked the large body of sociological and political-science literature known as "governmentality studies."

Governmentality studies has had relatively little impact in the United States, and within the United States less impact on the legal academy than in social science circles. However, it is not at all coincidental that two emi-nent historians of U.S. law, who have both done a great deal to revive the subject of "police" within legal history, are both careful readers of Foucault and of the Foucault-inspired work produced by Pasquale Pasquino, Niko-las Rose, Mitchell Dean, and others. One of these historians is Bill Novak, who contributed to the revival of interest in "police" in his influential argu-ment about the persistence, even at the height of laissez-faire, of a strong U.S. tradition authorizing coercive measures to build "the well-regulated community" (Novak 1996). The other is Chris Tomlins, who explored the contradictions between the regulatory logic of police and the rights-based logic of law in his influential work on the legal history of labor in the United States (Tomlins 1993).

Thus, the eighteenth-century meaning of "police"—as the regulatory power to take coercive measures to ensure the safety and the welfare of "the community"—became, in the 1990s, a topic for theoretical inquiries, via the work of historians with a theoretical bent. This took place most vis-ibly within Foucault-inspired work, work that was in any case more alert to the theoretical importance of historical research than is generally the case among theoretical schools. Later in the 1990s, and reaching a crescendo in the first years of the twenty-first century, the term "police" came into promi-nence in yet another literature. Along a somewhat separate parallel path, some very recent theoretical work of a more or less neo-Marxist character has on its part revived the subject of "police" as part of a retheorization of "sovereignty." Mitchell Dean's contribution to this volume may help U.S.

readers (especially within the legal academy) become familiar with this lively and, in Europe, highly influential, post-9/11 literature, whose most cited works include Hardt and Negri's *Empire* (Hardt and Negri 2000) and Giorgio Agamben's works on sovereignty, "bare life," and the state of exception (Agamben 1998, 2005). In chapter 7, Dean explores the argument made (rather a priori) by Hardt and Negri to the effect that the field of international relations has in recent years seen a disappearance of old-fashioned military actions in favor of quasi-police actions.

It is clear that recent developments in the United States have suddenly made this somewhat arcane and hyperbolically theoretical literature appear as highly relevant. Agamben's theorization of modern life as variations on the theme of the "camp," with the concentration camp regarded not as an exception but as the foundation of law and sovereignty, seemed like one of those radical rants that Italian Marxists are famous for—until Guantánamo. Legal scholars as well as progressive Americans in every field are now attempting to understand the U.S. government's insistence that Guantánamo inmates are not prisoners of war but something akin to that good old American category, outlaws. This is stimulating interest in the kind of political and legal theory that explores nonliberal systems and nonliberal rationales—e.g., the work of the German antiliberal thinker Carl Schmitt.

But whatever the future may hold for this exploration of theoretical resources useful for an understanding of new forms of legal and nonlegal coercion, it can be said that, in general, the literature that contrasts the logic of military struggle between sovereign nations to the policelike logic that would discount many states as "rogue" states in need of external paternal rule (explored by Levi and Hagan in chapter 8) has not made explicit the connections between "the international police power" of current UN armed actions and the "police" of eighteenth-century police regulations and police science—despite the interesting fact that Mitchell Dean's first book concerned itself centrally with "the police of the poor" (Dean 1991).

It is thus clear that if one is willing to cross disciplinary and theoretical boundaries, it is possible to draw new connections that show that it is not by a semantic accident that the word "police" has had such an interesting career, or, more accurately, set of careers. But it is perhaps less clear what should be done, intellectually, after having noted the hitherto hidden and often evanescent connections. Having brought together scholars from a variety of fields—mainly legal theory, legal history, political theory, and sociolegal studies—who had in their respective work explored the importance of "police," through the academic techniques of inviting people (most of whom did not know one another) to a workshop and asking them to produce papers, the question arose as to how to handle the one thing everyone noted, namely, the multivocality and ambiguity of the term "police." Some of the authors included here decided to attempt to develop something like a unified theory of "police" (Farmer and Neocleous, mainly, and Dubber to some extent). Others chose to pursue a different kind of theoretical inquiry, one that documents the affinities, borrowings, and similarities that link uses of "police" that may appear to be totally independent—but more by way of finding what Wittgenstein famously called "family resemblances" than by way of setting the groundwork for a unified theory of police as such. Clearly, the decision to either seek a unified theory or avoid general theorizing in favor of documenting "family resemblances" has little to do with one's substantive research into police matters and a great deal to do with one's attitude toward the general crisis of theoretical work today—what not long ago used to be called the question of postmodernism.

Whether one seeks a unified theory, or whether one prefers to document similarities, adaptations, analogies, and metaphorical borrowings, however, our book highlights the fruitfulness of including within a single work not only different literatures on "police" but also studies of the large variety of governing activities authorized by the term "police." By considering the various studies of "police" together, two fundamental theoretical points become clear:

1. *Police and temporalities of governance.* The policing work of constabularies is mainly devoted to finding offenders and getting them punished for specific deeds done in the past. This backward-looking logic famously distinguishes the criminal law from forward-looking exercises of the police power of the state (e.g., taking preventive public health measures or differentiating urban spaces through zoning law). But if the police power of the state—as exercised in fatherly measures to safeguard order and public health in advance—is linked to the enforcement of criminal laws by more than a semantic coincidence, as several of the chapters in this volume argue, then it becomes clear that "police" works as a sort of temporal-hinge word, allowing the governance of the past to be articulated with the governance of

the future. Prevention and punishment are very different as logics of governance; "police" is the middle term that links them.

2. *Police and the inevitability of discretion.* Blackstone's famous definition of police as the fatherly concern to ensure the present order, future prosperity, and general well-being of the national household isolates the patriarchal element of police. This element has been linked, as far back as Aristotle, to a certain kind of wisdom—the practical wisdom that knows which concrete measures will work in the particular circumstances, in a way that defeats the high theorists who would seek strict definitions in advance. Legal writers constantly complain that the police power is undefined, residual, very broad, and so forth; but this innumerability of police powers is less strange if the knowledge dimension is considered. The patriarch's prudential wisdom is precisely the ability to decide, in the particular instance, which specific measure will best promote prosperity, order, and well-being, without being bound by strict lawlike definitions.

The work of the officers entrusted with enforcing the criminal law is of course supposed to be governed strictly by the letter of the law—the opposite of the paternal, concrete, future-oriented prudence. But if we attend to the links between "police" in the sense of police force and "police" in the sense of police power we may be able to see the recurring problems of police discretion in a new light. Even when enforcing specific statutes, police forces still have some share in the discretionary logic of paternal prudence. Prevention has been part of police forces since their inception—Sir Robert Peel famously advocated prevention as the key purpose of police forces. And discretion is a necessary feature of all forms of governance that are oriented toward prevention and that do not limit themselves to punishing specified acts. Prevention and punishment being two contrasting modes of governance—as well as two different temporal orientations—it becomes clear that, yet again, "police" can be regarded as fulfilling a sort of "hinge" function. If police is the hinge between governing the past and governing the future, it is also, by the same token, a link between punishment and prevention.

If police articulates temporalities and modes of governing, it also works to articulate spaces of governing. Let us briefly outline these sites—socio-physical-legal spaces that may appear to be quite separate even though they all feature some version of police—before concluding the introduction with an overview of the chapters.

Police Power and Its Various Fields

1. *The local/the urban.* In U.S. law, the "police power of the state" is exercised by the state in some respects—e.g., liquor regulation—but it is often delegated to municipalities. In fact, "the police power" is sometimes imagined as essentially local. And this is not a peculiarity of the U.S. political system: in late eighteenth-century England and Scotland, advocates of strict police regulations targeting vagrants, itinerant merchants, prostitutes, and other marginal urban populations also assumed that such regulations were within the province of local magistrates or municipal corporations. As time went on, the "police of the poor" tended to give way to regulatory efforts targeting urban spaces and activities more than identifiable groups of persons, and this tendency of course reached its zenith in the United States and Canada in the 1970s, when "status offenses" were declared unconstitutional, something that forced local governments to concentrate on using time, space, and activity as the vectors of urban regulation and urban order—not persons.

2. *The colony.* If governing local spaces, especially urban spaces, has been and remains a fundamental site of police, this book shows that police is nevertheless not essentially local. First of all, as Chris Tomlins's concluding comments make clear and as Valverde's contribution highlights, the government of colonies has also been carried out using police rationales and police strategies. Those charter colonies that were set up by royal governments in the Americas, and endowed with delegated paternal powers, were often subject to minute regulation and micromanagement of a police-like character. In addition, aboriginal peoples, whether living in the white settlements, on reservations, or in their ancestral lands, were also brought under the jurisdiction of various forms of quasi-paternal coercive powers—the police of Indians and the police of the (domestic) poor shared many substantive and formal similarities, and, of course, in the United States, slaves were subject to their own form of police.

3. *The factory.* Regulations imposed on workers (and on nonworkers, such as vagrants) by states, municipalities, and parishes, and by private factory

owners often took the form of police regulations. Very generally, one can see the persistence of "the police of the poor" in today's complex rules for welfare recipients; but one can also see the survival of private police jurisdictions in the Byzantine regulations covering such matters as proper attire and proper workplace hair styles, regulations generally upheld by courts.

4. *The national household.* In the small German states of eighteenth-century police science it was perhaps easier to see the household-kingdom analogy than it is today, especially in today's large federal states. Nevertheless, Blackstone's famous definition of police as the internal ordering of the kingdom—contrasted with the outward looking logic of warfare—is still relevant, even in states that (like the United States) claim that the police power is not federal. The recent invention of "homeland security" is perhaps an indication of this long-standing link between the household and the state, not only because of the name of the new institution, but because of the fundamentally preventive logic that enables its officers to govern certain "suspect" people and certain spaces (e.g., airports) in a highly despotic fashion, all in the name of ensuring security, of course.

5. *The international.* Adam Smith and other classical theorists regarded "police" as intrinsically national and contrasted it with both warfare and diplomacy. In recent times, however, we have seen the rise of the idea that international spaces too can be governed through police logics— or even police forces, as in the case of UN peacekeepers and UN-sponsored foreign police working in "failing" or postconflict states. As Levi and Hagan show, Teddy Roosevelt borrowed some ideas and techniques of governance from his work as New York City Police Commissioner when he came up with the doctrine of "the international police power." And in recent years we have seen a veritable explosion of experiments in international police. It may be that, in the near future, it is the international that becomes the main venue or site for innovations in "police." If that is the case, a good understanding of the history and varied effects of different, earlier police projects will be particularly important.

Police Historiography

The first three chapters take a broadly historical approach to an investigation of the concept of police. In chapter 1, Mark Neocleous explores the theoretical foundations of police by revealing the broad and varied concept of police that was the subject of the old police science in pre-Enlightenment Europe and underlay social and institutional reforms not only on the Continent but—less familiarly—in the late eighteenth- and early nineteenth-century London of Patrick Colquhoun and his Thames River Police. While Colquhoun's police reforms today are regarded as the beginning of modern policing—and the creation of police as an institution of "law enforcement"— Neocleous instead exposes their roots in the police concept of the original police scientists. Countering the common tendency to associate police with restrictive, if not downright oppressive, state action, Neocleous stresses the affirmative aspect of police. In particular, he regards police as having been a means of fabricating order in general, and class order in particular, and having played a central role in the creation of the English working class. In his view, the policing of the poor was central to the project of crime control that is now generally associated with police work, as indigence—as an extreme form of poverty—was viewed as a major cause of crime.

This view of police as an institution that "has been central to the historically massive operation on the part of the state to consolidate the social power of capital and the wage form" allows Neocleous to put meat on the bones of the concept of police. To those who see police everywhere, he presents a more clearly delineated version of the concept that provides it with a crucial critical edge. It is this critical ambition that, in Neocleous's view, distinguishes the new police science from the old, whose practitioners functioned as expert facilitators of central policy making, regardless of whether a policy created, or oppressed, certain segments of its object population.

In the most explicitly historical chapter, Pasquale Pasquino uses two seventeenth-century works on the outskirts of the German police science tradition to capture the nature and scope of the police project. Through a close reading of *Biblische Policey* (Biblical Police) by Dietrich Reinkingk and *Teutscher Fürstenstaat* (German Prince State) by Veit Ludwig von Seckendorff, Pasquino reveals a vision of the early-modern police state that manages to retain theological foundations while making room for a police bureaucracy that executes the prince's administrative decisions and maintaining a subtle balance among the various social and political estates of the period. In this theory of the state, earthly government—exemplified by the figure of the expert advisor, the bureaucrat—interprets, translates, and manifests

God's often cryptic commands within a clearly defined piece of earth delineated by borders—the territory.

This, then, is the paradox of police—at one and the same time, government asserts itself as an administrative machine for the ordering of populations *and* legitimates itself as the maximizer of the welfare of its objects. It's a paradox that, in small Lutheran principalities in premodern Germany, remains hidden under a veneer of theological allegory but shines through clear enough in Pasquino's careful analysis. As a result, Reinkingk's and Seckendorff's texts can appear as both descriptive and critical. They provide accounts of the operation of the administrative police state, but in exposing its imperfections—be they political or administrative—they also open up a new critical space that makes room for critique from within the paradigm of police itself.

After this excursion into the land and time of *Polizeiwissenschaft*, Mariana Valverde refocuses our attention on the realm of the common law, which long has denied any traces of the "police state" in its institutions and traditions of government. As Neocleous also noted, of course, the concept of police figured prominently in English and Scottish governance of the late seventeenth and early nineteenth centuries before police as a means of governing disappeared in name, but not in fact, with the rise of the modern police department. Valverde leaves the confines of British domestic government behind and traces the role of police in colonial and, more recently, postcolonial governance. In the end, she employs the concept of police to lay out nothing less than a critical constitutional history of the Canadian state, powerfully illustrating the richness of the concept for historical analyses of law and government even—and perhaps especially—in states that have erased the police power from its political vocabulary. In fact, much of the history of the police power in Canadian government is the history of its denial. The power given to the Canadian federal government by the "peace, order, and good government" (POGG) clause of the British North America Act—a clause often identified with a cultural preference for peace and order, in contrast to the U.S. quest for individual freedom in the pursuit of happiness—has strong affinities with the U.S. police power. While the so-called POGG powers are primarily emergency powers, this clause nonetheless has also been used to authorize routine regulatory activity in such fields as environmental risks and narcotic sales. Thus, in contrast to standard Canadian legal textbooks, which locate the equivalent of the U.S. police power at the level of the Canadian provinces (including the functions delegated to municipalities by the provinces), Valverde argues that the police power is actually dispersed throughout the Canadian governmental structure. Without being named, it has been, in fact, deployed to govern at the national and imperial levels as well as domestically and locally.

Valverde shows that the logic of police has shaped, and continues to shape, not only the postcolonial relationship between England and Canada (revealed, for instance, by the long-standing practice of framing criminal offenses as violations of the Queen's—or King's—peace) but also the governing practices *within* Canada. As Valverde demonstrates, domestic Canadian governance of the Quebecois and of Canada's aboriginal peoples through the Department of Indian Affairs mirrors England's police-type governance of Canada the colony itself. Valverde thus challenges the common assumption that police power is local power. Police power is, above all, delegated power; the police power exercised by the Canadian government over aboriginal peoples does not represent the devolution of governmental power from England to the independent Canadian state, but a localized replication of imperial police power. The power of provinces and of municipalities to police their respective territories and populations is not the power of local self-government, but the local manifestation of central imperial police power. The distinction between local and central government is not qualitative, but quantitative only—the logic of police manifests itself in both.

Policing Crime

The next three chapters narrow the focus to the role of the power to police in criminal and quasi-criminal law. They also can be seen as shifting the emphasis from historical foundations to contemporary legal institutions and practices, without, however, abandoning a historical sensibility altogether; for the study of any legal or political relationship from the perspective of police always also implies a certain curiosity about origins and continuities even in the face of change and complexity. The new police science, by insisting on the continued relevance of long-denied rationales and methodologies of government, is both deeply historical and hopelessly anachronistic.

Its practitioners must have, in Neocleous's words, "the courage of our anachronisms."

Starting with the observation that the criminal law in the United States is regarded as a manifestation of the police power, Markus Dubber gives an account of the U.S. criminal process from the perspective of the rich concept of police as a rationality of governance whose historical foundation and significance was explored in the first three chapters of the book. Dubber places particular emphasis on the patriarchal posture of police governance, captured, for instance, in Blackstone's influential late eighteenth-century definition of "public police and oeconomy" as "the due regulation and domestic order of the kingdom: whereby the individuals of the state, like members of a well-governed family are bound to conform their general behaviour to the rules of propriety, good neighbourhood, and good manners: and to be decent, industrious, and inoffensive in their respective stations" (Blackstone 1769, 162), which he believes can be traced back to the Greek conception of *oikonomikos*, the governance of the household by the householder.

In this light, the criminal process emerges as a means for representing and enforcing the state-householder's authority vis-à-vis the constituents of the household defined by its (territorial) criminal jurisdiction. The Police Power Model of the criminal process thus stands in marked contrast to the Autonomy Model, which—even though it bears little resemblance to the criminal process in action—fulfills the key ideological function of bringing the criminal process in line with the fundamental principle of legitimacy in the modern democratic state: autonomy, or self-government.

Lindsay Farmer goes beyond Dubber's reading of the criminal process as a manifestation of police power; he seeks a new paradigm for the critical analysis of criminal law. Farmer's "jurisprudence of security" both recognizes and challenges the often-drawn distinction between the realms of police and of law, where the former is defined by difference and heteronomy and the latter by identity and autonomy. He arrives at his new paradigm by investigating the various—and not always consistent—conceptions of police that have appeared in police thought over the centuries and the accompanying attempts to differentiate between police and law. Rather than bringing the legitimacy constraints upon law to bear on prudential police governance, Farmer proposes to reformulate the legitimacy challenge posed by police in a state under the rule of law.

Following Adam Smith, Farmer calls for reuniting police and law within a broad conception of jurisprudence (which itself includes both *ius* and *prudentia*) in pursuit of security, where both jurisprudence and security, the means and the end, would require careful scrutiny. Insofar as security is—unlike police—not defined by its very indefinability and therefore may serve a function other than the evasion of principled constraint and critical analysis in the name of the pursuit of the undefined welfare of an undefined public, the project of giving meaning to the notoriously vague end of security bears the promise of constructive debate. It may emerge as the common ground where law theories of crime as an infliction of harm on persons and police theories of crime as an offense against the authority of the sovereign-householder can meet.

The police power not only has been cited as the source of all criminal law (insofar as *any* crime disturbs the sovereign's peace and is inconsistent with "the domestic order" of the state, to quote Blackstone), it also has been said to generate its very own class of offenses, known as regulatory offenses, public welfare offenses, *mala prohibita*, or simply police offenses. Chief among these are traffic offenses, which are almost universally ignored by criminal law scholarship even though they occupy a considerable portion of police officers' time, play a central role in the investigation and suppression of crime (notably drug crime), affect more persons on a daily basis than any other form of criminal regulation, and can result in sanctions of considerable severity (ranging from fines and license suspensions and public humiliation to jail and prison sentences and eventually—in the case of certain alcohol-related traffic offenses that result in a fatal accident—the death penalty [Christian 2000]).

In chapter 6, Alan Hunt undertakes a study of the regulation of traffic as an exercise of the power to police. Hunt documents how the enforcement of traffic regulation can be seen as part of the general project of civilization using the particular discourse of safety. The process of civilization can be seen as facilitating the modern state-householder's ability to perform the complex task of policing its vast, diverse, and diffuse population. Civilization simplifies administration by subjecting the object of government to a gradual and almost imperceptible process of uniformization in the name of progress toward an elusive and ever-moving goal. To be effective, rather than counterproductive, this process cannot rely exclusively, or even primarily, on direct oppression and violence; in contrast to the extraordinary measures of imprisonment, shaming, or even capital punishment, the vast bulk of traffic policing is accomplished through visual, aural, or verbal commands backed up with visible surveillance, the threat of sanctions, and, to the extent effective, mechanical devices such as traffic lights and cameras. Traffic criminal law thus illustrates a little-noticed, but crucially important, aspect of the paradigm of a jurisprudence of security. When, but only when, appropriate, traffic regulation is justified in terms of preventing harm to persons (most often fellow drivers, but also construction workers, pedestrians, and even police officers); otherwise it is carried on quietly, as one variant of the state project of police-through-civilization.

Police on Earth

Chapters 7 and 8 complete a move foreshadowed by Valverde's discussion of police in colonial and postcolonial governance in chapter 3; they explore the usefulness of the police concept for the analysis of international rather than internal affairs. Various critical theorists—Schmitt, Agamben, and Hardt and Negri—have remarked that international military conflicts have been transformed from wars into police actions. Mitchell Dean investigates this claim through a close analysis of the rhetoric and reality of military interventions by the United Nations and the United States in the Balkans and Iraq. Dean concludes that speaking about international military interventions in terms of police is illuminating provided one carefully differentiates between law, war, police, peacekeeping, and the confounding neologism "policekeeping." While the policization of war can imply the eradication of the distinction between combatants and civilians in a "total war" through the wholesale criminalization of the enemy, Dean warns against hyperbolic invocations of the police paradigm and draws attention to an altogether different image of police, "the use of carefully calibrated force and minimum violence to protect suffering humanity so that it might begin to build a civil society." The rhetoric of police governance, after all, always also included the efficient pursuit of good order; even the Greek *oikonomos* or the Roman *dominus* could be more or less competent in the management of his household's welfare. Police is not sinister or illegitimate by definition, neither in domestic nor in international affairs. It is rather alegitimate, at least insofar as it lies beyond the reach of the traditional legitimacy constraints placed on government through law.

The role of police in the international realm is further developed by Ron Levi and John Hagan. Returning to the more explicitly historical-foundational approach illustrated by the first three chapters, Levi and Hagan bring to light a long-standing tradition of police talk in international affairs. Rather than an essentially domestic rationality of governance, police is revealed as a central component of Theodore Roosevelt's approach to international relations. As New York City Police Commissioner, Roosevelt apparently grew frustrated with what he experienced as the constraints of law—and constitutional law in particular—on vigorous government in the name of the good police of its objects. Protections of the right to property, for instance, stood in the way of his efforts to clean up sweat shops, as rich landlords hired fancy lawyers to plead their constitutional case. As President, Roosevelt gave only halfhearted support to efforts to establish basic institutions of international law and justice and instead stressed the need for order maintenance not only domestically but internationally as well, with or without the grounding in some legalistic framework or other—if need be, any nation (and, most importantly, the most powerful nation on earth, the United States) must stand at the ready to provide global policing.

Roosevelt's much-derided "Policeman of the Hemisphere" (and eventually of the world) thus is less a police officer in the narrow modern sense of police as law enforcement than a police commissioner in the traditional sense of police as communal welfare. Against this backdrop of the primacy of police over law in international relations, it comes as no surprise that U.S. foreign policy so far has not been able to accommodate the idea of an international criminal law, not to mention the institution of an international criminal court, which would dramatically manifest and personify meaningful legal constraints on the discretionary exercise of an international police power for the good police of the global community.

Police Old and New

This book combines contributions from scholars from several countries (Canada, Australia, the United Kingdom, France, the United States) who work in various disciplines (history, sociology, criminology, politics, law) with the common aim of testing the critical and analytic potential today of a long-submerged concept that once sustained a massive project of inquiry into the nature of government: the police. For now, police has proved its mettle. The concept has shown remarkable versatility and power of illumination in a wide range of contexts, from critical historiographies of the English working class, the theory of statehood in early modern Germany, and post-colonial constitutionalism in Canada to analyses of the operation of the modern criminal process in the United States, the use of "Anti-Social Behaviour Orders" in the United Kingdom, the enforcement of traffic regulations in the United Kingdom and Canada, and, eventually, attempts to make sense of the ever-evolving New World Order defined by police actions, UN police-keeping, and the Police Commissioner of the World.

Clearly much remains to be done. The analytic usefulness of police must be tested on other issues and in other fields. It may well turn out that the concept will shed more heat than light when it is pushed to do work at greater levels of detail. Undoubtedly questions about the definition of police, which appear throughout this book and have plagued thought about police from the beginning, will continue to arise and trigger serious disagreements. The relationship between the Old and the New Police Science may need to be considered more carefully. Many, in fact, who appreciate the analytic usefulness of the concept of police may find the recovery of the project of a science of police more trouble than it's worth. But none of this matters for purposes of this book. An agenda for inquiry with great potential for research across disciplines and countries has been laid out and exemplified. Surely for the present it is enough to have shown that the New Police Science has a future. What that future will bring remains to be seen.

References

Agamben, G. 1998. Homo sacer: *Sovereignty and bare life*. Stanford, CA: Stanford University Press.
———. 2005. *State of exception*. Chicago: University of Chicago Press.
Blackstone, William. 1769. *Commentaries on the laws of England. Vol. 4.* Oxford: Oxford University Press.

Burchell, G., C. Gordon, and P. Miller, eds. 1991. *The Foucault effect: Essays on governmentality*. Chicago: University of Chicago Press.

Dean, M. 1991. *The constitution of poverty: Toward a genealogy of liberal governance*. London: Routledge.

Freund, E. 1904. *The police power*. Reprint, New York: Arno, 1976.

Hardt, M., and A. Negri. 2000. *Empire*. Cambridge, MA: Harvard University Press.

Novak, William. 1996. *The people's welfare: Law and regulation in nineteenth century America*. Chapel Hill: University of North Carolina Press.

Raeff, Marc. 1983. *The well-ordered police state*. New Haven: Yale University Press.

Small, A. 1909. *The cameralists*. Chicago: University of Chicago Press.

Tomlins, Christopher. 1993. *Law, labor and ideology in the early American republic*. New York: Cambridge University Press.

CHAPTER ONE

Theoretical Foundations of the "New Police Science"

MARK NEOCLEOUS

The concept of police has had a peculiar history. Where it once occupied a central place in the work of major thinkers on the grounds that policing was so obviously a central part of state power and thus integral to civilized life, for the bulk of the twentieth century the concept was relegated to the backwater of a very narrowly conceived "police studies." Within this backwater it suffered the fate of being transformed beyond anything recognizable to earlier writers on police powers, being reduced to the study of crime and law enforcement and thus absorbed into the discipline of criminology. Stuck in the discipline of criminology, most research on the police eschewed any attempt to make sense of the concept itself or to explore the possible diversity of police powers in terms of either their historical origins or political diversity.

On the other hand, recent years have seen the emergence and steady growth of what might now be called a new body of work on the police idea. Although much of this work has been developed by individuals working more or less in isolation, one of its common features is the desire and willingness to do more than simply replicate the empirical mode and policy-oriented focus of what has passed as "police studies." Taken together and thought of as a body, this work has led some to suggest that we can indeed begin to speak of a "new police science"—as the workshop that forms the basis of this volume suggested. For reasons that will become clear, I have a slight concern about the term "new police science," preferring instead to think of the work in question as a new and productive approach to the police idea and thus a critical interrogation of police power rather than a new police science. But whatever it is called, an obvious question arises: what are the theoretical foundations of this body of work? In this chapter I aim to suggest a number of possible dimensions that in my view ought to constitute the foundations of this new approach to police powers.

I take as a guiding assumption that the impetus behind this critical analysis of police powers is a desire to circumvent—or perhaps even undermine—the narrow, commonsensical, and essentially liberal notion of police in which it is taken to refer to a (mostly uniformed) body designed to prevent, detect, and solve crime, out of which emerges a set of debates concerning "reform." Rather, part of the *raison d'être* of this work is the need to explore the connections between police and a complex of related terms and technologies of power: law, order, "lawandorder," security, discipline, governance, welfare, state. This means navigating a way through not only the comparative organizational structures, methods for dealing with crime, role in stratified societies, and so on. It also means stepping back a little from the contemporary and aiming to unearth and explore the idea of police science in its original form. In effect, this drives the new police science toward unearthing and exploring (1) the broad powers and remit of police, (2) its essentially nonliberal connotations, and (3) its mode of functioning through a complex network of institutions. From the perspective of contemporary criminology this unearthing will make any new police science appear anachronistic, taking it back to ideas about police in the "first" police science and prior to the emergence of professional—that is, "proper"—policing as it emerged in the nineteenth century. I suggest that on this score we will have to have the courage of our anachronisms.

Before I begin, however, I want to mention four important issues that are hinted at by the anachronism in question, issues that are important because they will remain central to debates about police powers for some years to come.

The first issue concerns the question of disciplinarity. A personal comment is apposite here. My own attempt to develop a critical theory of police power has been influenced by and developed through a critique of three sources: Marx, Foucault, and Hegel. I have then tried to use these sources to interrogate writers I think important or interesting to the development of the police idea, such as Patrick Colquhoun and Adam Smith. This is, of course, a diverse bunch. But one thing they have in common is that they share what we might call a "predisciplinary" attitude. None of them sought to write a history or sociology or political theory or legal account, or whatever, of police powers. In this they are also at one with the original police science of the eighteenth century. What I suggest is that such predisciplinarity needs to be embraced, albeit in what is sometimes claimed to be a postdisciplinary world. The approach to police powers being developed in this book might well be described as predisciplinary in its historical inspiration and postdisciplinary in its current intellectual implications. Either way, to be coherent and effective it will have to be as far removed from the university-sponsored imposition of bourgeois "disciplinarity" as possible. (I prefer "predisciplinarity" to "interdisciplinarity" on the grounds that the latter presupposes the appropriateness and acceptability of the divisions in question and then aims to somehow link them. The former, however, simply sees no division in the first place. This approach might be thought of as relying on the concept of a social totality. It might also be thought of as another anachronism, which of course in some ways it is.) Part of the reason for the need to distance this project from disciplinarity will be obvious to anyone who has even started thinking about police: police powers are *so* general that they necessarily take us beyond any disciplinary limits. To think otherwise is to fall into either the trap of twentieth-century criminology, which tries to think of policing in isolation from other practices of power, or the trap of political science, which barely ever discusses police.

This in turn raises the second issue, concerning the specificity of the police idea. It is now well established that in its concern with "order" police originally held an incredibly broad compass, overseeing and administering a necessarily large and heterogeneous range of affairs. In some sense police power was without parameters, extending to the minutia of social life and including such a vast range of concerns as to make an explanation of "police" sound like the Borgesian Chinese encyclopedia entry for "animals" with which Foucault begins *The Order of Things*: the police oversee means of comfort; public health; food and wine adulteration; the production or distribution of key commodities; expenses at christenings, weddings, and funerals; the wearing of extravagant clothing; the behavior of citizens at church or during festivities; the maintenance of roads, bridges, and town buildings; public security; the regulation of the provision of goods and services; the performance of trades and occupations; moral questions such as Sunday observance, blasphemy, cursing, and perjury; the behavior of servants and domestics toward their masters; rules for the bringing up of children; sumptuary regulations; the status of Jews; overseeing educational institutions; and attention to families and their domestic problems ranging from unruly children to love triangles. This dimension of the origin of police powers draws attention to the idea that police powers were originally by their very nature both inevitable and limitless. This idea is a central part of the impetus driving the new police science and underpins much of the recent excellent work in this area. But if police powers are discussed as limitless—if police is absolutely everywhere—then as a conceptual tool "police" is in danger of looking like nothing more than a twenty-first-century version of "social control," "hegemony," or "discipline." Part of the problem with these concepts as they came to the fore in social sciences and political debate in the 1970s, 1980s, and 1990s was a lack of specificity. In each case the concept very quickly came to look as though it was being made to work in a catchall way, where any new social policy, institutional reform, or legal innovation could be read as contributing to the "control" of the lower orders, the "hegemony" of the ruling powers, or as a "disciplinary" technology. This lack of specificity—of either a conceptual or historical kind—therefore meant that each and every social, economic, or political institution could in some way be interpreted as an agency of social control/hegemony/discipline, with the result that the terms became used so broadly and loosely that they lost any real intellectual or political weight. I sense a similar danger within the attempt to develop a new police science. The danger can perhaps be seen in recent work on the sociology and politics of sexuality (for example, Watney 1997; Lees 1997; Cain 1989; Steinberg, Epstein, and Johnsen 1997), which uses the idea of police to make sense of some of the power struggles around sexuality—to explore, that is, the way sexuality is "policed." The problem is that the term is so taken for granted that no real explication of the concept ever takes place. It then becomes difficult if not impossible to distinguish between the practices of power through which, say, the state regulates ("polices") sexuality and the practices of power exercised in the school playground. My own view, not shared by all the authors of the chapters in this book, is that it is necessary to try and identify some kind of limit to the way we use the concept. For me, police as an institution has been central to the historically massive operation on the part of the state to consolidate the social power of capital and the wage form: the police mandate was to fabricate an order of wage labor and administer the class of poverty thereafter. "Police" is therefore an important conceptual tool in grappling with the way the state administers civil society in general and the working class in particular. I will develop the outline of this argument later, but for the moment it is worth registering that this tension over how and why we use the police idea draws attention to our third issue and a much wider problem: do we need a new police science at all?

The term "new police science" is a conscious echo of the original police science. But there is for me something uncomfortable about this echo. The original police science was a project designed to sustain, defend, and "improve" the powers of the state in ordering social life. Texts on police powers were rather like handbooks for princes but written for the bureaucrats of the modern state as much as for the prince himself. They were, to put it crudely, *on the side* of police powers. The "new" police science, however, has been launched with a much more *critical* frame of mind, seeking to *unearth* the mechanisms through which police powers operate rather than to offer guidelines on how to improve them. My own work, for example, has been an attempt to place the concept of police at the heart of critical social and political theory; others have used the police idea in critical genealogies of sumptuary laws, licensing procedures, patriarchal power, welfare, the civilizing process, and so on. To my mind this critical frame is what makes the new approach to police so interesting. But it also seems to make this new work much less a new police science and much more a body of work that seeks to use the notion of police to gauge and assess the production and reproduction of the processes and technologies through which the social world is perpetually ordered and transformed. The term "new police science" is therefore, to me at least, a discomforting one, failing to fully register on the critical dimension of the political scale and running the danger of making us sound more like advisors to police forces than intellectuals critically engaged in an examination of police power. (I realize that other authors in this volume do not share my unease, and I will, having made this comment, continue on occasion to use the phrase "new police science.") This takes us to the fourth preliminary issue: the question of politics.

One reason for the predisciplinary nature of the work of those thinkers or traditions originally interested in police powers was that what they had to say about police was driven by what they saw as the political issues inherent in or lying behind the police idea. That their own politics was wildly divergent—think of Smith's move away from a cameralist conception of police or Marx's critique of Hegel—is of less importance than the fact that they saw in police powers the key political question: the constitution of political order in the modern world. They recognized, in other words, that dealing with police powers and using the police idea is a deeply political act. I raise this issue here to highlight the reason this chapter finishes on a more explicit political note.

Having raised some of the general issues that animate some of the work in this volume, let me sketch out what I consider some of the key foundations of the developing new approach to the police idea and analysis of police powers.

Work: The First Principle of Police

From the late fifteenth century, political discourse in Europe centered very much around the concept of police. Originating in French-Burgundian *policie* in the fifteenth century, the word "police" spread across Continental Europe. Though the spelling of the word varied, the meaning remained constant, denoting the legislative and administrative regulation of the internal life of a community to promote general welfare and the condition of good order and the regimenting of social life. The instructions and activities considered necessary for the management of good order gave rise to the *Polizeistaat*; they referred, in effect, to the "well-ordered police state" (Raeff 1983).

In being directed to the idea of good order, police powers extended to the minutiae of social and economic life, overseeing the range of concerns I previously identified. One task for any new police science must be to excavate any coherence both in this mishmash of concerns and in the idea of "good order." It is clear from the other chapters in this book and from the discussion at the workshop from which it arose that three possible subjects suggest themselves: work, the city, and the colony. (I think of the latter as including the household [Dubber 2005] and as able to incorporate more recent work on the camp as the *nomos* of the modern [Agamben 1998].) Christopher Tomlins takes up the overlap between the three in his attempt to "frame the fragments" of this volume. I want to focus here on the question of work, which was integral to the original police project and, I suggest, needs to remain central to any new police science.

Historically, one of the fundamental concerns of policing was with the state of prosperity: the wealth of nations. Police theorists quickly came to argue that the state should secure a flourishing trade and devote its power to the preservation and increase of resources—of individuals and the state of prosperity in general—by overseeing the foundations of commerce. Even a writer such as Adam Smith, whose later rethinking of the police ideal would help impose a decidedly liberal reading on the police idea, was happy to describe police as "the proper means of introducing plenty and abundance into the country" (Smith 1982, 333). In this sense, it is clear that police powers were historically central to "the properly channeled growth of wealth" (Foucault 1980, 170) or the "maximization of resources" (Dubber 2005, 90). But such terms need some consideration. Behind such terms, and behind the concept of order as a whole, lies work. For prosperity could never be divorced from the concomitant concern with subsistence in general and the question of poverty. Behind the police of the state of prosperity as the basis of order was a more specific concern over the place of the poor and the potential threat posed by the new "class" of poverty to the emerging structures of private property. In other words, the administration of poverty was (and is) at the heart of the police project. Even genealogies of police that identify an alternative source and focus of police power, such as the patriarchal household (Dubber 2005), often highlight the importance of work and poverty (for example, via analyses of vagrancy as a threat to social order). This is perhaps unsurprising, given the intimate connection between the police of poverty and the policing of the family (see Dean 1991; Donzelot 1979). It is for this reason that the poor were present in text after text on police, from the most mundane handbooks for bureaucrats to the more philosophically demanding texts such as Hegel's *Philosophy of Right*. By virtue of its concern with the production of wealth, policing meant policing the class of poverty. The police of poverty was regarded as a necessity because of the perceived connection between poverty and "disorderly" behavior, such as begging, crime, gambling, and drinking—all understood as a threat to public propriety and the common good. Police came to rely on a distinction between groups according to the degree of danger they appeared to pose to the common good—domestic laborers, prostitutes, the young, religious, and political groups. But the most significant part of this enemy was the growing class of poverty and its social cousin, the "class" of vagrants.

Where poverty, vagrancy, and crime meet in police texts, there one will ultimately find the question of work. The ostensible concern over vagrancy and begging was a concern that those persons engaged in such activities were more likely to engage in criminal activity. Yet in some sense the greatest "crime" was thought to be idleness itself; "disorderly" is more often than not a euphemism for "workless." Though the police theorists invariably lacked a political economy finely tuned enough to pinpoint the precise nature of the relationship between poverty and wealth, they nonetheless knew what the broad connection was: when they looked at beggars and vagrants, they saw able-bodied (but lazy, ignorant, and potentially rebellious) workers withholding their labor and thus not producing wealth. This is why Blackstone regards vagrancy as the ultimate police problem. The solution to such a problem was clear: "the philosopher's stone, so long sought after, has been found—it is work" (Abbé Malvaux, cited in McStay Adams 1990, 240).

It might therefore be said the founding principle of police is the idea that every citizen-subject *ought to work*; or, more explicitly, that every citizen-subject ought *to be put to work*. Foucault (1967, 46) picks up on this:

> Police is the totality of measures that make work possible and necessary for all those who could not live without it; the question Voltaire would soon formulate, Colbert's contemporaries had already asked: "Since you have established yourselves as a people, have you not yet discovered the secret of

forcing all the rich to make all the poor work? Are you still ignorant of the first principles of the police?"

This means that while, broadly speaking, the object of police powers might be order, such a concept might be refined a little—given a little specificity—by pointing to the centrality of work to the idea of order and, concomitantly, the place of the class of poverty within that idea.

Two caveats. First, the argument might appear a little reductionist. It might be pointed out that the limitless reach of police powers means that police is concerned with all sorts of things that are in no way about work. I would suggest that the argument is not reductionist but that it is, however, essentialist. I am suggesting that part of the *essence* of the object of police is the working class. While police powers engage with many things that are a long way from work, these are not essential to their existence. For example, the fact that a great deal of police time is spent acting as a juridical-administrative arm of the insurance industry obscures the fact that police would continue to exist even if the insurance industry found an alternative means of verifying claims. The second caveat is to point out that this is not to fall into a version of the "repressive hypothesis." Rather, and to use a Foucauldian phrase, we need an approach that recognizes the *productive* nature of police powers. Let me sketch the contours of such an argument, developing as we go the idea that work is central to police; these contours will also help show how the idea of police powers can be used as a critical political tool.

Fabricating a Well-Ordered Civil Society

Historically, the project of the abolition of disorder shifted as policing developed in conjunction with the shifts in the nature of both state power and the transformation from feudalism to capitalism. One might divide the history of police into three stages. The first two are separated by the Thirty Years' War (1618–1648), while the third stage emerges in the late eighteenth century and is consolidated in the nineteenth century. The "stages" therefore parallel stages of state formation (crudely: early modern, absolutist, representative) and the rise and consolidation of a system of bourgeois rule. In its first stage, policing was characterized by ad hoc reactive measures. The police project was to maintain the structure of manners threatened by the decay of the existing estates and the crisis provoked by the Reformation. Because the major activity of policing in this phase was formed through a reaction to emerging social problems and crises it might be thought of as an early form of "emergency legislation," passed without breaking with legal tradition or usurping the power of the estates. Police legislation was thus "negative"—though this is not an entirely satisfactory term—in that unsatisfactory conditions and violations of existing laws were "corrected" to restore the normal and proper order. In its second stage policing changed from being an improvised set of legislative and administrative emergency responses to a more active and conscious interventionist form of social regulation grounded on the principle of good order and in search of the "general welfare" or "common good" of the population. In the course of the seventeenth and into the eighteenth centuries, then, police legislation and ordinances acquired a "positive"—again, a far from satisfactory term—cast. The aim was less to restore or correct abuses or defects and more to bring about changes, introduce innovations, and create new conditions of order. In other words, in its second stage police was less concerned with *re*-forming a social body of increasingly obsolete social estates and much more concerned with actively *shaping* the social body according to certain ends—the ends of the state and the production of the increasingly dominant new forms of wealth. This would pick up and develop Raeff's comment (1983, 50, 149) that the "positive" nature of this process is captured in the German notion of *Beste*, which has connotations of a hypothetical state to be pursued and a goal to be actively worked for, or what Christopher Tomlins (1993, 54) has identified as the important similarity between the language of *improvement* and the language of police.

If we accept this idea, then what becomes apparent is that police powers were increasingly aimed not just at the maintenance or reproduction of order but to its *fabrication*. The *Oxford English Dictionary* tells us that the use of fabrication to describe "the action or process of fabricating; construction, fashioning" is now rare. If we are indeed to have the courage of our anachronisms it might be especially appropriate to use this rare term. For the term helps in that it treats police power as a far more *productive* or *creative* force than many assume, pointing to policing as an *activity* rather than an institution, shaping order rather than passively responding to disorder: the fabrication of order (Neocleous 2000). I would suggest that writers and thinkers who grasped the importance of the police power also recognized this dimension. It is a theme that runs through cameralism, for example, and is central to Hegel's account of police. It is also this dimension, I suggest, that sustains Foucault's interest in police. In other words, I am suggesting that as well as work being one of its main objects, a "new police science" might also be founded on the idea that policing involves a process whereby society is shaped and order is fabricated. In this sense, I am suggesting that one way of maintaining a degree of specificity in the idea of police is to use it to grapple with the way the state administers civil society—where "administer" captures the processes and technologies through which the state fabricates order, fashions the market, generates new forms of subjectivity, and subsumes struggles.

To mention state and civil society in this way may make some people uncomfortable. Unnecessarily so, I think, but let me get at the problem in a slightly roundabout way, because any new police science will need some reflection on this conceptual pairing.

In *Commonwealth v. Alger* (1851), perhaps the most influential legal discussion and decision on the police power in the U.S. context, Chief Justice Shaw suggests three possible origins of the police power: royal prerogative, the Massachusetts constitution, and "the nature of well ordered civil society." William Novak (1996, 25) has pointed out that Shaw refers to the "well ordered" six times in one page, and it is easy for those of us writing about police powers to get carried away with such an idea. After all, was not "order" the animating idea of the original police theorists? But also present here is the idea of civil society, that problematic "other" of the state. Why problematic? It is notable that the original police science followed political thought in seeing state and civil society as interchangeable terms, identifying the welfare of the ruler, the state, and the subjects as one and the same. This identification is understandable, given the range of functions that fell under the label of "police" and the fact that state and civil society had yet to be drawn apart within political philosophy.

Now, this might be seen as good grounds for any new police science to reject the state–civil society couplet. Foucault, such an important figure in the recent work on police, might be called on here. In trying to move discussions of power "beyond the state," Foucault treats the state–civil society

distinction as obsolete, on the grounds that it is neither intellectually pertinent nor politically fruitful. The opposition was essentially a product of the
late eighteenth century, the role of which was to assist liberalism in limiting
the state's sphere of action. Having served that historical and political purpose it now merely functions as a way of afflicting the notion of "state" with
a pejorative connotation while idealizing "society" as a good, living, warm
whole (Foucault 1991, 163–64; 1988, 67–68). Thus "rather than embrace
the distinction between state and civil society as an historical and political
universal . . . one can attempt to see a form of schematization proper to the
particular technology of government" (Foucault 1981, 355). I think this is
one of the reasons for Foucault's interest in the cameralists and early police
science: that such work was not troubled by such "liberal" terminology. In
one sense Foucault might have been on to something. For civil society has
become something of a Left-liberal fetish in recent years—since 1989 in
fact. It might be thought that the crass liberalism that underpins most of the
recent work on civil society and that mythologizes this domain in its search
for, variously, a postsocialist alternative to traditional socialism, a communi-
tarian response to neoliberalism, a (neo?)liberal response to statism, and so
on, combined with Foucault's encouragement in this regard, should steer us
away from the conceptual couplet.

But there is no inherent reason an expanded concept of police requires a
rejection of the state-civil society distinction. The lesson here might well be
Hegel. Hegel's concept of police functions as a moment within civil society,
within a greater totality of the state; its main aim is the integration of the
individual economic agent into a wider network of social and political ties
and bonds in order that the isolation suffered by the individual does not lead
to the breakdown of the system. It is certainly the case that Hegel has a little
mythologizing of his own here—as the young Marx was right to ask, since
when is the police power the power *of* civil society? But disregarding this,
Hegel is on to something important. Hegel senses that civil society is not,
pace the eighteenth-century liberals, a self-generating sphere. He is much
closer to Sir James Steuart than Smith in this regard. Civil society needs to
be managed and organized: it needs a not-so-hidden hand to keep it from
collapse. Most importantly, it needs the class of poverty to be kept in order.
In other words: it needs policing. Police thus comes to figure for Hegel as
the mechanism whereby the state administers civil society and the class of
poverty. Using the state-civil society distinction, in other words, does not

have to be within the confines of a contemporary liberal fetish. Hegel's—
and, I should add, Marx's—use of the conceptual couplet illustrates that the
state-civil society distinction can be used to grapple with the ways the state
fabricates order within civil society.

The Making of the Working Class

If police involves the fabrication of order, however, then I would add that
we need to also recognize that it is fabricating a social order of wage labor.
Here I would push the specificity a little further. This fabrication of wage
labor might be thought of in terms of sheer coercion, in the way that, for
example, the declining peasantry was "forcibly expropriated from the soil,
driven from their homes, turned into vagabonds, and then whipped, branded
and tortured by grotesquely terroristic laws into accepting the discipline necessary for the system of wage-labor" (Marx 1976, 899). But it can also take the
far more mundane form of everyday political administration that comes to
the fore in the nineteenth century. Either way, we need to address and work
on the centrality of the historically massive police operation on the part of the
state to the consolidation of the social power of capital and the wage form:
as order became increasingly based on the bourgeois mode of production, so
the police mandate was to fabricate an order of wage labor and administer
the class of poverty. Having emerged as a response to the fear of "masterless
men," police helped *transform* these masterless men into rational calculating
individuals in pursuit of clearly defined economic goals. Its concern for the
prosperity of the state meant that it had to encourage wealth production, and
thus the productivity of labor, as the foundational activity of modern society. It therefore prioritized productive activity in the material and economic
sphere. That is, its mobilizing work was the mobilization *of* work.

Employing the idea of a fabricatory or productive role for police powers
might enable a creative rethinking of some of the key police categories. Let
me use as an extended example an idea central to police—*prevention*—and
one of the key early police theorists in Britain—Patrick Colquhoun—to illustrate the point. The idea of good police as "crime prevention" trips easily
off the tongue these days. It also has a long history. Many of the ideas and
arguments around prevention have their roots in late eighteenth-century
debates about crime and the function of the criminal law. Unearthing these

through the work of Colquhoun helps illustrate the pivotal role of police powers in the fabrication of an order of wage labor.

Colquhoun's starting point is the insecurity of property. Estimating that in 1795 there were some 150 offenses on the statute books with execution as their punishment, Colquhoun notes that the rationale for this is prevention, yet this is precisely what severe punishment *fails* to achieve. The main way to reduce crime, Colquhoun argues, is less through the style of punishment and more through the prevention of crimes in the first place. Thus "security [of property] does not proceed from *severe punishments*, for in very few countries are they more sanguinary than in England. It is to be attributed to a more correct and energetic system of Police." At its core is the belief that society needs not just sensible laws but also a police system to prevent crimes occurring in the first place. Wise legislatures know that it is better to prevent rather than punish crimes: "the prevention of crimes and misdemeanors is the true essence of Police" (1796, vi, 3–6, 14, 18, 45–47, 94, 95, 188, 259). Colquhoun works this problem of prevention into the much broader definition of police:

> Police in this country may be considered as a *new Science*; the properties of which consist not in the Judicial Powers which lead to *Punishment*, and which belong to Magistrates alone; but in the PREVENTION AND DETECTION OF CRIMES, and in those other Functions which relate to INTERNAL REGULATIONS for the well ordering and comfort of Civil Society. (1806a, preface)

The emphases are significant here. Civil society is something to be ordered. This ordering is the project of the "Criminal Police" on the one hand and the "Municipal Police" on the other, with the latter incorporating the usual mishmash of police concerns: paving, watching, lighting, removing nuisances, dealing with building regulations, dealing with fires, regulating coaches, carts, and other carriages, and so on. The crux of the conjunction between criminal police, municipal police, and the idea of prevention lies in the connection Colquhoun makes between crime, indigence, and poverty:

> *Poverty* is that state and condition in society where the individual has no surplus labor in store, and, consequently, no property but what is derived

from the constant exercise of industry in the various occupations of life; or, in other words, it is the state of every one who must labor for subsistence. . . . *Poverty* is therefore a most necessary and indispensable ingredient of society, without which nations and communities could not exist in a state of civilization. It is the lot of man—it is the source of *wealth*. . . . *Indigence* therefore, and not *poverty*, is the evil. . . . It is the state of any one who is destitute of the means of subsistence, and is unable to labor to procure it to the extent nature requires. The natural source of subsistence is the labor of the individual; while that remains with him he is denominated *poor*; when it fails in whole or in part he becomes *indigent*. (1806b, 7–8)

The key to Colquhoun's science of police is that the Criminal Police deals with the criminal "underclass"—those who have fallen from indigence into crime. The Municipal Police is there to prevent the class of poverty from falling into indigence. The *essence* of the police project is to identify and implement the mechanisms necessary to prevent the poverty-stricken class from falling into indigence and from there into crime. "The great desideratum, therefore, is to prop up *poverty* by judicious arrangements at those critical periods when it is in danger of descending into indigence. The barrier between these two conditions in society is often slender, and the public interest requires that it should be narrowly guarded" (1806b, 8–9). The key to prevention is thus not directly preventing crime, but preventing the class of poverty from falling into indigence (1799, 5, 8; 1806a, 95; 1806b, 43–49).

What this means, in effect, is that the main object and concern of police is the poor. The heart of the system of police is thus to "relieve the indigent requiring assistance [and] to prop up the industrious poor ready to descend into indigence." This is not an optional extra of police but its very essence, for it would have the effect of "returning to police its genuine character, unmixed with those judicial powers which lead to punishment, and properly belong to magistracy alone" (1799, 12–15; 1806b, 69, 82, 87, 90, 94, 109). Colquhoun thought he had shown the power of indigence as a cause of crime and disorder. In this sense the poor law (or *social security*) becomes a form of municipal police.

For Colquhoun, then, the major police problem is the tendency to idleness, immorality, and depravity among the indigent working class. The task of police is thus to employ a whole panoply of measures and techniques to manage idleness, extending well beyond the administration of relief into the morality, profligacy, and propriety of the working class. The working class needs to be taught the morality of work and thus the immorality of idleness, through what might be described as a moral economy of labor. The range of mechanisms subsumed under the police project—limiting, regulating, and persistently checking public houses; restricting gambling; introducing a moral code to be implemented in pawn shops; disseminating via the Police Gazette essays, articles, and selections from the moral sections of statutes to teach a strong sense of virtue, loyalty, and love of country; and using the educational system to teach the poor about good order and morality—are thus consciously rethought as methods for preventing the poor from falling into indigence and from there into crime. They are designed to put the poor to labor—to make the working class work.

Significant here is Colquhoun's first practical success in introducing a police for the Thames in the late 1790s and the role of this institution in consolidating the money wage as the form of subsistence for the workers in question. In the eighteenth century the worker was not yet fully tied to the money wage. Many workers during this period were paid partly in money wages and partly in kind, often in terms of "ancient entitlements": the thresher was partly paid with part of the harvest, the coal worker by part of the coal he handled. In the docks, carpenters were entitled to some of the spare timber, coal hewers and coal meters received an allowance of fuel, the mates of the West Indiamen had a right to the sweepings of sugar and coffee from the hold of the ship, gangsmen and coopers established a claim to the spilled sugar and molasses, and laborers in the corn ships believed themselves to be entitled to the grain that had been removed as samples. Though not a part of the actual wage, such customary rights formed an important part of a laborer's income and meant that it was more or less impossible to draw a line between "established right" and straightforward theft when workers appeared to be making sure that such "extras" were in plentiful supply.

Toward the end of the eighteenth century, however, and despite (or, rather, "against") the deeply embedded notion of customary right, employers began a more concerted attempt to enforce the moral sanction against such perks and to ensure that such activities were properly criminalized. The increasingly dominant bourgeois class felt that the activities in question jarred with the fundamental purpose of labor, which was to earn a wage and be paid in money. The thefts in general raised a fundamental question: are those who labor entitled to appropriate the products of their own labor other than through the wage? The answer given by capital was increasingly a firm no. Thus the increased prosecution for such "thefts" in the nineteenth century was explicitly designed to eliminate popular ideas about the legitimate taking of property, which the bourgeois class now wanted to be clearly defined as unlawful and liable to be punished.

In this context Colquhoun's arguments about "prevention"—and the police project more generally—became even more important. Colquhoun believed that the major task of the new preventive police was not just to halt losses to capital, but also to break the notion that the appropriation of goods on which workers labor was "sanctioned by custom." "The transition from innocence to acts of turpitude . . . is easy and obvious," he notes:

> An indulgent Master, at first, grants the privilege of a few samples or a tri-fling quantity of foul Corn, on the solicitation of an industrious servant, under the pretence of feeding a pig, or a few poultry. The stock of poultry or pigs is increased, and additional quantities of grain become necessary. The indulgence of the Master in a few instances is, at length, construed into a sanction to appropriate Sweepings of foul Grain. These Sweepings are presently increased by previous concert among the Laborers. Corn becomes foul, which might have been preserved in a clean and merchantable state. (1800, 80)

This process is then extended to other commodities and industries. For this reason, Colquhoun argues, workers agreed to work without wages because they knew this would provide them with opportunities for taking what they considered to be justifiably theirs: they would agree "to be admitted to work . . . without any pay, trusting to the chance of Plunder for remuneration" (1800, 63). In other words, they would prefer crime to the wage. A police for the Thames and its docks would therefore mean that not only would commodities being transported be better secured, but the improvement in the security of property would also have the deliberate effect of reducing "wastage" and "loss." More tellingly: the wage form could be consolidated. Thus 1798 saw the issuing of a new Marine Police Establishment by the West India merchants, charged with controlling dock labor. Eight hundred twenty lumpers were enlisted to perform their duties in accordance with instructions issued by the Marine Police, while "master lumpers" were appointed to restrain the others from pillage and willful breakage and to regularly search the lumpers with the help of other police. The Marine Police not only oversaw the unloading of ships, but also set rates of pay. Thus a force designed to protect property was also at the heart of imposing the money wage on the working class and of enforcing the discipline of labor on the same group.

I have been exploring Colquhoun's ideas about prevention to illustrate how a rethinking of some traditional "police categories" might bring out the active role of police powers in fabricating order rather than merely preventing—in the "negative" sense—crime or disorder. And this role, going back to the earlier points, is centrally concerned with work. The net effect of the first real instance of "preventive police" in England was the commodification of labor and the consolidation of the money wage. In this sense, police powers were at the heart of nothing less than the making of the English working class.

Police/Policy/Security

To talk of police powers in terms of their role in administering the class of poverty and the conditions of prosperity makes policing sound less like what is usually thought of as police and more like what might be called social policy. This idea can be pushed quite a bit further, in a number of ways.

I noted earlier that the term "police" appears to have originated in French-Burgundian *policie* in the fifteenth century. In spreading across Continental Europe it generated a range of words adopted from the French-Burgundian: "Policei," "Pollicei," "Policey," "Pollicey," "Pollizey," "Pollizei," "Politzey," "Pollucey," and "Pullucey." Though the spelling of the word varied, the meaning remained constant. It is sometimes said that the idea of "police" was long alien to British political discourse, a claim that often runs hand in hand with the suggestion that the interest in police is a quirk of the Continental mind (and that explains why modern "police states" are a European phenomenon). But in fact many of the practices associated with "police" were captured in an English equivalent, "policy," which also derives from the old French *policie*. "Police" and "policy" were thus used in rather un-differentiated but broadly parallel ways across Europe into the sixteenth century and after.

Noting this link between "police" and "policy" helps clarify something important about the nature of police powers and one of the foundations of the new police science. It captures, for example, the extent to which the original "police states" historically functioned as early "welfare states." Reinhold August Dorwart, in *The Prussian Welfare State before 1740*, suggests that the only reason we do not equate *Polizeistaat* with *Wohlfahrtsstaat* is because we are captives of twentieth-century definitions of police state and welfare state (1971, 4, 14, 310–11; also see Raeff 1983; Liang 1992; Dyson 1980). It is clear from its range of functions and powers, and its connotations of good order and security, that it would not be unreasonable to think of *Polizei* as synonymous with *Wohlfahrt*. Given that the twentieth-century "welfare state" is also characterized by and understood in terms of its wide-ranging *social policy*, it makes as much sense to think of the policing of the "common good" or "general welfare" as a form of policy, and to think of *Polizeistaat* as "policy state." The eighteenth-century "police states" might then be seen as the historical precursor to the nineteenth-century "administrative state" and the twentieth-century welfare state. (The term *Polizeistaat*, usually translated as "police state," came into general English usage in the 1930s as a means of conceptualizing the emerging totalitarian regimes and has many connotations that are probably inappropriate for the original "police states." That historical problem is compounded by a political one: underlying the modern term "police state" is a whole host of liberal assumptions about the supposedly "correct" limits on police powers, assumptions that do little to help our understanding of police and much to mythologize the nature of states in general and policing in particular.)

It strikes me that part of the basis of the new approach to police powers is an attempt to retain this link between police and policy as a feature of working with an extended concept of police. For it is clear that major figures in the field of police science were as concerned with what we now call "social policy" as they were concerned with what passes under the label "police." Retaining such a link suggests that those figures that emerged following the "birth of the welfare state" and that became central to *social policy*—poor-law and social security officers, social workers, probation officers, and the "official" administrators of policy—are on this view as much a part of the policing of the system as uniformed police officers; the "left hand" of police powers complementing the "right hand" wielding the weapons of state coercion. It also suggests that the new research on police powers recognizes the importance of policing as a form of political administration as much as a form of law-enforcement. If nothing else, this helps make sense of the definitive transformation in policing in the nineteenth century, which might then be read less as the century when the police found its "true vocation" focused on crime prevention and law enforcement, as police mythology has it, and more as the century in which policing was divided into a body that focused on crime and another much more varied set of institutions focused on the working class in its more mundane everyday existence—as workers administered through "social police." In this sense, policing and social security can be drawn together in a telling and compelling way: social security can be seen as a form of policing, but, conversely, policing might be read as the project of *social security*.

As well as pointing us in the direction of the relationship between police and policy, this connection also points us in the direction of security more generally. Let me, by way of finishing, turn to the question of security and make a more political suggestion about police powers in the current political climate.

Security is the supreme concept of civil society. This is truer now than when Marx first pointed it out in 1843 (Marx 1975, 230). We are constantly told that we live in insecure times: that the world is facing a huge calamitous threat from global terrorism and that the only possible response is to step up "security." Moreover, in recent years everything from AIDS to the environment, from migration to food production, has somehow become a security issue under the rubric of "societal security." Any argument concerning police powers now is surely compelled to deal with the question of security. A preoccupation with security was a founding principle of the first police science and core to principles such as the state of prosperity (Gordon 1991, 19). It remained central to accounts of police powers thereafter, from Hegel's claim that police exists to secure the livelihood and welfare of individuals through to Foucault's constant return to questions of security in his arguments about police. And Marx's full comment runs, "*Security* is the supreme concept of civil society, the concept of *police*." But the reason we need to take seriously the idea of security is not purely one of origin. Security discourse is now more than ever central to the way the state is transforming civil society, leading to the development of something like a fortress mentality, in both social and political terms.

Socially, the current obsession with security functions partly on an entirely individual level within the language of neoliberalism, as we are encouraged further into our privatized (but secure) universes. "Security" has become a positional good defined by income and access to private protective services, a prestige symbol concerned less with dealing with the social causes of insecurity and more with one's own private safety and personal insulation. This has helped sustain neoliberal assumptions about individual subjectivity and autonomy. Much of the contemporary sociological discourse on security, for example, assumes that its achievement can be found in a more productive relation to the self as a condition for liberty, requiring active participation in the schemes and plans put forward by those institutions of corporate finance that have come to replace the more traditional mechanisms of "social security." Thus "insecurity" comes to be used as an ideological strategy for encouraging investment in private health care schemes, private pensions, and the commodities that are said to make us more secure, turning us into consumers of the products of finance capital and the security industry; (in)security is nothing if not big business.

Politically, however, security discourse is also helping transform civil society through the intensification of surveillance programs. Such programs rely heavily on the search for absolute knowledge. I have elsewhere (Neocleous 2002, 2003) shown the integral link between security and knowledge, in the sense that security functions as knowledge, relies on knowledge, produces knowledge, and uses its claim to knowledge as license to render all aspects of life transparent to the state. Knowledge thus becomes the fulcrum around which security and police meet. Witness, to give just one recent example, the comment from Sir John Stevens, Commissioner of the Metropolitan Police in London, justifying the need for national ID cards in Britain: "we don't actually know who is in London at the moment" (cited in Johnston 2004). On these grounds the search for absolute knowledge becomes the grounds for infringing civil liberties: just imagine a system that allowed the state, police, and security services to know exactly who was in London at any one time.

It might therefore be argued that as part of the coinage of power, "security" has become a fundamental ideological tool not only of international relations, but also of internal political repression and social domination. The "securitization" of contemporary political discourse and practice is thus little more than a technique for grounding and legitimating the political regime, equating the political status quo with the desirable order and giving the state virtually carte blanche powers to protect it. It is now well-known that identifying acts of governance as an exercise of "police power" has long been a way to insulate such acts and powers from serious constitutional and legal scrutiny; the same point is also true of the way certain acts and powers are now identified as "security" measures. Securitizing questions of social and political power has the debilitating effect of allowing the state to subsume genuinely political action concerning the issues in question, consolidating the power of the existing forms of social domination, and justifying the short-circuiting of even the most minimal liberal democratic procedures. And I wonder whether we might not say *exactly the same about the concept of "police."* If, after all, police powers are thought to create the possibility of infringing civil liberties and acting beyond the law, then is this not also because police operate according to the security mandate? Security, after all, is always said to be achievable only through more and more police.

Mitchell Dean in chapter 7 and Ron Levi and John Hagan in chapter 8 have pointed to the difficulties and dangers of reading as "police action" the military intervention by one state on another, and I share their concerns—the lack of a genuine international police force is because there is no world state (regardless of all the talk of a new world order). Nonetheless, one of the features of security discourse is that like police it constantly elides the differences between the internal and external, domestic and foreign, inside and outside. And in that sense whatever one might think about using the concept of police to describe relations *between* states, it is clear that international military actions of all sorts always fold over into the domestic security realm—the realm of police. This may give some weight to Lindsay Farmer's suggestion (chapter 5) that the police project be thought of through the idea of a jurisprudence of security. But one might also make the converse point: that given that the U.S. Patriot Act and the U.K. Anti-Terrorism, Crime and Security Act (2001) are concerned with internal affairs—and thus with "police powers"—perhaps we need to start thinking of the project of national security in general and the "war on terror" in particular as police projects. And, of course, like all the other "wars" in which police powers have been mobilized—the war on drugs, the war on poverty, the war on crime, and so on—this is yet another mythic war that the state has no chance of winning. It is, however, a war in which the state is given the chance of transforming civil society in the interests of certain powers. And it is, of course, through the war against the mythic enemy that *all* of a society's institutions are expected to be mobilized.

I would therefore argue that any new police science has to not only address this connection between police and security, but to do so in a mode that is critical of the climate of fear generated by the political manufacture of insecurity. Otherwise any new police science would be seen as little more than another academic exercise. A critical engagement with the question of security, then, would help revive the original political dimension to debates about police powers, and would reinforce the critical project underpinning the "new police science."

References

Agamben, Giorgio. 1998. Homo sacer: *Sovereign power and bare life.* Stanford, CA: Stanford University Press.

Cain, Maureen, ed. 1989. *Growing up good: Policing the behaviour of girls in Europe.* London: Sage.

Colquhoun, Patrick. 1796. *A treatise on the police of the metropolis, etc.* 2d ed. London: H. Fry.

———. 1799. *The state of indigence and the situation of the casual poor in the metropolis, explained, etc.* London: H. Baldwin.

———. 1800. *A treatise on the commerce and police of the river Thames, etc.* London: Joseph Mawman.

———. 1806a. *A treatise on the police of the metropolis, etc.* 7th ed. London: Joseph Mawman.

———. 1806b. *A treatise on indigence, etc.* London: J. Hatchard.

Dean, Mitchell. 1991. *The constitution of poverty: Toward a genealogy of liberal governance.* London: Routledge.

Donzelot, Jacques. 1979. *The policing of families: Welfare versus the state.* London: Hutchinson.

Dorwart, Reinhold August. 1971. *The Prussian welfare state before 1740.* Cambridge, MA: Harvard University Press.

Dubber, Markus D. 2005. *The police power: Patriarchy and the foundations of American government*. New York: Columbia University Press.

Dyson, Kenneth. 1980. *The state tradition in western Europe: A study of an idea and institution*. Oxford: Martin Robertson.

Foucault, Michel. 1967. *Madness and civilization: A history of insanity in the age of reason*, trans. R. Howard. London: Tavistock.

———. 1970. *The order of things: An archaeology of the human sciences*. London: Routledge.

———. 1980. *Power/knowledge: Selected interviews and other writings 1972–1977*, ed. C. Gordon. Sussex, UK: Harvester.

———. 1981. History of systems of thought, 1979: Foucault at the College de France II: A course summary with an introduction by James Bernauer. *Philosophy and Social Criticism* 8(3): 350–59.

———. 1988. *Politics, philosophy, culture: Interviews and other writings 1977–1984*, ed. L. Kritzman. London: Routledge.

———. 1991. *Remarks on Marx*. New York: Semiotext(e).

Gordon, Colin. 1991. Governmental rationality: An introduction. In *The Foucault effect: Studies in governmentality*, ed. G. Burchell, C. Gordon, and P. Miller. Hemel Hempstead, UK: Harvester Wheatsheaf.

Johnston, Philip. 2004. Bill paves way for identity cards. *Daily Telegraph* (London), April 8.

Lees, Sue. 1997. *Ruling passions: Sexual violence, reputation and the law*. Buckingham, UK: Open University Press.

Liang, Hsi-Huey. 1992. *The rise of modern police and the European state system from Metternich to the Second World War*. Cambridge, UK: Cambridge University Press.

Marx, Karl. 1975. *Early writings*, trans. R. Livingstone and G. Benton. Harmondsworth, UK: Penguin.

———. 1867. *Capital: A critique of political economy*. Vol. 1, trans. B. Fowkes. Reprint, Harmondsworth, UK: Penguin, 1976.

McStay Adams, Thomas. 1990. *Bureaucrats and beggars: French social policy in the age of enlightenment*. Oxford: Oxford University Press.

Neocleous, Mark. 2000. *The fabrication of social order: a critical theory of police power*. Pluto Press: London.

———. 2002. Secrecy, privacy, idiocy. *Social Research* 69(1): 85–110.

———. 2003. *Imagining the state*. Maidenhead, UK: Open University/McGraw-Hill.

Novak, William. 1996. *The people's welfare: Law and regulation in nineteenth-century America*. Chapel Hill: University of North Carolina Press.

Raeff, Marc. 1983. *The well-ordered police state: social and institutional change through law in the Germanies and Russia, 1600–1800*. New Haven, CT: Yale University Press.

Smith, Adam. 1982. *Lectures on jurisprudence*, ed. R. L. Meek, D. D. Raphael, and P. G. Stein. Indianapolis, IN: Liberty Fund.

Steinberg, Deborah Lynn, Debbie Epstein, and Richard Johnsen, eds. 1997. *Border patrols: Policing the boundaries of heterosexuality.* London: Cassell.

Tomlins, Christopher. 1993. *Law, labor and ideology in the early American republic.* Cambridge, UK: Cambridge University Press.

Watney, Simon. 1997. *Policing desire: Aids, pornography and the media.* 3d ed. London: Cassell.

CHAPTER TWO

Spiritual and Earthly Police

Theories of the State in Early-Modern Europe

PASQUALE PASQUINO

"The term 'politics,'" wrote H. Heller in 1928, "derives from 'polis' and not from 'polemos,' though the common root of both words remains significant." Its central problem is "the unity of territorial decision" (*Einheit der Gebietsentscheidung*),[1] or rather, "the formation and the maintenance of this unity . . . in the multiplicity of voluntary acts which constitute it" (Heller 1971, 423–24). "Police" (*Policey*, *Polizia*) was the name of politics at the start of the modern period throughout most of the European continent (Oestreich 1976; Schmitt 1972, 91 and n. 3).[2] This chapter is intended as a contribution from the perspective of conceptual and constitutional history[3] to the relationship between the concept of police and the theory of the state by focusing on Protestant Germany during the second half of the seventeenth century.

In 1653 and 1656 two texts were published in Frankfurt-on-Main, which are forgotten today but created a stir at the time: these are the *Biblische Policey*[4] and the *Teutscher Fürstenstaat*[5]; their authors were, respectively, Dietrich (Theodorus) Reinkingk[6] and Veit Ludwig von Seckendorff. Recent interest in these works cannot simply be explained by an interest in the reconstruction of the history of ideas; rather, it is born out of the judgment of O. Brunner, which sheds light on the problematics of my research: "The history of doctrines of the state can be written from two perspectives. On the one hand, by taking into consideration structure and theoretical content: in this case, the original thinkers and creators [like Machiavelli, Bodin, and Hobbes] will have a central role. We can, on the other hand, interrogate those authors who, without being the leading thinkers of their age, nevertheless had considerable importance on account of their wide-ranging influence, and who exerted considerable influence on political actors by transmitting to them the fundamental categories of their way of conceiving reality. We can include among the members of this second group D. Reinkingk. . . . He was a technician [*Praktiker*] of politics and administration rather than primarily a theoretician" (Brunner 1963).

Now, if it is true that men make their own history and if it is also true—as far as this can offend the contemporary democratic conscience and historians of the popular classes—that the history of modern Europe was primarily made by "dominant groups," it would not be futile for the historian to occupy himself with those texts that must have helped shape the "political opinions" of ruling groups during this period.[7]

Beyond the significant differences between these two books, to which I will return later, it is possible to highlight several shared features:

1. Above all, there is what I would call their double practical character. These are, indeed, texts written by civil servants, more precisely high-ranking civil servants, active in various political centers (courts or cities) of northern Germany, and aimed at those in power and other civil servants. In the subtitle of the *Teutscher Fürstenstaat*, we read, for example:

> Written for the benefit, use and profit of persons of high rank and their children, and of illustrious gentlemen, counselors and advisers who labor in princely courts or other courts or in tribunals and other bodies engaged in territorial administration.

This is one of the reasons these two texts were written in German and not in Latin, as were treatises with theoretical content, including, for example,

Reinkingk's *Tractatus de regimine seculari et ecclesiastico.*[8] Furthermore, their goal was not to lay the theoretical foundations of a "political science," as H. Conring attempted,[9] or to describe a "politica generalis," or even a doctrine of public law similar to that of J. Limnaeus,[10] but rather the very practical one of formulating rules for the art of governing, that is to say, a "Policey." Reinkingk wrote in a preface to his work, "One will in the end find in it [that is, in Holy Scripture] the right *Polizey*, salutary and agreeable to God. One should learn from it the right rule of government or the art of government, and it will be by no means inconvenient to form, on the basis of it, political axioms and a policy [*Polizey*], and arranging them in order."

2. *Politica christiana* versus *ratio status*. Both authors refuse the *raison d'état* as a criterion for their Policey. This refusal would merit further discussion elsewhere. In the context of this chapter, I will limit myself to acknowledging it[11] and to pointing out that they place themselves explicitly at the heart of the anti-, or, rather, non-Aristotelian, Protestant religious tradition.

3. Finally, neither text has as its spatial frame of reference the Empire but rather political units of smaller dimensions. This implies nothing with regard to the position of the authors in relation to the Empire and the relationship between the Empire and the territorial states, issues with which I will not preoccupy myself.

Political Iconography

I would like to begin by analyzing the half titles of these two books. The frontispiece of the *Biblische Policey* (figure 2.1)[12] shows in its lower part a representation of human society begotten by a divine triple *fiat*. It appears structured and divided in three estates, which the Lutheran orthodoxy of the period (Carpzov, Stephani, and Cothmann, besides Reinkingk) calls "status ecclesiasticus," "status politicus," and "status popularis," or, in German in the *Biblische Policey*, "die drey Haupt-Stände: der Geistliche, der Weltliche, der Häussliche."

If we observe the detail of figure 2.1, we can recognize, from left to right, under the inscriptions *Deo Honor—cuique suum—sine labore nihil*, the objects that characterize the three states (i.e., the three different social conditions)

Figure 2.1

respectively set before a church apse, palace room, and humble abode. In the first image, a Bible rests on an altar; to its sides are a chalice and paten, with the hosts. In the second, a crown, sword, and scepter rest on a table covered by a precious piece of cloth. In the third, finally, some sort of bread (?), a distaff, and a third object (on the left), which I have not identified, rest on a table covered by a simple tablecloth. Here, furthermore, on the right side of the small room, an open window allows us to make out fields where a peasant is busy working (and a village in the distance).

In the intermediate space between God and creation, above, and human society, below, on both sides of the title, we find the figures of Moses and Aaron. That the latter is indeed the character depicted on the left becomes apparent if we recall the detailed description of his appearance that is given in Ecclesiasticus 45:8ff (see Reau 1956, 213).[13] It is significant that we find the same pair of figures, Moses and Aaron, in the small frame below on the left, on the primitive frontispiece of the work (see figure 2.2) and also above and left on the frontispiece of the *Tractatus* (figure 2.3).

It is in a contemporary text (1651) and a very different one on many levels, the *Leviathan* by Thomas Hobbes, that we can find useful indications on the symbolic significance of these two figures of the legislator and guide of the people—Moses—and of the prophet and high priest—Aaron. In chapter 36, "Of the word of God, and of prophets," Hobbes writes,

> the name of PROPHET, signifieth in Scripture sometimes *Prolocutor*; that is, he that speaketh from God to Man, or from man to God: And sometimes *Predictor*, or a foreteller of things to come. . . . It is most frequently used in the sense of speaking from God to the People. So Moses . . . and others were Prophets. . . . In the like sense it is, that God saith to Moses [Exod. 4:16] concerning Aaron, "He shall be thy Spokes-man to the People; and he shall be to thee a mouth, and thou shalt be to him in stead of God;" that which here is Spokes-man, is interpreted Prophet [Exod. 7:1]; "See (saith God) I have made thee a God to Pharaoh, and Aaron thy Brother shall be thy Prophet." (Emphases in the original)

The two figures on the frontispieces represent here the two incarnations of the mediator between divine law and worldly order. Moses governs in conformity with the law; Aaron interprets it and knows how to make it

Figure 2.2

Figure 2.3

speak with regard to the concrete cases of life. I would like to suggest that Reinkingk uses here an antique allegory to place the image of the prince's counselor (Aaron), in a certain way his self-portrait, alongside that of the sovereign (Moses).

The half title of the *Teutscher Fürstenstaat* published in 1656 (figure 2.4; it can in fact be found in all editions) shows an iconographic landscape quite removed from what I have just described. Beneath a solar and mute God (here, the sun could also be the symbol of the "The Royal Science of the Art of Governing the State"),[14] we find in the forefront a two-headed eagle, symbol of the Holy Roman Empire of the German Nation. In the lower half, we find the image and allegories of the power of the modern territorial state, for which the treatise of the chancellor of Gotha is intended as a model of constitution (*Verfassung*) and of government (*Regierung*) (see *Teutscher Fürstenstaat*, 2, 32). Here, the estates (understood in the orthodox Lutheran doctrinal meaning) have disappeared. In their stead, we see a geographic space and four female figures. The first holds a sword, the third a wand around which a snake is coiled, the fourth a book. The second holds an object that cannot be identified so easily but appears to be a measuring implement. There is no particular difficulty in identifying the allegories expressed by at least three of the four figures. From left to right, the first, which bears the sword and points to the image of a fortification below, refers to the task of defending and protecting and, at the same time, to the laws of war and peace. The third (I will come back shortly to the second) holds in her hand the iconographic symbol of *prudentia-Klugheit*. Ripa, in his classic *Iconologia* (1593), writes under the heading "*Prudenza*," "She [Prudence] holds in her right hand an arrow around which is wrapped a fish called remora by the Latins, and which, according to Plinius, attaches itself to ships and thus delays their progress" (Ripa 1764–1767, 4:428). Finally, the fourth figure, with an open book and the image of a church, stands for instruction and at the same time for the *cura religionis*.

As for the second female figure, I can only formulate hypotheses. The object that the woman holds could allude to justice if it were identified with a fasces (Ripa 1764–1767, 3:202),[15] but this seems improbable. The object in question, incised with notches, looks rather like a measuring implement. If such is indeed the case, it might be understood as a symbol of equity, and thus of justice, but I have found neither in Ripa nor elsewhere iconographic evidence along those lines. Even if I am not absolutely convinced by the hypothesis that I propose, I believe that we can see it as an allusion to the limits of the state, or perhaps to a specific knowledge of it, such as that dealt with in the beginning of Seckendorff's book, which was called *Statistik* in Germany (Pasquino 1986). (Our author gives it the name "materialische

Figure 2.4

Beschreibung" [*Teutscher Fürstenstaat*, 2].) An ulterior hypothesis, that it symbolizes commerce, naturally remains possible.

The fact that the four allegorical figures refer to the characters and qualities of public power, of the "Obrigkeit," is confirmed by the image that appears on the half title of a book by J. B. von Rohr, published in Leipzig

Wenn ein Regente will des Landes Wolfarth bauen,
Mus er auff Gottesfurcht, Justiz und Klugheit schauen

Figure 2.5

in 1718 under the title *Einleitung zur Staats-Klugheit*[16] and that forms part
of the *Wirkungsgeschichte* of Seckendorff's treatise. Here we find four female
figures surrounding a sovereign seated on his throne (figure 2.5). Moreover,
the image is accompanied by the following caption: "If a sovereign wants to

build prosperity in a kingdom, he must be in fear of God and practice justice and prudence."[17]

From left to right, we can immediately identify the three virtues mentioned in the caption: the first blindfolded figure, who holds a sword and balance, can be identified with justice; the second, who holds a cross and Bible, with the fear of God. The last, who holds in her hands a serpent and mirror, iconographic symbols to which Ripa also makes reference (the passage cited above also mentions that "she holds a mirror in her left hand"; Ripa 1764–1767, 4:92), can be identified with prudence. In comparison with Seckendorff's own half title, here we find justice in the place of defense and again a fourth figure whose significance is less clear. I would nevertheless suggest that this figure, third from the left, can be identified with the goal of government, *Wohlfahrt*, given that she holds in one hand a palm frond, which generally represents peace, as R. van Marle has pointed out (Marle 1932, 166–67). She gestures with her arm toward the *Land*, outside the frame, meanwhile casting her gaze on the sovereign.

Let us finally return to the false title of the *Fürstenstaat* (see figure 2.4); we see, in the background, cities, hills, forests, fields, and a sea crisscrossed by ships. Broadly speaking, it is the space on which the prince exercises his power: the territory.

Let us end here this analysis of seventeenth-century iconography by simply observing that a systematic inquiry into such an unexplored field could prove interesting to historians for several reasons. The material is not lacking, and we have but to think of the important bibliography compiled by M. Praz in his *Studies in Seventeenth-Century Imagery* (Praz 1964; see also Brandt 1982), in which there are numerous texts that refer to the political imagination, among which we find the *Emblemata Politica* of the cameralist Jakob Bornitz.[18]

D. Reinkingk and His "Contribution to the Historical Foundation of the German Lutheran State"[19]

Martin Heckel has very aptly demonstrated, in his study on doctrines pertaining to the relationship between state and Church among the German

Protestant jurists of the first half of the seventeenth century (Heckel 1968), that the orthodox-Lutheran doctrine of "drei Stände" does not simply constitute a version of the medieval concept of a *Dreiständegesellschaft*. On the contrary, it represents a reaction of the orthodoxy to the extraordinary diffusion, perceived as menacing in the world of Protestant culture, of political Aristotelianism (see Maier 1980, 134); we have but to think of the considerable role played during this century by the University of Helmstedt and by Henning Arnisaeus[20] and Hermann Conring.[21] It is a reaction, accordingly, to Aristotelianism but also to the *raison d'état* that was penetrating Germany, thanks in no small part to the Aristotelians.[22] This doctrine of the "drei Stände" assumes in the works of Reinkingk a double function and oscillates in a certain way between two poles. On one hand, it is an organizational principle for the Church ("Kirchenverfassungsprinzip"), particularly in his first important book, the *Tractatus de regimine (Policey) seculari et ecclesiastico*. On the other, in *Biblische Policey*, it is a fundamental category of social order (see Heckel 1968, 156: "The three estates appear here [in *Biblische Policey*] as social orders without being considered solely in their ecclesiastical position," id. n. 835). Heckel observes opportunely, "This shifting use of the theory of the three orders is at the same time the reason why in the orthodox ecclesiastic law the boundary between the worldly juridical sphere and that of the Church remains ill-defined and ambiguous" (157). In *Biblische Policey*, the accent is in fact placed on the second of these terms.

It is not on this second aspect, the doctrine of the three estates (*Dreiständelehre*), that I now wish to pause. I have brought it up simply because this structure corresponds to the tripartition and the formal pattern of Reinkingk's book, which deals in its three major subdivisions with the "Geistlicher," "Weltlicher," and "Hauss-und-Ehe Stand."

The frontispieces that we have examined seem to suggest two very different images of social order: the religious and traditional one of a society with three estates ("Ständegesellschaft," Reinkingk) and the more modern and mundane one of the territorial state, the legal-material space on which the authority of the prince-sovereign is exercised (Seckendorff). At this point, it is necessary to go beyond the image, at least as far as the words, to see if Reinkingk's book contains nothing more and nothing other than what is featured in its frontispiece; to verify—as Christoph Link has suggested—

"whether some new wine is flowing within the old wineskin of Lutheran orthodoxy."[23]

I have mentioned the fact that the book is divided into three parts relating to the three "Stände"; notwithstanding the affirmation of the first *Axioma* ("the ecclesiastical order is the most ancient and the most important and has a certain superiority"), over two thirds of the 650 pages of the book are devoted by the author to the "Weltlicher Stand." This part is in turn subdivided into eight sections among which figure most prominently those relating to (a) the "role of the supreme authority, the king and the one who governs,"[24] (b) "the counselors, functionaries, and employees of the State," and finally (c) the "subjects."

Here the division according to estates has disappeared. At the core of the social doctrine we find a political doctrine, the image of a form of power, of a *Herrschaftsstruktur*, with determined hierarchical criteria (*Über-* and *Unterordnung*).[25] If we go beyond the monotonous and repetitive framework of the *exempla* that are inscribed in a specifically medieval ethical-rhetorical tradition within which the axioms, the rules of behavior, are nothing else than *exempla*,[26] a careful reading identifies two elements that deserve to be highlighted here:

1. Above all, the central or middle axis of the tripartition in estates, the "Weltlicher Stand," shows, as we have seen, an internal hierarchy where we find, besides and around the sovereign, what would later be called the "public service" ("Beamtentum," *Beamtenstand*). In front of it appears the figure of the subject. The territorial sovereign and the subjects (Landeshoheit and Untertänigkeit) are here already central political categories (Link 1977, 92). I would like to add two further considerations. The first is that a fairly peculiar book by an author about whom we know nothing and which H. Maier (Maier 1980, 119–22) has brought to our attention (*Christliche Policey oder Prudentia Politica Christiana* by C. W. Friedlieb, published in Goslar in 1614) had already insisted in a chapter on government ("Von der Regierung") that a sovereign (Regent) cannot govern alone (chap. 2, ¶ 1, p. 50ff). Reinkingk addresses this point in *Biblische Policey*:

> The greater a lord, the larger the country, and the greater the number of persons that he must govern, the larger will be the number of counselors,

functionaries and servants that he will need. A sovereign is only one man
and at each moment he can only be in one place, and therefore must, in his
governing activity, see the majority of things through the eyes of others and
hear the majority of, things through the ears of others, and for that reason
needs to rely on faithful counselors, functionaries and servants. (bk. 2,
axioma 59, p. 255)

The second consideration: Reinkingk, in the *Tractatus* of 1619, already
assigns to the territorial sovereign authority ("Landeshohenobrigkeit," in
the chapter "De actibus correspectivis superioritatis territorialis") the four
functions of *protectio, justitiae administratio, onerum exactio et praestatio,* and
religionis curae (bk. 1, § 5, chap. 4, ¶¶ 43, 97, 130, 227).[27]

2. In the sections of the *Biblische Policey* relating to themes that we could
call "cameralist" (see Maier 1980, 138) and that deal in some way or other
with the good administration and order of society, Reinkingk feels the need
to draw his *axiomata* and his *exempla* not only from the Bible but, for example, from Landgrave Philip of Hesse's *Testament* (see *Biblische Policey,* bk.
2, axioma 56, p. 249, and axioma 80, p. 293). Here, the Christian prince
appears alongside the scriptures as an authorized source for the proper rules
of world order.

It is useful to recall that Reinkingk descended from a family of civil servants and that he spent nearly his entire life in the service of different German
princes. His experience as a statesman, or rather as a counselor of the prince,
is apparent throughout his book. He is a soldier of *ratio Dei,* which he op-
poses to *ratio status* or to *Ratio Diaboli,* as he calls it, and he rises up against
its so-called "taceat Deus in politicis" (*Biblische Policey,* bk. 2, axioma 38, p.
206). Nonetheless, he knows perfectly well, like Seckendorff, who also considers the art of governing—the most noble of all sciences—to be of divine
origin (*Teutscher Fürstenstaat,* Dedicatio), that the commandments of God,
but also those of Philip of Hesse, are mute and accordingly impracticable
without someone like him—Aaron, the civil servant counselor (the Rat, the
Beamte)—who knows how to interpret the tables of the law (*Biblische Policey,*
bk. 2, axioma 30, p. 161: "The other table deals with good police."). "Silete
theologi in munere alieno," as Alberico Gentili had put it. And Reinkingk

has his *ratio status* say, "God and his word are appropriate for the altar, but not for the government's or the state's secret deliberations, and much less for councils of war" (*Biblische Policey*, bk. 2, axioma 38, p. 206). Still Reinkingk, under the mantle of the divine word, does not speak from the pulpit of the Church but rather from the council chambers, the chancery.[28] Consider *axioma* 52 as but one example: "Well-appointed archives and an office [bureau] that is in charge of recording daily events are both very necessary and useful for all governments, chancelleries and tribunals" (*Biblische Policey*, 240).

Here we can measure accurately the distance between the *Biblische Policey* and the oldest "mirrors of princes" (*Fürstenspiegel*) literature (Jessen 1962, 61). For Reinkingk, the order of government is not possible without its "plan" and its "memory." In his works, the "virtues" of the prince begin to transform themselves into techniques of governing, into political prudence (*Staatsklugheit*), but also into the first rudimentary elements of an administrative science.

V. L. von Seckendorff: Protestant Ethics and the Birth of the State

Seckendorff too belongs to the group of men, profoundly imbued with Lutheran religious tradition, who were politically active in the north of Germany toward the second half of the seventeenth century.[29] This is attested by his late *Christen-Staat* (1685) and his intense relationship with Spener and the pietistic movement, but primarily in his monumental history of the Reformation, the *Commentarius historicus et apologeticus de lutheranismo* (Francofurti et Lipsiae, 1688–1694), then considered to be his major work, written in Latin and translated not only into German but, unlike his other writings, also into Dutch and French during the eighteenth century.[30] I will nevertheless focus here only on the *Teutscher Fürstenstaat*, published three years after Reinkingk's *Biblische Policey*, when the author was twenty-nine years old[31] and worked as a civil servant (*consiliarus*) at the court of Duke Ernest the Pious in Gotha (1656).

We have a fairly peculiar autobiographical account by Seckendorff that deserves our attention. It consists of a letter written to Leibniz in March 1683 from his retreat at Meuselwitz.[32] He recounts in his elegant Latin that, although he had been interested since a young age only in theological studies, he had been forced at the age of sixteen, by those whom he had to obey [his parents], to take up studies in jurisprudence. He further described how, four years later, while war raged against Sweden, after having abandoned the universities of Strasburg and then Marburg, he had to agree to work at the court of Ernest of Saxony to earn a living because his father had died and the means of subsistence of his family were reduced to nearly nothing. In the same letter, Seckendorff speaks of a book written in German concerning the true felicity of man and the way one can and must govern with it in mind, the three estates of society, the civil, the ecclesiastical, and the domestic. The book was written in a clear style and with simple, not esoteric, arguments. This is evidently the *Christen-Staat*,[33] in which not surprisingly we find Reinkingk's doctrine of the three estates (*Dreiständelehre*). He makes no reference, however, to the work of his youth, the *Fürstenstaat*, other than perhaps in a passing and implicit manner when, speaking of his time spent in Gotha and of his legal and theological studies, facilitated by the local "Bibliotheca" and by "doctorum virorum conversatione," he adds almost with regret, but at the same time as a sort of Lutheran declaration of the civil servant's ethics (Beamtenethik)[34]: "It is nevertheless necessary to carry out the task that was entrusted to me by Monsignor." This silence regarding the *Fürstenstaat* is surprising if we consider not only the opinion of his contemporaries (to which I will turn shortly) and the twelve editions of the book, but also Leibniz's comments in his letter of January 1683, evidently referring to Seckendorff's first book:

> I do not see who can give true and deep advice, any more than you: you who know the affairs of the German princes and who was the first to organize in scientific form a topic that had remained very vague until that time. . . . You have not merely put together a compilation, as many others have, or gathered together general prescriptions that one hears here and there, in the universities; rather, on the contrary, you have given precise examples taken from direct experience of both reality and reflection. (Leibniz 1938, letter no. 459, p. 557 [cited by Lüdtke 1939, p. 56, n. 2, and p. 60, n. 1, and Miglio 1957, p. 22])

My objective here is not to analyze Leibniz's laudatory appraisal, nor the relationship between the author, Seckendorff, and his various books (see

Maier 1980, 140). The question to which I will try to find an answer is simply, what is the *Teutscher Fürstenstaat*?

Let us begin by citing the opinions of several contemporaries. C. Thomas, in his *Funeral Oration*, delivered at Halle on December 22, 1692, states, "The *Fürstenstaat*, written while he was still young, is nothing less than a doctrine that is synthetic and well founded upon the manner in which temporal lords and their advisors must conduct with prudence and wisdom their government, for their tranquility and for the satisfaction of their subjects."[35] Schreber, in his *Historia vitae ac meritorum Seckendorffii* (Leipzig, 1733), summarized in turn the content of the *Fürstenstaat*:

> The work is organized in the following manner: the first part presents the general doctrine of "statistics" [or the knowledge of states], the second part expounds the right rule for governing states properly, and the third, finally, shows what one must know regarding the patrimony, taxation, and the splendor of princes, the latter with the aid of much advice that is good and sound. (142)

Later still, in 1776, Pütter wrote in his *Literatur des teutschen Staatsrechts*,

> This was a man experienced in the affairs of government and of state who, in 1655, at the age of 29, wrote, at the request of his prince, the book entitled Teutscher Fürstenstaat, in which he presented a practical view of what is required for the well-ordered government of a country and what is appropriate for it, especially for the constitution of a German principality.[36]

Rather than consider other testimonies (see Schreber 1733, 143ff, and Ludewig 1753), it is time to analyze the book itself. In the *Dedicatio*, the author depicts the "prudentia gubernandi," "the knowledge through which the kingdoms, principalities and territories are happily governed" in the guise of an "indispensable sun." It represents a sort of *ars artium, scientia scientarum,* or *summa* of practical knowledge that

> encompasses in its amplitude and its generality everything that is in a fragmented state in other sciences . . . it can be compared to a vast sea upon

which discharge the streams of all other forms of knowledge and sciences, and which thus reappears, once again united, throughout all countries, for the common good.

And to highlight the practical character and the specific destination of the knowledge with which he deals, he adds, "They are mad, those who without the company and the favor of this goddess [the art of government] penetrate the secrets of governing."

The most pertinent observations, from the perspective that interests us here, can be found in the "preface to the reader." In it, the author reflects above all on the external and internal reasons that led him to write and publish this treatise. Among the first, we find essentially the request of the duke of Gotha to the young civil servant to provide a description of his principality's concrete situation (*Zustand*).

It is necessary, in this respect, to take into account the fact that Seckendorff's book fits not only into his concrete activity as a civil servant, but also into a complex and precise historical context: the reconstruction of the principality of Gotha undertaken by Ernest the Pious toward the end of the Thirty Years' War (see Patze and Schlesinger 1982, 209–44). Ernest, having acquired power in 1640 as a result of a partition of the Ernestins family territories, immediately began, after having chosen Gotha as his *Residenzstadt*, to reorganize, during the last years of the war, the central administration and to set in order the government of the land that was subjected to the massive depredations of Swedish, French, Bavarian, and Imperial troops until 1647. The duke set out to involve in his government numerous prominent civil servants such as Christoph von Hagen, Johan Christoph Lobhartzberg, and the jurist Strauss. Besides its specifically administrative activity, two traits best characterize the government of the duke and of his civil servants: on one hand, the close collaboration of the central administration with the representatives of the estates (*Landstände*), and on the other the strong Lutheran religious imprint stamped on the land, to which the theologian Salomon Glassius was an important early contributor. The young Seckendorff belonged to the civil service of the principality from 1646 to 1664. It is in the context of this process of reconstruction and rationalization of the principality of Gotha's government undertaken by Ernest the Pious and, in particular, in the context of the reorganization of the land (*Generallandes-*

visitationen) that we must place the preparatory work on which Seckendorff relied to write his treatise.

This set of circumstances, of which we have long been aware, has often resulted in a failure to appreciate the significance of the *Fürstenstaat*. "Its descriptive character," W. Lüdtke wrote in 1939, "gave the work practical value over the following 100 years, and now gives it historical value for the researcher" (Lüdtke 1939, 60). The most extensive—though not the most significant—book devoted to Seckendorff's works bears the telling title *The Small German State of the Seventeenth Century in Light of Seckendorff's "Teutscher Fürstenstaat"* (Krämer 1922–1924). This view of the book seems to me inevitably reductionist and bound to result in the sort of negative appraisal formulated with all the weight of his authority by F. Meinecke in his *Idee der Staatsräson*: "The patriarchal traditions of the territorial state, be they Protestant or Catholic, had for their political principle the force of inertia and quietude, the maintenance of ancient legal principles, and the care taken by local authorities in charge of religion and in charge of the administration of justice; these traditions expressed themselves in the 'Mirror of Princes' type of literature, especially the work of V.L. von Seckendorff, only knew the traditional rights and duties of Christian sovereigns and did not imagine they were creating rights or conquering new powers."[37]

Now, aside from the fact that Meinecke's work today is entirely inadequate for an understanding of political thought in the modern period—particularly with respect to Germany, as noted by B. Croce (1925) and C. Schmitt (1940) in the 1920s and by M. Stolleis more recently (1981)—his statements reflect an outdated conception of modern constitutional history that was elaborated during the nineteenth century based on the model of Prussia's absolutist development. Research by T. Mayer (1964), W. Näf (1951; see also Hartung 1952), and G. Oestreich (1969) has cast some doubt on this model and has rejected its schematic generalization.

Rather than absolutism[38]—which seemingly was imposed upon the estates—and the *Machtpolitik*, the bipartite ellipse (prince and estates) of the *Ständestaat* (Näf 1951), on one hand, and the construction of the modern political unit through religious and military *Sozialdisziplinierung* (Oestreich 1969, in particular "Strukturprobleme des europäischen Absolutismus," 179–97), on the other, today seem to be more characteristic of the political "ideal type" of the early modern period. It is only in the light of this new constitutional history that it is possible to reread the *Teutscher Fürstenstaat* with the hope of dispelling the prejudice and deformations that over time have accumulated concerning this book, in particular following the birth of the doctrine of *Rechtsstaat*.

From the perspective of this project of rereading, it may be appropriate to reverse the question that, from Bluntschli to Meinecke and Hans Maier, has been asked within the German doctrine of the state: why did modern Germany not produce texts like Machiavelli's *The Prince* or Hobbes's *Leviathan*? We instead might ask ourselves why nothing comparable to the *Teutscher Fürstenstaat* was published in England or Italy.

Let us, however, return for a moment to our author's preface. Besides the request made by Duke Ernest, Seckendorff evokes a second—more internal, personal—type of reason that resulted not so much in the book's writing as in its publication. He remarks, "There is insufficient information about these matters." He then proceeds to state negatively the goal of the book: "neither the whole organization of the Empire, nor a general description of either temporal or spiritual government, nor an explanation of royal rights and other similar things." Among the authors who have written on the subject of politics/police (Politik), he points out, "Few are those who have truly taken into consideration the various manifestations of a policy [Polizey] and the way in which, as it were, these modes of existence appear concretely, in real life."

The "Policey," then, is the general theme of the treatise. "Policey" is a term and a concept with a broad and complex significance until the latter decades of the eighteenth century, as noted by S. Kaplan: "'Police' encompasses . . . everything that concerns the public welfare. One could even say that police is the public welfare because police is an end as well as a means, an ideal type as well as the method for achieving it, a concept that is as much political as administrative. As verb, as noun and as adjective, the word is used to describe the manner in which civil and social life ought to be organized" (Kaplan 1979, 17).

Therefore, in Seckendorff's own words, he is not writing "a general politics or a set of specific rules for governing," but rather "the way in which German principalities are usually [*pflegen*] governed and preserved."

These statements have often been understood as an explicit declaration on the part of the author of the descriptive character of his book. Yet, by reading the text a little further, one discovers a significant specification:

> If anyone thought that only some or even none of the German territories were governed according to the description I have presented, despite the fact that here I have been writing not normatively but taking into account the real state of things, he should reflect, without prejudice, on the fact that it is much more useful to know the good of each thing rather than the possible harm that it contains. . . . I have often held my pen during the writing of this treatise and I have resolved to write *as if* I did not find any mistakes within our German governments, *as if* I did not want to substitute my own rule in place of the rule that obtains in reality; may God grant that, thanks to my feeble effort and the moderation I have used, he who has the occasion to read my book may, through the description of good practices, come to know the abuses. (Preface, ¶ 4; emphases mine)

We are now in a position to identify an essential dimension of the book. If we find in Seckendorff's work a renunciation of critique of that which exists, this reflects neither an apolitical and descriptive attitude nor the conditions of censorship under which the words of a seventeenth-century civil servant were published. Rather, in this particular case, it reflects the fact that critique resides in the distance, which from time to time can be perceived by the reader of the treatise, between Seckendorff's thesis of good government ("Gute Policey") on one hand and the practices existing in reality on the other. In other words, the author knows well, when he states, "difficile est Satyras non scribere" (*Teutscher Fürstenstaat*, preface, ¶ 4), that the reality of German principalities represents only a more or less rough approximation of the model described. Yet it is precisely in this "distance" that the meaning and value of the book are found; in other words, it is what makes it a "Politischer Tractat" (*Teutscher Fürstenstaat*, preface, ¶ 2). It is this distance and the relationship with reality that transform his political views into a feasible project.[39]

Neither simple description nor pure prescription, the particular dimension of the *Teutscher Fürstenstaat* is that of the realistically possible, of the "*Was sein kann*" (see Lüdtke 1939, 62).

We cannot take into consideration here—however briefly—all the essential elements that constitute the Seckendorffian model. I will restrict myself to pointing out those that appear to deserve a more thorough examination for purposes of the present inquiry. If we put aside the relation between *landesfürstliche Hoheit* and Empire, on one hand, and the relation between prince and estates, on the other, it seems to me that the material constitution described by Seckendorff in the second part of his treatise ("*Von der Regierung und Verfassung eines Landes und Fürstenthums*") revolves around three pivots:

1.   The territory and *Landsässigkeit*
2.   The figure of the subject
3.   The concept of sovereignty (*Bottmässigkeit* is the German term adopted by Seckendorff)

G. K. Schmelzeisen, in what is certainly the most important contribution to the analysis of the book that interests us here, observed that "the princely state appears in Seckendorff's work as a territorial state. The impact of the prince's power extends over a state area" (Schmelzeisen 1970, 193). This territory is not only the geographic space whose "material description" opens the treatise; it constitutes here the political-juridical milieu where, without being the property of the prince,[40] his power is exercised and applied. The relationships between prince and subjects are not personal ones of a feudal type; they are "mediated" by the territory. The subject is the *Landsässiger*, and he is subject only because he resides on the territory. Sovereignty itself (*Bottmässigkeit*) is exercised over the territory and its inhabitants.

The constitutional structure of the *Fürstenstaat* can be illustrated by a triangle:

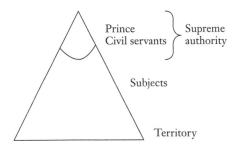

In this sense the *Fürstenstaat* is not the prince's state. Seckendorff is thus very far removed from a patrimonial conception of political power. The *Fürstenstaat* is rather, as Grimm's dictionary has it, "ein von einem Fürsten regierter Staat" (a state governed by a prince) (Grimm and Grimm, col. 880).

We must moreover also take into account that even though the person of the sovereign plays a leading role, it begins to sustain a process of irreversible transformation that brings us back to the central themes of theory and of constitutional history. The prince's government asserts itself more and more as a government of civil servants (see *Teutscher Fürstenstaat*, vol. 2, ¶ ¶ 5, 7, at 82–83), a government, thus, of the administrative machine. And at the same time, the sovereignty—as in Hobbes—tends to transform itself into an "office":

> The government of the territory's prince in the German principalities and territories, as is the case in every system of just and well-ordered police, is nothing but the supreme and eminent sovereignty of a prince who governs the territory legitimately [that is, not after a usurpation] and it is exercised by him over the estates and the subjects of the principality as well as over the territory and what belongs to it in order to achieve and realize the common utility and well-being concerning spiritual and material matters and to administer justice. (*Teutscher Fürstenstaat*, vol. 2, ¶ ¶ 1, 2, at 33)

Whether with a social contract, as in Hobbes, or without it, as in the present case, such is the principle of the *Herrschaft*'s material legitimation. "Oboedientia facit imperantem,"[41] wrote Spinoza. Through the production of well-being (*Wohlfahrtsleistung*), the *oboedientia* transforms itself here into political obligation.

As Jean Calvin put it in *L'institution de la religion chrétienne* (1541), "The Church of God . . . requires a certain spiritual police which is quite different from earthly police" (bk. 4, chap. 2, ¶ 1).

Reinkingk's *politica christiana* appears as the government of God (*göttliches Regiment*). On this point, Knemeyer has observed that

> besides the Aristotelian concept of 'politeia' there appeared another concept with a theological dimension that very closely resembles the Christian doctrine of estates of the late Middle Ages. "Police" here mean the same as the

order of estates [*Ständeordnung*]. This Christian police concept associated with the society of estates, the "description of a Christian police, useful and good" [Friedlieb], manifested itself most clearly in Reinkingk's *Biblische Policey*. (Knemeyer 1978, 883 [s.v. Polizei])

I have in turn sought to show that Reinkingk's "Policey" is something more than a *Ständeordnung*. Beginning with the impossible gamble of elaborating a political theory drawn from the Holy Scriptures (*Biblische Policey*, preface), he manages to identify the first elements in a protostate form of social discipline. Although his book may remain largely inscribed, as illustrated by the frontispiece, in the framework of the doctrine of a society of three estates (*Dreiständegesellschaft*), the organization and form of the "Weltlicher Stand" emerge as the central theme, comprising within the three figures of the prince, the civil servant, and the subject.

In Seckendorff's book, these three segments have become, alongside the territory, the hinges and gears of a machine that functions and acquires a significance of its own. The question that I had asked myself—what is Seckendorff's *Fürstenstaat?*—can now be reformulated in the following way. If the question with which the modern period opens is, as Michel Foucault put it, "How is it possible to govern?" then the answer we find in Seckendorff would be, "Thanks to the political-administrative machine that links sovereignty (the government), subjects and territory, and results in their unity." Ever since, we have called this machine the territorial state, and the *Teutscher Fürstenstaat* was its first systematic treatise. With it begins what we could call, following H. Heller, a social, and not only legal, doctrine of the state.

Notes

1. All translations are mine.
2. On the connection between *Politik* and *Policey* in the seventeenth century, see Justi 1756, ¶ ¶ 1, 2, and 3.
3. Along these lines, see the definitive work by O. Brunner (1964); see also Koselleck 1983.
4. The complete title of the work is *Biblische Policey, das ist: Gewisse auss Heiliger Göttlicher Schrift zusammen gebrachte auff die drey Haupt-Stände, als den Geistlichen, Weltlichen, und Häusslichen, gerichtete Axiomata, oder Schluss-Reden, sonderlich mit biblischen*

Sprüchen und Exempeln, auch andern bestärcket, in allen Ständen nützlich, dienlich und anmuthig zu lesen. Seven editions of this text appeared between 1653 and 1736 (Jöcher 1819, cl. 1726–29). I have used the sixth edition of 1701, subsequently referred to as *Biblische Policey*.

5. The title of the first edition is *Fürsten-Staat.* Twelve subsequent editions of this work appeared, the last one published in Jena in 1754 (Schmelzeisen 1970). There are two recent facsimile editions, one from 1972 and one from 1976. Schmelzeisen also reports a comment by R. Stinzing to the effect that the *Teutscher Fürstenstaat* "was until the 18th century the basis for political instruction at German universities." One finds the same judgment in Ranke 1847 (cited by Stolleis 1977).

6. D. Reinkingk (1590–1664) attended the universities of Cologne and Giessen and was for a brief period "Extraordinary Professor of Roman law, feudal law, and public law" in the latter. It was in Giessen that he began his career as a functionary, under the title of *Hofrat*. This led to the position of vice-chancellor in Marburg, chancellor in Schwerin, and finally, in 1636, as counselor to the archbishop in Bremen. He followed this latter personage when he was called to the throne of Denmark, under the title of Frederick III, and later became chancellor of the duchy of Schleswig-Holstein and, finally, president of the local Oberappellationsgericht (Supreme Court of Appeals) (Link 1977). The only study devoted to the *Biblische Policey* is a dissertation by a student of E. Wolf (Jessen 1962).

7. R. Vierhaus has written in one of his studies on Germany during the absolutist period, "The social system, of which we must speak here, was hierarchically ordered and profoundly characterized by a principle of authority; the economic, political, and cultural power was distributed in such a way that a research which began with ruling groups will have a better chance of capturing reality than a research which would begin 'from below'" (Vierhaus 1978, 52).

8. This appeared in Giessen in 1619 and was reissued numerous times.

9. In Conring's Latin this is known as *prudentia politica* or *prudentia civilis*. On Conring, see Dreitzel 1983 and Willoweit 1977.

10. Author of *Juris Publici Imperii Romano-Germanici*, published in Giessen in 1629 (Hoke 1968).

11. See *Biblische Policey*, preface and bk. 2, axiomata 36–39, pp. 162–212, and *Teutscher Fürstenstaat*, preface: "Nevertheless, I do not want the word 'state' (Staat) to be understood in the manner in which it is generally used today, not wanting to justify any meanness, ignominy and libertinism by referring to words such as 'state', *ratione status* [raison d'état] or 'affairs of state', as is done in certain perverted countries" (5th ed., 1687, unpaginated). On the concept of *ratione status*, see Stolleis 1980a.

12. I am discussing the fifth edition. Even though this frontispiece is not found in the first two editions, it figures almost certainly in the third, published in 1653, prior to Reinkingk's death. A very brief analysis of this frontispiece is provided by Maier (1980, 132), who has some pages devoted to Reinkingk.

13. One statue representing Aaron dressed in this way exists in the palace of the archbishop of Milan.

14. See Lüdtke 1939, 61–62, where he refers to the dedication of the work and suggests, briefly, an interpretation of the false title that is somewhat different from mine here.

15. But see also figure 2.3, where the female image at the bottom left represents Concord.

16. The title continues as follows: Oder: Vorstellung wie Christliche und weise Regenten zur Beförderung ihrer eigenen und ihres Landes Glückseeligkeit ihre Untertanen zu beherrschen pflegen. The author explicitly refers to *Teutscher Fürstenstaat* in the preface to this work. On Julius Bernhard von Rohr (1688–1742), see Small 1909, 185–205.

17. "Wenn ein Regente will des Landes Wolfhart bauen, Mus er auff Gottesfurcht Justiz und Klugheit schauen."

18. The exact title of the work is *Emblematum sacrorum et civilium miscellaneorum, sylloge prior-posterior* (Heidelberg, 1659); on this author, see Stolleis 1983a.

19. The expression is from Link 1977, 81.

20. On Helmstedt and Arnisaeus, see Dreitzel 1970.

21. See note 9.

22. See, e.g., Conring 1970–1973 and 1662, chap. 2. On this point, see Stolleis, 1983b.

23. Link, in "Dietrich Reinkingk", 79. See also the interpretation by H. Jessen: "Beneath the ancient form something new is beginning to stir . . . mysticism is connected in a surprising manner to rationalism. A profound pity is mixed with a sense of realism." *Biblische Polizei*, op. cit., 24–25, n. 6.

24. The activity of governing is here clearly conceived as a public function. This is also the case in *De regimine seculari et ecclesiastico* (by the same author), a work of 1,120 pages in which only 130 deal with ecclesiastical government (Brunner 1963, 95).

25. This is the second of three definitions of "absoluter Verfassungsbegriff" in Schmitt 1928, 4–5.

26. On this problem see Le Goff 1981.

27. I have consulted the sixth edition of 1659 (see Willoweit 1975).

28. See *Biblische Policey*, bk. 1, axioma 34, p. 65: "The clergy should not concern itself with political questions, it ought not to have one foot on the lectern and another in the cabinet [of government]." Similarly, H. Jessen remarks, "The clergy ought not to mix in government affairs" (Jessen 1962, 92).

29. V. L. von Seckendorff (1629–1692), after having studied in Strasbourg with Boecler, began his career as a functionary in Gotha in 1646, in the service of Ernest of Saxony, where he remained until 1664, occupying increasingly important positions, culminating in chancellor. He then entered the service of Maurice of Saxe-Zeit, later becoming Kurbrandenburgischer Geheimrat, and, just before his death,

chancellor of the new university of Halle (see Stolleis 1977; Small 1909, 60–106; Miglio 1957; Schiera 1968, 140ff.; Brückner 1977, 9–32; Schreber 1733).

30. The first German translation was published in Leipzig in 1714, with a second one in Tübingen in 1781–1782. The first Dutch translation was published in Delft in 1728–1730, in three volumes, and finally, a French translation appeared in Basel in 1784–1785.

31. This is underlined by the author himself in the preface to the work.

32. This text is found in Leibniz's correspondence (Leibniz 1938, letter no. 505, pp. 565–67).

33. Republished in 1693 and in 1716.

34. M. Stolleis observes that "in general, the tendency toward a rational organization of the bureaucracy diminished the importance of the confessional problem. The 'police' of the state was secularized. The religious beliefs of the functionaries thus lost much of their importance" (Stolleis 1980b).

35. In *Allerhand bissher publicirte kleine teutsche Schrifften* (Halle, 1701, 547–66, 551): "The *Fürstenstaat*, written in his blooming years, is nothing but a short and well founded dissertation on how the princes of this world and their councilors are to govern wisely and knowledgeably for their own tranquility as well as for the delight of their subjects."

36. Erster Theil, Göttingen, 1776, p. 226: "He thus already was a man of experience in the affairs of state and government when he in 1655, as a 29-year-old, wrote the so-called *Teutscher Fürstenstaat* at the direction of his prince, wherein he provided a very practical concept of that which is required for a well-ordered government of a territory [Land] and in particular is appropriate for the constitution of a German principality."

37. The first edition was published in 1924; the quotation is from p. 124 of the French translation published by Droz, 1973.

38. See the entry "Absolutismus" in Vierhaus 1966.

39. On the theme of practicability in modern German thought, see Pasquino 1982.

40. A refutation of the patrimonial concept of the state is found as early as 1622 in a text by G. E. Löhneyß (Löhneyß 1622).

41. See Heller 1971, 2:57; the citation is from Spinoza 1670.

References

Bornitz, Jakob. 1659. *Emblematum sacrorum et civilium miscellaneorum, sylloge prior-posterior*. Heidelberg: apud Clementem Ammonium.

Brandt, Reinhardt. 1982. Das Titelblatt des Leviathan und Goyas El Gigante. In *Furcht und Freiheit: Leviathan—Diskussion 300 Jahre nach Th. Hobbes*, ed. U. Bermbach and K. M. Kodalle, 203–31. Opladen: Westdeutscher Verlag.

Brückner, Jutta. 1977. *Staatswissenschaften, Kameralismus und Naturrecht: Ein Beitrag zur Geschichte der politischen Wissenschaft im Deutschland des späten 17. und frühen 18. Jahrhunderts.* Munich: Beck.

Brunner, Otto. 1963. Dietrich Reinkingk: Ein Beitrag zum Reichsgedanken des 17. Jahrhunderts. *Jahrbuch der Akademie der Wissenschaften und Literatur*, 94–95.

———. 1964. Moderner Verfassungsbegriff und mittelalterliche Verfassungsgeschichte [1939]. In *Herrschaft und Staat im Mittelalter*, ed. H. Kämpf, 1–19. Darmstadt: H. Gentner.

Brunner, Otto, and Werner Conze, eds. 1978. *Geschichtliche Grundbegriffe. Historisches Lexikon zur politisch-sozialen Sprache in Deutschland.* Stuttgart: E. Klett.

Conring, Hermann. 1662. *De civili prudentia liber unus.* Helmstedt: Typis & sumptibus Henningi Muileri.

———. 1970–1973. Dissertatio de ratione Status [1651]. In *Opera* 4:549–80, ed. W. Göbel. Aalen: Scientia Verlag.

Croce, Benedetto. 1925. *La Critica* 23:50–75.

Dreitzel, Horst. 1970. *Protestantischer Aristotelismus und absoluter Staat: Die "Politica" des Henning Arnisaeus (ca. 1575–1636).* Wiesbaden: F. Steiner.

———. 1983. Hermann Conring und die Politische Wissenschaft seiner Zeit. In *Hermann Conring (1606–1681): Beiträge zu Leben und Werk*, ed. M. Stolleis, 135–72. Berlin: Duncker & Humblot.

Grimm, Jacob, and Wilhelm Grimm, eds. 1878. *Deutsches Wörterbuch.* Vol. 4, part 1, no. 1. Leipzig: S. Hirzel.

Hartung, Fritz. 1952. Herrschaftsverträge und ständischer Dualismus in den deutschen Territorien. In *Schweizer Beiträge zur Allgemeinen Geschichte* 10:163–77.

Heckel, Martin. 1968. *Staat und Kirche nach den Lehren der evangelischen Juristen Deutschlands in der ersten Hälfte des 17. Jahrhunderts (Jus Ecclesiasticum, Bd. 6).* Munich: Claudius-Verlag.

Heller, Hermann. 1971. Politische Demokratie und soziale Homogenität. In *Gesammelte Schriften.* Vol. 2:421–33. Leiden: Sijthoff (first published in *Probleme der Demokratie*, I. Reihe (1928): 35–47).

Hoke, Rudolf. 1968. *Die Reichsstaatsrechtslehre des J. Limnaeus.* Aalen: Scientia Verlag.

Jessen, Hauke. 1962. *"Biblische Policey": Zum Naturrechtsdenken Dietrich Reinkings.* Diss. jur., Freiburg i.B.

Jöcher, Christian Gottlieb. 1819. *Allgemeines Gelehrten-Lexikon, 6. Ergänzungsband.* Bremen: Heyse.

Justi, Johann Heinrich Gottlob von. 1756. *Grundsätze der Policey-Wissenschaft.* Göttingen: A. van den Hoecks.

Kaplan, Steven. 1979. Réflexions sur la police du monde du travail, 1700–1815. *Revue historique* 261:17–77.

Knemeyer, Franz-Ludwig. 1978. Polizei. In *Geschichtliche Grundbegriffe: Historisches Lexikon zur politisch-sozialen Sprache in Deutschland.* Vol. 6, ed. O. Brunner, W. Conze, and R. Koselleck, 875–97. Stuttgart: Klett-Cotta.

Koselleck, Reinhart. 1983. Begriffsgeschichtliche Probleme der Verfassungsge-schichtsschreibung. In *Der Staat. Beiheft* 6:7–21.

Krämer, Horst. 1922–1924. Der deutsche Kleinstaat des 17. Jahrhunderts im Spiegel von Seckendorffs "Teutschem Fürstenstaat." *Zeitschrift des Vereins für Thüringische Geschichte und Altertumskunde, N.F.* 25:1–98.

Le Goff, Jacques. 1981. *La naissance du purgatoire*. Paris: Gallimard.

Leibniz, Gottfried Wilhelm. 1938. *Sämtliche Schriften und Briefe, Erste Reihe: Allgemeiner politischer und historischer Briefwechsel, Dritter Band: 1680–1683*. Leipzig: Preußische Akademie der Wissenschaften.

Link, Christoph. 1977. Dietrich Reinkingk. In *Staatsdenker im 17. und 18. Jahrhundert*, ed. M. Stolleis, 78–79. Frankfurt a.m.: Metzner.

Löhneyß, Georg Engelhard von. 1622. *Aulico-Politica*. Remlingen: Löhneysen.

Ludewig, Johann Peter von, 1753. *Oeconomische Anmerckungen über Seckendorffs Fürsten-Staat*, ed. C. E. Klotz. Frankfurt, Leipzig: Wagner.

Lüdtke, Wilhelm. 1939. V. L. von Seckendorff, ein deutscher Staatsmann und Volkserzieher des 17. Jahrhunderts. *Jahrbücher der Akademie gemeinnütziger Wissenschaften zu Erfurt, N.F.* 54:39–137.

Maier, Hans. 1980. *Die ältere deutsche Staats- und Verwaltungslehre*, 2d ed. Munich: Beck.

Marle, Raimond van. 1932. *Iconographie de l'art profane au Moyen Age et à la Renaissance. II: Allégories et symboles*. The Hague: M. Nijhoff.

Mayer, Theodor. 1964. Die Ausbildung der Grundlagen des modernen deutschen Staates im hohen Mittelalter [1939]. In *Herrschaft und Staat im Mittelalter*, ed. H. Kämpf, 284–316. Darmstadt: H. Gentner.

Miglio, G. 1957. Le Origini della scienza dell'amministrazione. In *Atti del primo convegno di studi di scienza dell'amministrazione (1955)*, 20–34. Milan: Giuffrè.

Näf, Werner. 1951. Frühformen des "modernen Staates" im Spätmittelalter. *Historische Zeitschrift* 171:225–43.

Oestreich, Gerhard. 1969. *Geist und Gestalt des frühmodernen Staates: Ausgewählte Aufsätze*. Berlin: Duncker & Humblot.

———. 1976. Policey und Prudentia civilis in der barocken Gesellschaft von Stadt und Staat. In *Stadt, Schule, Universität, Buchwesen und die deutsche Literatur im 17. Jahrhundert*, ed. A. Schöne, 10–21. Munich: Beck.

———. 1980. *Verfassungsgeschichte vom Ende des Mittelalters bis zum Ende des alten Reiches*. Munich: Deutscher Taschenbuch Verlag.

Pasquino, Pasquale. 1982. L'utopia praticabile: Governo ed Economia nel cameralismo tedesco del' 700. *Quaderni della Fondazione G. G. Feltrinelli* 20.

———. 1986. Politisches und historisches Interesse: "Statistik" und historische Staatslehre bei Gottfried Achenwall (1719–1772). In *Aufklärung und Geschichte: Studien zur deutschen Geschichtswissenschaft im 18. Jahrhundert*, ed. H. E. Bödeker et al., 144–68. Göttingen: Vandenhoeck & Ruprecht.

Patze, H., and W. Schlesinger, eds. 1982. *Geschichte Thüringens*. Vol. 5: *Politische Geschichte in der Neuzeit, I. Teil. I. Teilband*. Cologne: Böhlau.

Praz, Mario. 1964. *Studies in seventeenth-century imagery*. Vol. 2: *A bibliography of emblems books*, 2d ed. Rome: Edizioni di storia e letteratura.

Pütter, Johann Stephan. 1776. *Literatur des teutschen Staatsrechts, Erster Theil*. Göttingen: Verlag der Witwe Vandenhoek.

Ranke, Leopold von. 1847. *Neun Bücher preußischer Geschichte*. Berlin: Veit und Co.

Reau, Louis. 1956. *L'iconographie de l'art chrétien*. Vol. 2: *Iconographie de la Bible, l'Ancien Testament*. Paris: Presses universitaires de France.

Reinkingk, Dietrich. 1632. *De regimine seculari et ecclesiastico*. Marburg: Typis & sumptibus N. Hampelii.

Ripa, Cesare. 1764–1767. *Iconologia* [1593], ed. C. Orlandi. Perugia.

Schiera, Pierangelo. 1968. *Il cameralismo e l'assolutismo tedesco: Dall'arte di governo alle scienze dello Stato*. Milan: Giuffré.

Schmelzeisen, Gustav Klemens. 1970. *Der verfassungsrechtliche Grundriss*. In V. L. von Seckendorff's "Teutschem Fürstenstaat." *Zeitschrift der Savigny-Stiftung für Rechtsgeschichte (Germ. Abt.)* 87:190–223.

Schmitt, Carl. 1928. *Verfassungslehre*. Munich, Leipzig: Duncker & Humblot.

———. 1940. Zu F. Meineckes "Idee der Staatsräson" [1926]. In *Positionen und Begriffe im Kampf mit Weimar-Genf-Versailles, 1923–1939*, 45–52. Hamburg: Hanseatische Verlagsanstalt.

———. 1972. *Le categorie del "politico,"* ed. G. Miglio and P. Schiera. Bologna: Il Mulino.

Schreber, Daniel Gottfried. 1733. *Historia vitae ac meritorum perillustris quondam domini, Domini Viti Ludovici a Seckendorff*. Leipzig: In Officina Brauniana.

Small, Albion W. 1909. *The Cameralists: The pioneers of German social polity*. Chicago: University of Chicago Press.

Spinoza, Benedictus de. 1670. *Tractatus theologico-politicus*.

Stolleis, Michael. 1977. V. L. von Seckendorff. In *Staatsdenker im 17. und 18. Jahrhundert*, ed. M. Stolleis, 148–71. Frankfurt a.M.: Metzner.

———. 1980a. *Arcana imperii und Ratio status: Bemerkungen zur politischen Theorie des frühen 17. Jahrhunderts*. Göttingen: Vandenhoeck & Ruprecht.

———. 1980b. Grundzüge der Beamtenethik, 1550–1650. *Die Verwaltung* 13: 447–75.

———. 1981. Friedrich Meinecke: Die Idee der Staatsräson und die neuere Forschung. In *Friedrich Meinecke heute*, ed. M. Erbe, 50–75. Berlin: Colloquium Verlag.

———. 1983a. Jacob Bornitz. In *Pecunia nervus rerum: Zur Staatsfinanzierung in der frühen Neuzeit*. Frankfurt a.M.: V. Klostermann.

———. 1983b. Machiavellismus und Staatsräson: Ein Beitrag zu Conrings politischem Denken. In *Hermann Conring (1606–1681): Beiträge zu Leben und Werk*, ed. M. Stolleis, 173–99. Berlin: Duncker & Humblot.

Vierhaus, R. 1966. Absolutismus. In *Sowjetsystem und demokratische Gesellschaft*. Vol. 1, cols. 17–37. Freiburg Basel, Vienna: Herder.

———. 1978. *Deutschland im Zeitalter des Absolutismus (1648–1763)*. Göttingen: Vandenhoeck & Ruprecht.

Willoweit, Dietmar. 1975. *Rechtsgrundlagen der Territorialgewalt: Landesobrigkeit, Herrschaftsrechte und Territorium in der Rechtswissenschaft der Neuzeit*. Cologne: Böhlau.

———. 1977. Hermann Conring. In *Staatsdenker im 17. und 18. Jahrhundert*, ed. M. Stolleis, 129–47. Frankfurt a.M.: Metzner.

CHAPTER THREE

"Peace, Order, and Good Government"

Policelike Powers in Postcolonial Perspective

MARIANA VALVERDE

Like England, Canada officially disavows the specific legal entity known in the United States as the police power. Searching Canadian legal databases for "police power" turns up only decisions on the powers of the uniformed police to detain, search, and seize; and a widely used textbook in Canadian constitutional law, Peter Hogg's *Constitutional Law of Canada*, has no entry for "police power."

The very absence from Canadian law of a specific jurisprudence of the "police power" can be, somewhat paradoxically, a resource both for research and for theory—and not only for Canadians. The fact that one cannot quickly turn to a particular chapter in legal textbooks to obtain an answer to the question, If Canada, like England, does not have a "police power," what does it have instead? is initially frustrating. However, examining the legal and political history of Canada from the standpoint of police science and police power and being forced to go outside black-letter legal doctrine given the dearth of case law has uncovered some stories that, apart from having some intrinsic interest, shed new light on the perennial historiographical and theoretical questions about power flows in contemporary liberal states and about the not yet fully mapped legacies of colonialism.

The postcolonial theme may seem odd, since police science emerged as a specifically domestic, intrastate knowledge, as Neocleous's contribution to this volume (chapter 1) and other literature clearly show. When beginning to do research for this chapter, I certainly did not anticipate being drawn into the field of British colonial law. But colonial technologies for governing colonies, states, provinces, and aboriginal groups turn out to be intertwined in a variety of complex ways with other more or less paternalist legal and political technologies used to promote what eighteenth-century police science called "the general welfare." Thus, while my original aim was to investigate the fortunes of governmental powers to regulate economic and social life in the Canadian polity with a view to providing some comparative insights for this volume, the research showed that much can be learned if one refuses to take the distinction between the domestic and the international as given.

Historians of the British Empire have told us that officials and governors traveled frequently from London to far-flung colonies and then to other colonies: but theorists of legal processes and of national political cultures have yet to fully analyze the significance and the effects, at home and abroad, of this constant flow of legal and political techniques and innovations across oceans and across institutions. To this end, I will take an admittedly partial look at a contemporary non-Canadian case—a lawsuit, decided by an English court of Queen's Bench in 2001, undertaken by the exiled inhabitants of Diego Garcia against the British government. It turns out that, despite the huge geographic and sociolegal differences separating Ottawa from the U.S. military base on the island in the Indian Ocean that is now Diego Garcia, there are only two legal degrees of separation between the exile of the islanders and the development of a distinctly Canadian political culture. Political doctrines and legal technologies presented to Canadians as unique to Canada's "civilized" system of government (especially the peace, order, and good government powers given to the federal government under the British North America Act [BNA Act]) are, unbeknownst to Canadian constitutional experts, flexible colonial technologies with the continuing capacity to perform and justify highly illiberal state actions elsewhere in the world—as well as in Canada. The substantive analysis of what I call "police-type" powers (a deliberately ambiguous but in this context appropriate term) leads me to some still-tentative general thoughts about the way political and legal powers, including illiberal coercive powers, instead of competing in a zero-sum game, in which power is assumed to go down in one container as an automatic result of the level of power going up in another linked container, sometimes proliferate, multiply, incite, and feed off one another.

Methodologically, this paper is designed to show that one need not abandon research on legal texts to generate nonlegalistic analysis. In the work of mapping police-type knowledges of disorder and risk and the corresponding police-type powers exercised by a variety of state bodies, it is possible to focus on legal texts and to be concerned about such "legalistic" issues as the structure of judicial review, but nevertheless write one's analysis with a view to illuminating not "law" in its formal sense but rather the flows, exchanges, and transformations of knowledge and power that are the lifeblood of both "high" law and everyday law enforcement.[1] Such dynamic analyses hold promise not only for sociolegal scholarship but more generally for those interested in going beyond zero-sum and static models of knowledge and power forms.

Playing Billiards after 7 p.m.: Canadian Federalism and Police Regulations

Despite the somewhat centralist character of the governmental architecture created by the 1867 BNA Act, political scientists have pointed out that Canada is unusual, comparatively, in that the provinces have experienced a growth in autonomy rather than a diminution throughout the twentieth century (Panitch 1977). Health care, education, social assistance, most natural resources, liquor and beer sales, and, most importantly, "property and civil rights" are within provincial jurisdiction. While the criminal law is federal, provinces have their own system of private law, with the province of Quebec using a civilian rather than a common-law system. This peculiar bilegalism is rooted in the historic settlement of the long-standing war between England and France in 1763, a settlement by which the British flag was planted in Quebec (formerly the capital of New France) but with assurances that neither the Catholic Church nor French civil law would be replaced.

One of the very few Canadian constitutional cases to explicitly mention the police power concept (*Hodge v. The Queen* 1883) saw the Judicial Committee of the Privy Council (JCPC)—until 1949 the supreme authority on

Canadian constitutional law—uphold provincial liquor licensing law, which at that time gave municipalities control over licenses and over the conditions attached to licenses. The case arose when a tavernkeeper in Toronto, Mr. Hodge, decided to challenge the power of the local license commissioners. The local authorities had not only drawn up detailed liquor sale regulations—in keeping with municipal police regulations everywhere in the Protestant world—but had also decreed that if liquor could not be sold in the tavern after 7 p.m. on a Saturday, then neither could customers play billiards, even though Mr. Hodge had a separate municipal license to operate and rent out a billiard table (just one).

It is perhaps characteristic of the sledgehammer-against-fly logic of the police power, visible in many of the papers in this volume, that the operation, after liquor-selling hours, of a solitary billiard table at the Toronto Saint James Hotel caused legal ripples to travel all the way across the ocean. These ripples resulted in Lord FitzGerald, Sir Barnes Peacock, Sir Robert Collier, Sir Richard Couch, and Sir Arthur Hobhouse gathering as the JCPC to rule on three questions: (1) whether Canadian provinces had the right to regulate liquor sales—given that the federal government had and still has, under the BNA Act, the power to regulate all commerce, including "the liquor traffic"; (2) whether the provinces, if they did have such a power, could delegate it wholly to municipalities; and (3) whether the power to regulate liquor sales, even if legally exercised by municipalities, could be used to regulate not only drinking but also the phenomenologically and legally distinct action of billiard playing.

American scholars familiar with the "slaughterhouse cases" and other police power law (see chapter 4) will recognize the *Hodge* case as a classic police power one. So did the JCPC, despite the absence of specific common-law precedents. The lords asserted, without any references to previous case law, that "the liquor trade, like all other trades, is subject to local regulation for purposes of police" (120) and that "regulations in the nature of police or municipal regulations of a local character for the good government of taverns etc., licensed for the sale of liquors by retail, are calculated to preserve, in the municipality, peace and public decency" (131). The fact that the federal government has exclusive jurisdiction over intraprovincial trade and international commerce was thus deemed irrelevant. The sale of liquor at the Saint James Hotel was not being regulated qua commerce, the judges stated, but qua source of potential disorder. It was thus permissible for the license commissioners—a municipal body, but one created by provincial statute—to govern billiard playing indirectly, specifically, through its link to alcohol (cf. Valverde 1998, 2003). Billiard playing elsewhere could perhaps still proceed of a Saturday evening; but at the Saint James Hotel, the playing of billiards was legally hardwired to drinking and its disorders. The license commissioners were thus acting lawfully when using the liquor license as a tool to prohibit the otherwise innocuous—and independently licensed—activity of billiard playing. The court concluded that the commissioners charged with managing liquor and its disorders were not exceeding their jurisdiction, since they "do not attempt to regulate billiard tables; it is as liquor licensee not as billiard licensee that the appellant is required to close his billiard saloon" (120).

The case was then and still is taken to mean that provinces have the kind of jurisdiction, under the "property and civil rights" clause of the 1867 BNA Act that U.S. states have under the doctrine of police power. This was confirmed a few years later by Lord Watson in the *Local Prohibition Case* (1896).[2]

And yet, because the authority being challenged by Mr. Hodge was, on the front line, that of the local license commissioners, not that of the provincial government, the case also sheds light on the way Canadian provinces, like U.S. states, are able to empower and sometimes compel municipalities to undertake the micromanagement of urban spaces and activities considered as potentially disorderly—but without thereby giving up any of their own powers.

We shall see later that this is illustrative of a more general feature of contemporary political governance. The empowering of lower levels of government—from Indian bands to municipalities—to govern certain disorders and risks is best described as a multiplication or proliferation of power rather than as a giving up of power by the higher authority. There are important theoretical implications involved in the fact that, in addition to the extensive "power of promoting the public welfare by restraining and regulating the use of liberty and property" (Freund 1904, iii) wielded by the provinces, municipalities in Canada exercise the same kind of regulatory powers enjoyed by local government in the United Kingdom and municipalities in the United States, but that they can do so only as empowered by the provinces. Nuisance law, zoning, business licensing, the granting of permits for use of public spaces, animal control, urban parks bylaws, public health inspection, trash disposal, and the regulation of both private-vehicle traffic and public transport are only some of myriad municipal functions. And yet, minor changes in the use of municipal legal technologies often require provincial government approval, in many cases involving a change in the provincial statutes constituting and regulating municipal powers.

Thus, any study of the genealogy and current features, in Canada, of the sort of governance undertaken under the banner of the police power in other countries can only begin by noting that the governmental power to ensure the "people's welfare" (Novak 1996), by preemptive coercive measures if necessary, is dispersed and uncoordinated and often shows a logic of multiplication. While most Canadians imagine that provinces have less power if municipalities gain this or that legal power, and they also assume that the federal government is giving up some of its colonial powers if Indian bands obtain the right to govern their own health care, close examination reveals that empowerment is not a zero-sum game. The multiplication and the dispersion of policelike powers are simultaneously facilitated and obscured from view by the fact that the future-oriented government of order and disorder is not named in law as "the police power."

"Some Few Tarzans or Men Fridays": Peace, Order, and Good Government in Canada and in the Empire

One of the keystones of the Canadian constitution, section 91 of the BNA Act—the act that brought into being most of the components of the contemporary postcolonial Canadian state—states that the monarch has the full power to legislate, on the advice and consent of the Canadian Parliament, to ensure "peace, order and good government in Canada." (Interestingly, from the police science point of view, some French-language constitutional texts use the term "administration" as a translation of "good government.")

These so-called POGG powers, held exclusively by the federal government, are not specifically enumerated. (In that regard they are similar, in form, to the U.S. police power.) Courts have understood these powers as covering (a) extraordinary measures to deal with emergencies, such as "apprehended insurrection"; and (b) areas of regulatory activity not specifically allocated to the provinces—such as atomic energy, some labor relations, offshore minerals, and illegal drugs.

As is the case with U.S. police powers, POGG powers are largely residual, which means that their specific content has been determined by a combination of case law and federal statutes rather than by explicit constitutional texts. Comparatively, it is very important that the Canadian version of federalism—unlike the U.S. and Australian versions—assigns to the federal government all residual powers: indeed, some commentators have gone as far as to say that Canada is not truly federal because the central government did not arise out of a kind of social contract among the existing colonies, but was created, at the same time that provinces were also created, by an imperial act (Kennedy 1922, 408–9).

The POGG powers granted to the federal government by the constitution are therefore arguably related to the U.S. police power, among other reasons because they are both rooted in the venerable paternalistic logic of governance most famously outlined by Blackstone (Dubber 2005; Novak 1996). For that reason, and because the form of POGG powers is also discretionary and residual rather than specified, they can be said to be policelike. But in internal Canadian legal and political practice, they have been used more to uphold and reconstruct sovereignty than to further the logic of economy, domestic order, and efficiency developed by eighteenth-century writers on police science (Foucault 1991; Pasquino 1991).[3]

For example, wage and price controls imposed by the federal government in 1975 were said by the courts to be constitutional under the POGG clause: but these were presented as temporary measures made necessary by abnormally high inflation construed as a national emergency. The controls were not presented as routine regulatory measures similar to the eighteenth-century assize of bread. And, to cite another key twentieth-century case about how to interpret the POGG clause, the federal government, in its efforts to address the Great Depression, had to fight hard before the JCPC—until 1949 the highest court of appeal for Canada—to obtain the power to institute national unemployment insurance. The 1940 Unemployment Insurance Act was intended by the Mackenzie King government as part of a broad program to create a welfare state (Struthers 1983); but in the end it turned out to be an almost unique event, since public health insurance and all other social programs other than veterans' pensions and mothers' allowances developed and remain under the control of the provinces. Indeed, the 1867 BNA Act had to be amended (in Westminster) to enable Ottawa to put in place unemployment insurance.

The twentieth-century trend favoring provincial governments as key sites of social policy and policelike regulation was partly a matter of internal Canadian politics, but it was also greatly facilitated by the fact that, for reasons of their own, the JCPC, from the 1890s onward, tended to side with the provinces in matters involving jurisdictional disputes. The leading member of the JCPC in the 1910s and 1920s, Lord Haldane, took the position that the POGG powers were in Canada solely national emergency powers. Everyday police powers, the lords insisted, were provincial. While this—as we saw in the case of federal unemployment insurance—changed somewhat during World War II, and while federal governments have been able to wield much regulatory power by waving the carrots and sticks of federal block grants to provinces, nevertheless, we can conclude that the POGG clause has served primarily to transfer some of the imperial government's military logics and emergency powers to Ottawa and only secondarily to exercise what Foucault would call biopolitical power.

If the POGG powers are a central element in Canadian constitutional law, they also lead another life in Canadian political culture. Recently, noted Canadian intellectual Michael Ignatieff, professor of human rights at Harvard University and now a federal Liberal member of parliament (and whose father, George Ignatieff, was a prominent Canadian diplomat), gave a speech for the Department of External Affairs in Ottawa invoking what is a cliché of Canadian political culture: namely, the idea that Americans are devoted to life, liberty, and the pursuit of happiness; the French are devoted to liberty, equality, and fraternity; and Canadians are, by contrast, devoted to peace, order, and good government. Few Canadians can give the exact reference for the POGG phrase, but most are familiar with it and see it as expressing the distinctly Canadian approach to political relations. Acknowledging that the pursuit of happiness is also worthwhile ("but when we want happiness, we go to Florida," he quipped), Ignatieff went on to develop a grandiose rationale for a new international-ordering body that would be led by Canadians and would take peace, order, and good government—rather than either liberty or happiness—as its mission statement. This body of specialized personnel would help failed states build up good institutions, presumably better than the Americans have been doing. And it would have some real power to bring about good government: elsewhere in the speech he remarked that international aid is worse than useless unless the recipient states have received the Canadian seal of approval, a statement that suggests that this international POGG police or POGG-keepers body would have sticks as well as carrots at its disposal (Ignatieff 2004).

Ignatieff's ambitious plan for a Canadian-led state-ordering force is his own, one that has not been taken up by any arm of the Canadian government as far as I know: but his view of the meaning of the POGG phrase is widely shared. In general, we Canadians think of ourselves as more conciliatory, more orderly, more respectful of authority, and less litigious and less individualist than Americans. That mythical distinction between the two otherwise culturally similar states is often seen as crystallized in the two constitutional phrases highlighted by Ignatieff (liberty and the pursuit of happiness versus peace, order, and good government).

British colonial law shows, however, that POGG is not, contrary to Ignatieff's claim, distinctively Canadian. It is actually a fixture of British colonial law, found in constitutional documents across the former British Empire. In that broader context, it is a legal technology enabling very great and highly discretionary powers, first for the imperial sovereign and then for the subsequent government—of the colony or of the postcolony—to which the sovereign delegates or grants the POGG power.

According to twentieth-century JCPC decisions (*Ibralebbe v. The Queen* 1964; *Liyanage v. The Queen* 1967; *Winfat Enterprises v. Attorney General of Hong Kong* 1985), "The words 'peace, order, and good government' connote, in British constitutional language, the widest law-making powers appropriate to a sovereign" (*Ibralebbe*, 923). The *Liyanage* case, for instance, had been a challenge to a Ceylon law that removed procedural rights in the case of certain kinds of criminal prosecutions and even abolished that keystone of the common law, the right to be criminally tried by a jury. The JCPC found that trials without jury offended against Ceylon's written constitution: but they upheld the right of the Ceylon parliament to pass pretty much any laws it wanted within the broad parameters of its own constitution. This and the other decisions all speak of POGG in positively Hobbesian terms.

Interestingly, from a Canadian perspective, a key precedent for many of these decisions was the 1885 appeal to the JCPC in regard to the treason conviction of the noted Canadian aboriginal leader Louis Riel. The process involved in Riel's conviction and death sentence was full of arbitrary government action—including the use of a six-person rather than twelve-person jury and the removal of the trial to a more government-friendly town in another province—and Riel's lawyers challenged both the process and the treason law itself. The JCPC denied leave to appeal, stating that both treason law and the procedure used to convict (and later hang) Riel might well be at odds with the common law of England but that the Canadian Parliament had the right to be the sole judge of what is in fact necessary for the "peace, order, and good government" of Canada. The POGG words, Lord Halsbury stated, "are apt to authorize the utmost discretion. . . . They are words under which the widest departure from criminal procedure as it is known and practiced in this country have been authorized in Her Majesty's Indian Empire" (*Riel v. The Queen* 1885). In keeping with this, as recently as 2000 a Queen's Bench judge hearing a colonial-law case (about which more later), who as a regular judge and not a JCPC member could not overturn established colonial law, stated as an unmovable fact that "the authorities demonstrate beyond the possibility of argument that a colonial legislature empowered to make law for the peace, order, and good government of its territory is the sole judge of what those considerations factually require" (*The Queen [Bancoult] v. Foreign and Commonwealth Office* 2001, 1103).

Postcolonial legal scholars have documented at great length how subjects of the British crown in various latitudes were subjected to all manner of coercive mechanisms by imperial officials. What is interesting, however, about the JCPC decisions regarding POGG powers is that they do not involve imperial officials but rather postcolonial national legislatures. In a move in keeping with Nasser Hussain's argument about how English imperial rule, including liberal as well as coercive legal mechanisms, shaped many features of current Pakistani "emergency" law (Hussain 2003), in these texts the illiberal mechanisms of rule associated with Empire are literally transferred to the emerging governments. Of course, many local elites were busy trying to accumulate power for themselves under the mantle of nationalism, as the subaltern-studies literature has shown; but what is much less known is that this process of creating new forms of domination was also undertaken, independently, by English judges. The judges no doubt believed that they were helping the "young" nations within the Empire and Commonwealth become autonomous and mature. But in authorizing the government of Canada to hang Riel without due process, and later using that as precedent to authorize the government of Ceylon to remove the right to trial by jury from certain criminal offenders, English judges were arguably promoting the continued effectiveness of colonial coerciveness by enveloping old colonial legal tools in a more or less nationalist container. In Canada this is not as evident as, say, in Pakistan, given the JCPC's curious regard for provincial powers. But in nonfederal centralized states the POGG powers are not so circumscribed.

The devolution of coercive illiberal powers to postcolonial legislatures did not, however, imply the end of the Colonial Office's reign. Creating new powers in postcolonial parliaments does not by itself reduce the power of Westminster or the power of colonial officials. A striking instance of the continuing existence of the Empire in the 1960s and 1970s is found in the re-cently revealed story of how officials in London—officials no longer called "colonial"—developed a legal strategy for forcibly removing the whole pop-ulation of the Chagos archipelago, whose main island is Diego Garcia (see *Bancoult* 2001, 1067; Tomkins 2001; Mahmoud 2003). The officials first split off the archipelago from the newly independent state of Mauritius, paying the government of Mauritius three million pounds (but paying nothing to the inhabitants) and coming up with the name of "British Indian Ocean Territory" (BIOT) for the new entity. The sole purpose of doing this was to hand the new territory over to the United States for military purposes. Then they devised various ways to empty the islands of people over a period of a few years (even though the U.S. military had not explicitly requested that the territory they wanted to lease needed to be *terra nullius*). The island of Diego Garcia not having health and other services, the inhabitants regularly traveled to other islands, and the British government simply cancelled boat service back to the archipelago on a number of occasions—thus stranding people, mainly in Mauritius but some also in the Seychelles. The last remain-ing inhabitants were forcibly removed from the BIOT in 1971 and dumped in Mauritius, whose government apparently did not object (possibly because Mauritius has made a claim to sovereignty over the archipelago).

The legal basis for this action was said to be found in a section of the BIOT Order (a quasi-constitutional document) that allowed the Commis-sioner of the BIOT—an official in London—to "make laws for the peace, order, and good government of the territory." This clause meant that the

Commissioner in the Foreign and Commonwealth office had as much power to decide what factually constituted order and good government for the hapless inhabitants of Diego Garcia and the other tiny islands as the Canadian Parliament had to institute a procedure for a treason trial in conflict with the common law. Indeed, the Commissioner had quite a bit more power than the legislature of Canada, or even the legislature and the Canadian federal executive combined. This is because Canada is regarded in colonial law as a "colony of settlement" (despite the historical fact that New France was ceded to England in 1763), not a colony of conquest or what English law calls a "ceded colony." Colonies of settlement—white colonies, basically—are thought to have become permeated with English legal principles and procedures, unlike conquered or ceded colonies, in which more despotic methods for governing the population are taken to be justified.

Some decades after their expulsion, the former Diego Garcia islanders, known as the Ilois people, managed to get a senior English barrister to take the government to court on their behalf, with a Mr. Bancoult being the official complainant. The judge hearing the case in 2000, the aptly named Justice Laws, faced with a mountain of Colonial Office documents showing blatant racism in the British government as well as blatant official disregard both for Parliament and for UN rules applying to colonial powers, was clearly sympathetic to the islanders. His lengthy decision reproduces many excerpts from internal government letters and memos that are absolutely embarrassing for both the Wilson and the Heath governments, excerpts that do not serve much of a legal purpose but which have a rather damning political effect. To cite just one example, Justice Laws quotes from a 1966 note by Permanent Under-Secretary of the Colonial Office, Paul Gore-Booth: "We must surely be very tough about this. The object of the exercise was to get some rocks which will remain ours; there will be no indigenous population except seagulls, who have not yet got a committee (the Status of Women committee does not cover the rights of birds)" (*Bancoult*, 1083). Justice Laws then quotes the reply to this note by another official: "Unfortunately along with the birds go some few Tarzans or Men Fridays whose origins are obscure, and who are being hopefully wished on to Mauritius etc."

While distancing himself from the Men-Fridays discourse, Justice Laws was nevertheless obliged to admit that the Magna Carta's section prohibiting governments from exiling their own peoples—one of the few legal texts that the Ilois people could use—did not apply in the BIOT. Few lawyers today would think of resorting to the Magna Carta; but it so happens that there is a prohibition against monarchs sending their subjects into exile in this hallowed document. However, the judge decided—probably quite correctly—that, like other British constitutional documents and principles, Magna Carta applies only to colonies of settlement, not ceded colonies. (Relevant colonial case law repeats the rather ambiguous statement that the "Magna Carta follows the flag," but in practice this seems to have been taken to mean that the rights of the English apply only in colonies settled by a large number of them.) Thus, the prohibition against exile contained in Magna Carta did not apply. And to make matters worse, one of the very few legally effective phrases in the short text of the BIOT Order was that the Commissioner of the BIOT was empowered to make laws for the "peace, order, and good government" of the BIOT. Therefore, Laws concluded, in a statement I have partially already quoted, that "the authorities demonstrate beyond the possibility of argument that a colonial legislature empowered to make law for the *peace, order, and good government* of its territory is the sole judge of what those considerations factually require. It is not obliged to respect precepts of the common law, or English traditions of fair treatment. This conclusion marches with the cases on the Colonial Laws Validity Act of 1865" (*Bancoult*, 1104).

But in a desperate attempt to distance himself and the English judiciary from the embarrassing comments about Tarzans surreptitiously dispatched to Mauritius, Justice Laws decided that even the despotic rule that English law allows in places like the BIOT—a despotic rule that the *Bancoult* decision actually confirms—presupposes that there are some subjects to be ruled. He concluded,

> Section 4 of the [BIOT] Ordinance effectively exiles the Ilois from the territory where they are belongers and forbids their return. But the "peace, order, and good government" of any territory means nothing, surely, save by reference to the territory's population. They are to be governed; not removed. . . . The people may be taxed . . . laws will criminalize some of the things they do; maybe they will be tried with no juries, and subject to severe brutal penalties; the laws made for their marriages, their property, and much besides may be far different from what obtains in England. . . . [But] I entertain considerable doubt whether the prerogative power extends so far as to permit the Queen in Council to exile her subjects from the territory where they belong. (1104–5)

However embarrassing to past and present British government officials, then, the *Bancoult* decision is hardly a major statement of equality rights. Indeed, the decision admits, somewhat regretfully, that the hapless ex-inhabitants of the archipelago have extremely limited rights, given that the territory from which they were expelled happened to be a ceded colony, and was, in addition, one without a legislature or a constitution or any other potential resource for rights claimants. In the end, the dispossessed Ilois are said to be unable to exercise most of the rights that British citizens take for granted; the only point granted to Bancoult and his people is that, in a chilling example of English legal understatement, the judge expresses "considerable doubt" about the legality of a government order permanently exiling people who had engaged in no treason or even any misdemeanor.

And indeed, when Bancoult and his friends tried to follow up on Justice Laws's decision striking down the original exile order to seek monetary compensation and the right to at least visit their former home, they were unsuccessful. As of this writing, the U.S. government has stated that they will allow the Ilois to visit, only temporarily, the minor islands in the archipelago but not Diego Garcia, the one that most of them came from, which is currently a U.S. military base on land leased from the British government. The British government seems unwilling to reconsider the lease or otherwise press the matter (Harwood, 2002).[4]

Colonial Governmentality and the Queen in Right of Canada

If the police power is, as Dubber's work has shown, intimately connected with the monarch's power to order his kingdom as fathers order their households, it makes sense in a collection on the police power to reflect on how devolving the paternal power to order the national household to emerging democratic nation-states has not necessarily brought about an end to monarchical rule, in Canada at any rate. Now, the royal prerogative that was used to bring into being the BIOT as an illiberally governed colony and was then used to empty that territory of people takes a different form in Canada. This is mainly because Canada has its own legislature and its own courts. But just as the POGG phrase has been shown to link situations and polities that seem worlds apart, so too the monarch, specifically the English monarch, continues to link and bond a variety of despotic and democratic regimes and to exercise certain ordering effects not only in those territories that are still colonies but even in independent states such as Canada.

American and French visitors to Canada often ask, "Why is Canada still a monarchy?" And Australians ask, "Why is there no republican movement in Canada?" In response, most Canadians speak about respect for authority, deference, and so forth, along the lines of the Ignatieff speech previously mentioned.

But instead of invoking a Canadian deferential culture to explain paternalist legal and political techniques, I think it is much more useful to continue the sketch of colonial governmentality and its fortunes on Canadian soil.

Why colonial "governmentality"? "Governmentality" here refers not to a set of beliefs but to a toolbox of governing technologies and institutional habits that emerged in the context of modern state formation but that are not monopolized or even invented by state actors (Foucault 1991; Dean 1999; Rose 1999). To speak of a "colonial governmentality" thus refers to certain techniques of governance—some liberal, some illiberal—that, whether invented by colonial officials or by extrastate actors, became part of the toolbox of governing tools available for the governance of European empires. The fact that London constantly transferred officials and governors from India to Jamaica to Canada, and from the colonial service to other state bodies, facilitated the rapid recycling of a whole range of governmental techniques. Legal techniques used to govern both white and nonwhite colonial populations proved to be mobile and very flexible (e.g., Hussain 2003; Karsten 2003). More studies of particular colonial and postcolonial settings are necessary before one can generalize about the effects of colonialism on the legal systems of various Anglophone nations; but provisionally, the brief historical sketch that follows concludes that although multiculturalism and liberal rights are certainly very important features of the Canadian state, multicultural liberalism [5] has not displaced, but has been added on top of, a governing structure that is still colonial both internally and externally. To summarize briefly the key findings of the historical sketch that follows, it can be said that, internally, Ottawa (a) succeeded to the imperial government's paternal power over aboriginal peoples, and also (b) inherited other colonial mechanisms, e.g., the power of "disallowing" provincial statutes.

These two legal avenues for internal colonialism are connected to and supported by the more visible remnants of Empire—the most visible of these being of course the monarch, whose face is featured on every coin and banknote in Canada, on most stamps, and in every post office and school. While in official discourse the head of state is known as the Queen of Canada (or the Queen "in right of Canada," as federal government documents obscurely put it), she is nevertheless the same person—though possibly not the same sole corporation, to use Frederick Maitland's categories (Maitland 2003, 45)—as the Queen of England. This is worth reflecting upon, however briefly.

The persistence of the monarchy into the present is an indication of something more than Anglo-Saxon nostalgia. There are many reasons for the notable lack of republican agitation in Canada (by contrast with Australia). But part of the answer lies in something that is geographically specific to the North American continent, something that worried British colonial authorities in the 1830s and worries Canadian cultural nationalists today: the ever-recurring fear that a geographically absurd state, the vast majority of whose population is much closer to U.S. markets than to the rest of Canada, may cease to exist, given a continent utterly dominated by a superpower. That this superpower happens to be a republic is more crucial for the preservation of the monarchy in Canada than any internal factor, in my view. It is notable in this regard that Canadian left-wing nationalists who are not particularly keen on the monarchy also share the English view about the evils of U.S.-style republicanism and are more likely to denounce reform proposals that seem to copy the United States (e.g., parliamentary oversight of Supreme Court appointments) than to raise the issue of the monarchy. Thus, the multipronged project to distinguish Canada from the United States—a project shared historically by London and by conservative Canadian advocates of Empire and, today, by progressive nationalists—acts as a powerful, multistrand governmental sinew connecting the more visible legacy of Empire (the ubiquitous face of the Queen) to the less visible but more powerful mechanisms for internal rule that are based on colonial ruling technologies.

HISTORICAL SKETCH OF A COLONIAL GOVERNMENTALITY

The usual story of Canadian nation building is a perfect Whig narrative of the slow and peaceful development of a national federalist sovereignty.

Like all Whig stories, this narrative assumes that power is a zero-sum game. Thus, if the government in Ottawa is acquiring more powers, this is regarded as automatically proving that the Empire's force is diminishing; and the division of powers between Ottawa and the provinces is also regarded as a zero-sum game in which one side's political or judicial win automatically means that the other side has less power.

Here I will trace a brief sketch of some key events, rereading the story of political power without making the zero-sum assumption that is foundational to liberal thought and liberal governance. In this light, it becomes apparent that the colonial governmentality of early nineteenth-century Canada did not depart the scene, to be replaced by autonomy and self-government. At one level, colonialism simply *continued*: acts of the Canadian Parliament still need royal assent, to this day, and new Canadian citizens have to swear allegiance to "the Queen and her heirs," not to the Canadian state or the constitution. But more importantly, colonial governmentality was *transformed* by being folded into the inner fabric of the colony, as Gilles Deleuze might say.[6]

Through this infolding, the federal government created in 1867 was given neocolonial powers (a) over the aboriginal peoples of Canada, many of whom had signed treaties with the Crown (unlike the situation in Australia), that Ottawa now inherited; and (b) over the provinces. The provinces did eventually gain more autonomy and power. But aboriginal peoples remain colonial subjects, now of the Canadian government rather than of the British Crown.

Municipalities are part of the story too, even though they are not considered a level of government but rather "creatures of the province." The Whig (and English) narrative that tells of backward French Canadian peasants being liberated from feudal relations by the enlightened proponents of liberal colonialism is usually read as a tale in which municipalities became a key tool of popular "self-government." But it is plausible to read the story of municipal government in Canada as one in which, to use Engin Isin's words, colonial authorities and Canadian state authorities did not give up any power but simply chose to govern "through" cities (Isin 1992). Despotic government was regarded from the 1830s onward as an impossible option for Canada, for many reasons, the key one being that the main conquered population—the French colonists—were white. But the much-touted self-government imposed on localities in the mid-nineteenth century, while in part a response both to local Reform agitation and to Reform in England, cannot be regarded as basically a concession to democratic aspirations; on the contrary, it was a technology for effecting central-government objectives "at a distance" (to use Jeremy Bentham's famous phrase).

The story of Canada's political machinery is one in which central state authority certainly shifted and moved around—from the Colonial Office to Ottawa, and from there, in some respects, to the provincial capitals (though much of that was facilitated by the JCPC rather than by democratic movements). Municipal self-government was also a key building block of the overall colonial and postcolonial structure. But neither democracy nor individual rights were major characters in this story. Individual rights were entrenched only in the 1982 Charter of Rights and Freedoms. Let us now go over a few of the key steps in this story.

1763

As mentioned in the Diego Garcia context, British colonial jurisprudence creates an opposition dividing largely white "colonies of settlement" from largely nonwhite colonies acquired through conquest or through horse-trading among imperial powers. The British Settlements Act of 1887 states that a "'British settlement' means any British possession which has not been acquired by cession or conquest," a negative definition explained in the preamble: "Whereas divers of Her Majesty's subjects have resorted to and settled in, and may hereafter resort to and settle in, divers places where there is no civilized government, and such settlements have become or may hereafter become possessions of Her Majesty, and it is expedient to extend the power of Her Majesty to provide for the government of such settlements."

Australia and Canada are the most important colonies of settlement. The fates of both countries were bound together in numerous imperial legal events, such as the Colonial Laws Validity Act of 1865 and the Statute of Westminster of 1931. The status of both states in international law is premised on the alleged "fact" that British subjects went to "divers places where there is no civilized government" (as the 1887 Settlements Act puts it).

Western Canada was indeed settled in a manner not dissimilar from Australia, that is, through the repression and marginalization of aboriginal peoples and their land claims. But Eastern Canada became British by the conquest and cession of an existing European settlement: New France. In existence since the mid-seventeenth century, New France came to an abrupt end with the 1763 Treaty of Paris, which confirmed the English military conquest of Quebec City and of various French forts and settlements in the Atlantic colonies. This should have made Eastern Canada into a "ceded" or "conquered" colony—which would have meant that neither British constitutional principles nor the words of the Magna Carta would have applied (Tomkins 2001). But for reasons that are not made apparent in the standard texts on Canadian constitutional history, there seems to have been a consensus to pretend that Canada was a single colony—rather than an assemblage of sites and peoples with very different legal statuses—and to furthermore pretend that it could be regarded as a "colony of settlement" on the same lines as Australia. (One additional and related difference is that in the late eighteenth century and up to the American-British war of 1812, many Indian nations—Mohawk, Iroquois, etc.—were recognized by the British crown as sovereign in various bilateral treaties and in war-related alliances, in contrast to the *terra nullius* approach taken in Australia.)

In the years after 1763, British governors in Canada and colonial officials in London alternated between using the more liberal but still paternal legal tools used in "settlement colonies" and using the harsher tools, including martial law, that make up that important dimension of British law recently characterized as "the jurisprudence of emergency" (Hussain 2003). The British political decision to restore Quebec's civil law in the 1770s, after the French military defeat, is often cited as exemplifying the more benevolent governmentality of "settlement" in relation to the French colonists. Constitutional law texts, however, neglect to mention the wholesale expulsion of the Francophone Acadians that took place in 1755, a key moment in Canadian jurisprudence of emergency in keeping with the methods deployed in nonsettler colonies.

Eventually, the harsher tools of ceded and conquered colony law were shelved. This was not because English rulers had learned to appreciate Francophone culture and politics, but (to oversimplify for a moment) for the pragmatic and entirely nonlocal reason that they had decided that it was best for the British Empire to not alienate the United States. Lord Durham, whose famous 1839 report is universally taken as the founding document of both liberal colonialism *and* Canadian nationhood (those two rather different entities being reduced to the same thing in standard Canadian political historiography) stated as a fact that, if the governance of Quebec and Canada were to be based on local factors, French Canadians would be governed "despotically"—as J. S. Mill recommended in regard to backward nations. But despotism, while appropriate for the irrevocably superstitious and unprogressive French population,[7] would not suit imperial objectives in North America, Durham added. If they saw despotic monarchical rule just over their northern border, the United States would stir up trouble against the Empire.[8] This would not do: "I rate the preservation of the present general sympathy of the United States with the policy of our government in Lower Canada [Quebec] as a matter of the greatest importance" (Durham 1912, 2:297). That imperial authorities did not repeat the ethnic cleansing imposed upon the Acadians, or the martial law imposed throughout Quebec after the 1837 Rebellion, was thus not necessarily due to the relentless march of enlightenment that Canadian liberal historiography deploys and celebrates (cf. Isin 1992).

1839

As part of the process of bringing "responsible" government to Canada— "responsible government" meaning not "democracy" but ministerial responsibility to the House of Commons on the Westminster model—Lord Durham promoted municipal government institutions. These existed to varying degrees in English Canada but not in French Canada. The anti-English and anti-Empire movement that had culminated in the Rebellion of 1837 (the immediate reason Lord Durham was sent off on his colonial reform mission) was not interested in municipal self-government; in French Canada parish priests performed most of the functions associated with clerks and town authorities elsewhere, and there were few if any municipal taxes. The French Canadians' main political vehicle had been, and remained, the provincial legislature—today known as the National Assembly of Quebec.[9]

Lord Durham envisaged his task as assembling governing technologies that would undercut the provincial legislature without quite effecting despotism. First, he proposed—successfully—merging Upper Canada (Ontario) with Lower Canada and Quebec. While in the short run French Canadians would still be the majority in the new, united province, immigration from the United Kingdom would produce Anglicization and the complete assimilation of the French in the medium term (Louisiana was his model). Second, he insisted that municipal self-government be forced onto the reluctant French Canadians.[10] And, last but not least, he advised future colonial officials and governors that continued use of the royal prerogative be maintained:

> The establishment of a good system of municipal institutions throughout these Provinces is a matter of vital importance. A general legislature, which manages the private business of every parish, in addition to the common business of the country, wields a power that no single body, however popular in its constitution, ought to have. . . . *The true principle of limiting popular power* is that apportionment of it in many different depositaries which has been adopted in all the most free and stable States of the Union. . . . The establishment of municipal institutions for the whole country should be made a part of every colonial institution; and *the prerogative of the Crown* should be constantly interposed to check any encroachment on the functions of the local bodies, until the people should become alive . . . to the necessity of protecting their local privileges." (Durham 1912, 2:287; emphases added)

Pursuant to Lord Durham's plan to use municipal government to "limit popular power" (which mainstream political scientists insist on reading as giving Canada local democracy), the government of the United Province of Canada formed in 1840 passed a District Councils Act, in 1841. But this was simply ignored in French Canada. Bruce Curtis's book on the rise of Canadian state science tells us that the all-Canada Census of 1841 failed miserably precisely because its fate was tied to that of "the larger liberal project of local representative self-government" (Curtis 2001, 56). The whole project was refused by French Canadians, who wanted a strong legislature instead and who saw the new local councils as "taxation machines" rooted in English ideas about locality.

1867

Most Canadians think that July 1, 1867, is the birthday of Canada as an independent country. But the by no means radical constitutional legal scholar Peter Hogg states that the BNA Act of 1867 "did not mark any break with the colonial past. Independence from the United Kingdom was not desired or even contemplated for the future" (Hogg 1985, 2). Hogg goes on, "The best-known example of the colonists' reliance on the old regime is the absence of any general amending clause in the BNA Act . . . the framers must have known that the absence of an amending clause would mean that amendments would have to be enacted by the imperial Parliament" (3).

The ritual fireworks lit every year on July 1 disguise the fact that the BNA Act strictly avoided not only the language of "independence" that constantly threatened to seep into Canada from the United States (and from the few but vocal Irish nationalists in Canada), but even the less strident language of state formation. The BNA Act is precisely *not* the "Canada" Act. "British North America" is one constitutional name for the entity that is elsewhere in the document called "The Dominion of Canada."

"Dominion" was a clever neologism whose effect was and is simultaneously to travel and to erase the considerable distance between a Crown colony, on the one hand, and an independent state on the other. It is a performative, as the linguists say, that performs colonialism but simultaneously differentiates the self-governing white settler colonies from the Other, the despotically ruled white-minority colonies. It is notable that, like Lord Durham's views of the French as a race unsuited for liberal governance, the term "dominion" was quickly and happily reproduced in and by Canadian ruling circles. Indeed, July 1 was known until the 1970s as "Dominion Day," not "Canada Day," even in popular speech.

The BNA Act, among other things, maintained for the imperial parliament not only the power to amend the Canadian constitution (the BNA Act and its successors), but also the powers of "reservation and disallowance." "Reservation" is the practice whereby a colonial governor neither signs a bill nor refuses assent, but refers it to the imperial government for decision. "Disallowance," a power that was used more frequently, is the practice by which a dominion bill is declared null and void by the imperial government, even though the governor (representing the Crown) had given royal assent. (Disallowance is found in other colonial and postcolonial founding laws, incidentally; it is not specifically Canadian.)

Most of these colonial legal technologies acquired a more made-in-Canada look over time, but without being actually repealed. By the time the 1931 Statute of Westminster limited the Empire's power to strike down Canadian laws or impose imperial laws, London had not exercised the powers of reservation and disallowance for some time. Along the same lines, the Canadian Department of Indian Affairs took over the work of paternally governing Canada's aboriginal peoples—even though First Nations that signed treaties with the Crown before 1867, and that did not consent to the infolding of colonial governmentality carried out through the 1867 BNA Act and the 1875 Indian Act, insist that the Crown in London is still a valid interlocutor and a potential defender of their interests vis-à-vis Ottawa.

The infolding of colonial governmentality had another dimension. Besides assuming responsibility for the governance of aboriginal peoples and lands, Ottawa also acquired the colonial power to declare provincial statutes invalid, invoking the same power of "reservation" that was previously a strictly imperial legal tool. A constitutional law text tells us that "early Lieutenant Governors of various provinces often reserved bills for a final decision by the federal government. Although the practice was controversial, and soon became unnecessary as communications improved between Ottawa and the provincial capitals, a Saskatchewan bill was unexpectedly reserved as late as 1961" (Stevenson 2004).

The imperial legal tool that was the twin of "reservation," namely "disallowance," was also extended to Ottawa, without being thereby taken out of the imperial relationship. Federal disallowance was used extensively immediately after Confederation and through the early twentieth century (see Kennedy 1922, 415–22). This did not escape the notice of A. V. Dicey, who, when contrasting Ottawa's powers to the much more restricted powers of Congress in Washington, stated, "In nothing is this more noticeable than in the authority given to the Dominion Government to disallow provincial Acts" (Dicey 1910, 166). The last provincial statute disallowed by the federal government was the 1943 Alberta Act. However, there is no reason to think that the federal government would never dust off this tempting legal tool, perhaps if Quebec were to decide to secede from the federation.

These quasi-colonial powers are admittedly marginal in the general scheme of federal-provincial relations in Canada. But the key point is that the creation of these internal-colonial powers in Ottawa did not mean the end—or even the automatic diminishment—of Westminster's continuing ability to override Canadian statutes or the end of the JCPC's continuing ability to hear appeals not only from the Supreme Court of Canada but also from provincial governments.

Colonial governmentality can thus change shape, give birth to new offspring without itself dying, and unexpectedly proliferate, through processes understood by liberal thinkers of zero-sum power as "progress toward national autonomy." More generally, techniques of governance (such as the highly illiberal practice of disallowance) could and did acquire a new life in a new space, while continuing, as formally available techniques at any rate, in their original space. This process seems to have taken place not only in federal-provincial relations but also in regard to aboriginal First Nations, which have over the years received some new powers (through court decisions as well as amendments to the Indian Act), but without these new powers being necessarily accompanied by a corresponding decrease in Ottawa's paternalist powers.

1931

The Statute of Westminster, which declared that no statute of the United Kingdom would extend to a Dominion unless that Dominion explicitly requested and consented to the enactment, largely decolonialized the Australian political system—but not the Canadian one. The Statute gave all Dominions the power to repeal or amend those imperial statutes that were also part of the law of the Dominion in question; and, more importantly, it stated that no Dominion statute would be found to be void because it contradicted any existing or future act of the imperial parliament. However, the Statute of Westminster contained an exception: Canada's constitution, the BNA Act, was explicitly excluded from its reach. It seems that the Canadian federal government was unable to obtain provincial consent for anything like an amending formula, and since Ottawa was unable to present a replacement mechanism for Westminster approval, Westminster's power to amend the Canadian constitution had to continue. As a result, the Canadian government would continue to go cap in hand to request Westminster to amend the BNA Act.

1982

In the 1970s Prime Minister Trudeau undertook a campaign to complete what the Statute of Westminster had left undone—in part because he felt that a more postcolonial, more modern Canadian state (including an entrenched Charter of Rights) was the only real answer to the growing threat of Quebec separatism. Trudeau had recently become Prime Minister when the Front de Liberation de Quebec (FLQ) provoked an unprecedented political crisis in 1970, with a British diplomat being kidnapped and murdered and a Quebec cabinet minister being also kidnapped. Invoking the World War I War Measures Act (passed during the Red Scare pursuant to the federal POGG powers), he caused hundreds of people—very few of whom were FLQ members—to be detained without charges and without legal counsel, something that had the predictable effect of increasing support for separatism, though more for the mainstream, nonviolent Parti Quebecois, not for the FLQ's revolutionary project.

The Parti Quebecois came to power provincially in 1976. When Trudeau and his cabinet devised the idea of "patriating the Constitution," the project was as much—or more—a response to Quebec complaints about the lingering effects of *English-Canadian* dominance within Canada as a nationalist attack upon London. Trudeau was never able to obtain Quebec approval for his particular approach to what he called patriating the constitution, however, and so ended up, ironically, increasing Quebec's marginalization, constitutionally at any rate.[11] To make a very long story short, Westminster was asked to pass the 1982 Constitution Act by the federal government and by nine out of ten provinces. And this Westminster did—despite the fact that an appeal to the Supreme Court of Canada from the Quebec government was still pending.

Despite several changes in government both in Ottawa and in Quebec, Quebec has still not formally agreed to the Constitution Act. The act contains a formula for amending the constitution requiring the approval of more than two thirds of the provinces, with those provinces having more than half the population among them. This formula means that Quebec—with close to a third of the population of Canada—does not have to be included. This flies in the face of previous constitutional history. The United Province of Canada, for example, created in 1840, had two premiers and two attorneys general, one English and one French. Along similar lines, the Supreme Court Act requires that three out of the nine Justices of the Supreme Court be from Quebec. Other regional quotas are merely conventional, but the Quebec representation is enshrined in statute. A host of other governmental practices also treat the Francophone population—and the province of Quebec, the distinction between these two being often fudged—as a special and essential component, rather than as merely another province or an important minority.

Thus, the province of Quebec has been forced into constitutional arrangements not of their own making and has thus become differentiated, to its disadvantage, from the other, largely Anglophone, provinces.

The other dimension of Ottawa internal colonialism has not undergone any basic change in form. While Trudeau was proclaiming that "today, at long last, Canada is acquiring full and complete national sovereignty" (Trudeau 1982), aboriginal leaders had this to say:

> April 17, 1982 was proclaimed as a day of mourning for the aboriginal peoples of Canada. It was the day the British crown irreversibly betrayed every treaty, proclamation agreement, trust and promise made with the Indian Nations of Canada. . . .[12] For the last three years, Chiefs, Indian organizations and leaders, and ordinary Indians have written to the Queen to inform her that the treaties were endangered by a new settler government constitution. ("The patriation of the Canadian Constitution" 1982)

The Constitution Act has a phrase stating that "existing aboriginal rights" will be maintained and recognized; but the problem lies precisely in determining just what "existing" rights amount to. Subsequent federal governments have not remedied the glaring omission of aboriginal representatives from the "patriation" process: the regular federal-provincial conferences on constitutional issues include only the Prime Minister and the ten premiers, not aboriginal representatives. The federal government did attempt to modernize the colonial Indian Act in 1985, by devolving many responsibilities and powers to local Indian bands and ending the overtly colonial institution of the "Indian agent," the white personage who for many decades exercised proconsul power over Indian bands. This responsibilization of status Indians for their own problems has met with mixed reviews, but the only point that need be mentioned here is that many aboriginal organizations continue to call for the wholesale repeal of the Indian Act.

Comparative Parenthesis

Constitutional litigation was for most of Canada's history limited to fights between the federal government and the provinces. It was only in 1982 that a Charter of Rights was added to Canada's constitutional documents (there was a Bill of Rights from the 1960s on, but this was an ordinary statute). Jennifer Nedelsky, whose expertise is comparative U.S.-Canadian constitutional law, addresses this question in a detailed study of nuisance cases, from 1880–1930, which led her to a conclusion that sheds much light on the issue of police-type powers: "Canadians do not seem to have shared the long-standing American distrust of democratic legislatures as threats to private property" (Nedelsky 1981, 310). One example of this is that in the early 1900s there was a major split among the ruling classes that, in the United States, could have led to constitutional challenges to the police power: internationally oriented financiers in Ontario wanted to be exempt from certain provincial regulatory mechanisms that applied to the finance sector. The financiers tried a twofold, typically Canadian route. First they made an unsuccessful attempt to persuade the federal government to use its power of disallowance against the Ontario rules, then they resorted to the courts. But the "challenge was dismissed with Justice Riddell's remark that 'The prohibition "Thou shalt not steal" has no legal force against a sovereign body'" (310). A starker statement of the police power of the state could scarcely be imagined.

This is not to say that Canadians are so respectful of authority that they never thought to challenge takings and similar practices. Nedelsky may be exaggerating the famous "deferential culture" of Canada as an explanatory factor and underestimating the importance of the political structure. When challenges to regulatory provincial legislation interfering with property and other rights were launched, in the long period up to 1982, the challengers either convinced the federal government to use its illiberal power to disallow provincial statutes (as happened many times in the early twentieth century, in regard to provincial regulatory statutes) or else took their case to a judicial system whose ultimate authority was not the Supreme Court of Canada but—until 1949—the JCPC. Neither federal disallowance nor Law Lords judgments were suitable vehicles for the kind of rights consciousness (especially property rights consciousness) and the kind of legal doctrines that emerged in the United States in and around police power cases, since disallowance is a transparently colonial paternalistic and illiberal political tool, and the Law Lords in England, whatever their views on property rights, were not empowered to make substantive decisions about Canadian property law but only to solve federal-provincial disputes. Thus, against Nedelsky's culturalist perspective, it could be argued that property owners in Canada did not play the individual-rights game simply because it was not available to them. They had to play the game of trying to take advantage of federal-provincial disputes to pursue their goals.

The Infolding of a Colonial Governmentality

As against the usual liberal and Anglo-centric account of the inexorable march of the Canadian state toward full autonomy, I have suggested here that we can better understand the particular genealogy of the Canadian constitutional framework by highlighting that the monarchy and other techniques of old-fashioned Empire are not anachronisms that are tolerated for sentimental reasons but are the visible tips of a rather large iceberg, an iceberg that includes a series of often-ignored tools of internal colonialism. Ottawa's frankly colonial rule over "Indians" and its quasi-colonial relationship with the provinces—in evidence in the disallowance cases and, today, in the continuing absence of both Quebec and First Nations representatives from the constitutional table—has been historically produced and maintained by means of legal mechanisms borrowed from the Empire's toolbox and adapted for new uses. The historical connections between Canada and other colonies have been disavowed and obscured by nationalist constitutional law scholars who have failed to investigate such issues as the fate of POGG powers in other climates. To understand the infolding of colonial governmental techniques, we need to first clear the mistaken assumptions about power as a zero-sum game that are integral to liberal thought generally. Ottawa's power has not been and is not now in a zero-sum relation with powers held in London, in Quebec City, or in First Nations' band councils. The zero-sum model is not adequate. Power relations can multiply through the borrowing and adapting of governmental techniques, an activity that does not necessarily mean they are not still in force in their original setting.

Colonial and Postcolonial Governmentality and the Paternal Model of Government

Blackstone's famous discussion of the police power features the benevolent but all-powerful father as the key metaphor of government. This same diagram of paternal power was very important in the spread—and the legitimation—of British imperial relations around the world. While from the legal point of view one can locate police-type powers in various parts of the Canadian political-legal system, and mainly in the provinces' control over property and civil rights and in certain statutory and common-law municipal technologies for governing disorder and guarding against risks, from a nonlegal perspective one could speak of a generalized Canadian paternalism that flows all through the system, including through and in the federal government's POGG powers. The POGG powers are supposed to be used only to deal with emergencies, but their logic is the same as that embedded in the Indian Act, as revealed in such contexts as the 1964 *Ibralebbe* decision of the JCPC, in which the removal of juries from criminal trials in Ceylon was thought to be well within the POGG powers of the Ceylon government (and in which the Law Lords took the time to chastise the Chief Justice of Ceylon for daring to opine that having Ceylon constitutional law decided by the Law Lords was inconsistent with independence).

Once constructed, in part by analogy with paternal power, the colonial relation could and did in turn serve as model for other illiberal relations. To give but one example: research I have carried out on the twentieth-century process of "interdicting" chronic alcoholics shows that, just as Indians were once denied the right to drink because they were thought to be like children, so too, in the 1950s and 1960s, chronic alcoholics in Ontario were banned from possessing alcohol in their own homes by the legal mechanism of being placed on what was popularly known as "the Indian list." This was not a list of Indians but a list of people not allowed to buy or possess alcohol. Turned into symbolic Indians, violent husbands and street winos could be denied rights with legal tools seldom found outside "ceded or conquered colonies" (Valverde 2004). Other examples could undoubtedly be produced of this creative recycling of colonial paternal technologies for governing problem people and problem activities.

Toward a Dynamic Analysis of Knowledge Processes in Law

Political science, like law, privileges static structures, e.g., of federal-provincial relations, rather than trying to map recurring moves—that is, more or less habitual ways of getting from one set of claims or resources to another place, to another configuration of power and knowledge. In static models, struggles appear only as little stories about how the structure developed or changed. In standard English Canadian political history, struggles such as that waged by the people of Quebec in the years after the conquest appear only as evanescent video clips that disappear as one focuses on the resulting fixed structure. There was the 1837 Rebellion, but then the British brought in responsible government, which is what we have now—that's the type of account to which we are accustomed.

My approach, however, privileges the struggles (in keeping with the Nietzsche-Foucault thesis that peace is what has to be explained, not struggle). In this way more dynamic analyses are encouraged. A fully dynamic analysis of struggles in their open-endedness is not possible, given that the very act of writing forces life into a more or less static format. But certain analytic tools—governmentality (the less structuralist versions of it) and Actor-Network analytic tools (Latour 1987, 1993, 2002) can help to make our analyses more dynamic.

In such analyses, the goal is not to generate better, more refined typologies of government structures or legal tools. The goal is rather to show how methodological insights from a variety of fields can be creatively used to understand the workings of law in ways that are always site-specific. This is what I understand by "doing the history of the present," a task which necessarily includes the past.

Notes

I could not have ventured into Canadian constitutional history without help and guidance from David Schneidermann, to whom I am very grateful. Tayyab Mahmoud's important work in progress on the Diego Garcia cases and colonial governmentality has also been a crucial resource, and I am grateful for conversations and the exchange of papers.

1. Ron Levi and I are developing a methodological argument that deconstructs the usual law-and-society split between lawyers who study texts and social scientists who study people, using analytic resources from Actor Network Theory. We will develop this in a book titled *Legal Labs*, now in the preliminary stages.

2. European readers might wonder whether my own interest in liquor laws is affecting my choice of cases here; but the fact is that liquor licensing and prohibition figure very largely in constitutional history because in no other field did the

Canadian state interfere so harshly with property rights, in the late nineteenth and early twentieth century at any rate. Today zoning and environmental law are much more powerful tools to exercise police-type regulatory power, but these did not exist until well into the twentieth century.

3. I do not mean here to invoke a binary opposition between "sovereignty" and "discipline," as if government could be reduced to a simple binary and as if analytic tools (like the idea of sovereignty) were more real than the practices that we ultimately seek to understand. I prefer to use "sovereign" and "disciplinary" as adjectives modifying nouns, and, preferably, historically concrete nouns. Compulsory military service, just to take a random example, acts upon the subjectivity of the relevant population in ways that evoke and inscribe the sovereign dimensions of state power: but in modern times, when random physical seizures of young men by press-gangs would look like a failure of state capacities, classic disciplinary techniques, from censuses and compulsory birth registration to medical inspection, are necessary to carry out the sovereign goal of building up the army. Conscription, then, like most other techniques of governance, is not properly analyzed if it is merely put in a pigeonhole marked "sovereignty." Concrete analyses of actually existing techniques of governance usually reveal a mix of logics.

4. *The Guardian* has covered the continuing saga of the Ilois after the *Bancoult* decision quite regularly, and many of the relevant articles can be found online.

5. "Multicultural liberalism" is the term I use to gesture not only toward governmental moves that recognize the importance of minority cultures—e.g., multilingual education in public schools—but a broader mentality of governance through which minority communities are seen as making up Canada rather than (as in many U.S. state mechanisms) being threats to it. Most recently, multicultural-type agitation has resulted in the federal government's reluctant agreement to change federal marriage law to allow gays and lesbians to marry, despite the Prime Minister at the time and a very large number of members of parliament being Catholic.

6. Inspired by Foucault's genealogy of modern subjectivity, Deleuze argued that rather than counterpose inner psychic identity to observable behavior, it is more useful to think of subjectivity as a process of "infolding," a process through which inside and outside turn into one another (Deleuze 1988).

7. "They clung to ancient prejudices, ancient customs and ancient laws, not from any strong sense of their beneficial effects, but with the unreasoning tenacity of an uneducated and unprogressive people" (Durham 1912, 2:30).

8. W. M. Kennedy quotes colonial official dispatches showing that the decision to reintroduce French civil law (*la coutume de Paris*) into Quebec in the mid-1770s was mainly a bit of political advertising aimed at showing Boston audiences that the British Empire could be liberal (Kennedy 1922).

9. Translations into English often conceal the nationalist claims embedded in Quebec political terminology; just to cite one example that illustrates, literally,

Bruno Latour's point about the importance of translations, the leader of the Quebec provincial government is known in English as "the premier," but French-language newscasts, including those on the federally funded CBC, describe him as "le premier ministre du Quebec."

10. Lord Durham's views were by no means exclusive to colonial authorities. The leading political scientist of late nineteenth-century Canada, John G. Bourinot, reiterated the English tale about childlike French peasants unable and unwilling to exercise local self-government—despite his French last name. Explaining Canada to the United States in the important series on Local Government sponsored in the 1880s by Johns Hopkins University, Bourinot wrote that "when the French Canadian became a subject of the British crown, he was, literally, a child who had never been taught to think for himself in public affairs," who lacked the "spirit of self-reliance and free action" found in—as a matter of essence—"peoples brought up under Teutonic and English institutions" (Bourinot 1887, 29).

11. On other fronts the Trudeau government made many important steps to remedy the internal colonialism of English Canadians over French Canadians, official bilingualism being the key tool of this project.

12. There is somewhat of a split among Canadian aboriginal peoples between "Treaty Indians," on the one hand, whose voice is heard in the excerpt cited here, and those aboriginal people who are Métis or belong to nations that never signed treaties with the Crown. The word "Indian" is used to indicate persons who are recognized members of recognized "bands"—"status Indian" is the term used, in popular as well as government discourse, for this smaller group, which is entitled to a variety of benefits. Nonstatus aboriginal peoples are not official Indians; their legal status varies widely. The term "First Nations" includes both treaty and nontreaty aboriginal peoples.

References

Bourinot, John G. 1887. *Local government in Canada: An historical study*. Baltimore: Johns Hopkins University Press.

Dean, Mitchell M. 1999. *Governmentality: Power and rule in modern society*. London: Sage.

Deleuze, Gilles. 1988. *Foucault*. Minneapolis: University of Minnesota Press.

Dicey, Albert V. 1910. *The law of the constitution: A digest of the law of England with reference to the conflict of laws*. Boston: Boston Book Co.

Dubber, Markus Dirk. 2005. *The police power: Patriarchy and the foundations of American government*. New York: Columbia University Press.

Durham, John G. L. 1912. *Lord Durham's report on the affairs of British North America*, ed. C. P. Lucas. Oxford: Clarendon Press.

Foucault, Michel. 1991. Governmentality. In *The Foucault effect: Studies in govern-mentality*, ed. G. Burchell, C. Graham, and P. Miller. Chicago: University of Chicago Press.

Freund, Ernst. 1904. *The police power: Public policy and constitutional rights.* Chicago: Callaghan & Company.

Harwood, Charles J., Jr. 2002. *Diego Garcia: The "criminal question" doctrine.* http://homepage.ntlworld.com/jksonc/5_DiegoGarcia.html.

Hodge v. The Queen 1883. 9 App Cas 117.

Hogg, Peter W. 1985. *Constitutional law of Canada,* 2d ed. Toronto: Carswell.

Hussain, Nasser. 2003. *The jurisprudence of emergency: Colonialism and the rule of law.* Ann Arbor: University of Michigan Press.

Ibralebbe v. The Queen 1964. [1964] AC 900.

Ignatieff, Michael. 2004. Peace, order and good government: A foreign policy for Canada. OD Skelton Lecture, Department of Foreign Affairs and International Trade, Ottawa, March 12.

Isin, Engin F. 1992. *Cities without citizens: Modernity of the city as corporation.* Montreal: Black Rose Books.

Karsten, Peter. 2003. *Between law and custom: "High" and "low" legal cultures in the lands of the British diaspora—the United States, Canada, Australia, and New Zealand, 1600–1900.* Cambridge, UK: Cambridge University Press.

Kennedy, W. M. 1922. *The constitution of Canada: An introduction to its development and law.* London: Oxford University Press.

Latour, Bruno. 1987. *Science in action: How to follow scientists and engineers.* Cambridge, MA: Harvard University Press

———. 1993. *We have never been modern.* Cambridge, MA: Harvard University Press.

———. 2002. *La fabrique du droit: Une ethnologie du Conseil d'Etat.* Paris: La Découverte.

Liyanage v. The Queen 1967. 1 AC 259.

Local Prohibition Case 1896. [1896] AC 348.

Mahmoud, Tayyab. 2003. Exceptionalism as the norm. Paper presented at Sovereignty and the Right of Death Conference, Cleveland-Marshall College of Law, Cleveland, Ohio, October 2003.

Maitland, Frederick W. 2003. *State, trust, and corporation,* ed. D. Runciman and M. Ryan. Cambridge, UK: Cambridge University Press.

Nedelsky, Jennifer. 1981. Judicial conservatism in an age of innovation: Comparative perspectives on Canadian nuisance law, 1880–1930. In *Essays in the history of Canadian law,* ed. D. Flaherty. Toronto: University of Toronto Press.

Novak, William J. 1996. *The people's welfare: Law and regulation in nineteenth-century America.* Chapel Hill: University of North Carolina Press.

Panitch, Leo. 1977. *The Canadian state: Political economy and political power.* Toronto: University of Toronto Press.

Pasquino, Pasquale. 1991. Theatrum Politicum: The Genealogy of Capital—Police and the State of Prosperity. In *The Foucault effect: Studies in governmentality*, ed. G. Burchell, C. Graham, and P. Miller. Chicago: University of Chicago Press.

"The patriation of the Canadian Constitution: Not an auspicious occasion." 1982. *Saskatchewan Indian* 12(4): 10. http://collections.ic.gc.ca/saskindian/a82may10 .htm.

The Queen [Bancoult] v. Foreign and Commonwealth Office 2001. [2001] QB 1067.

Riel v. The Queen 1885. 10 App Cas 675.

Rose, Nikolas S. 1999. *Powers of freedom: Reframing political thought*. Cambridge, UK: Cambridge University Press.

Stevenson, Garth. 2004. Reservation and disallowance, *Constitutional keywords*. http://www.law.ualberta.ca/ccskeywords/reservation_dis.html.

Struthers, James. 1983. *No fault of their own: Unemployment and the Canadian welfare state 1914–1941*. Toronto: University of Toronto Press.

Tomkins, Adam. 2001. Magna Carta, crown and colonies. *Public Law*, Autumn 2001, 571–85.

Trudeau, Pierre Elliott. 1982. Patriation of constitution. Remarks at Proclamation Ceremony, Ottawa, April 17. http://northernblue.ca/canchan/cantext/speech3/ 1982trco.html.

Valverde. Mariana. 1998. *Diseases of the will: Alcohol and the dilemmas of freedom*. Cambridge, UK: Cambridge University Press.

———. 2003. Police science, British style: Pub licensing and knowledges of urban disorder. *Economy and Society* 32(2): 234–53.

———. 2004. A postcolonial women's law? Domestic violence and the Ontario Liquor Board's "Indian list", 1950s–1980. *Feminist Studies* 30(3): 566–88.

Winfat Enterprises v. Attorney General of Hong Kong 1985. [1985] AC 733.

CHAPTER FOUR

The New Police Science and the Police Power Model
of the Criminal Process

MARKUS D. DUBBER

There was once a unified concept of police. Police was the means and the end of patriarchal governance. Policing meant governing the state as a household for the sake of its "public police and oeconomy" (Blackstone 1769, 162; see also Rousseau 1755; see generally Dubber 2005b). Police science was devoted to the study of police thus understood.

Today the concept of police has fallen apart. On one side lies the police of "police power," pure and simple, as exemplified by the police officer. On the other lies the police of "the police power," as exemplified by the police regulation. Police science survives as police officer science: the study of investigative techniques and "police management."[1] Police science as the study of the police power has disappeared. The police that the police officer protects, and the police power that she personifies, no longer exist. Instead, the police officer has been reconceptualized as a law enforcement officer, just as police science has become a subcategory of the field of criminal justice (see, e.g., John Jay College of Criminal Justice 2004).

The New Police Science seeks to recover the unified concept of police as an object of study (on the predisciplinary ambitions of this project, see Neocleous 2005). It concerns itself with the police power as a general mode of governance, rather than with one of its specific institutional manifestations, the police department, or one of the specific personal components of that institutional manifestation, the police officer. Clearly, a comprehensive theory of the police would have to find room for the police department and its members, but one cannot hope to come to grips with the concept of police by focusing exclusively on the duties and skills of the cop on the beat. Occasionally, one can catch a glimpse of the old concept of police in discussions of the functions of a police officer. Police officers are, after all, also often referred to as "peace officers." As U.S. Supreme Court Justice Clarence Thomas recently pointed out, dissenting in *Chicago v. Morales*, "the idea that the police are also *peace officers* [is not] simply a quaint anachronism. In most American jurisdictions, police officers continue to be obligated, by law, to maintain the public peace" (*Chicago v. Morales* 1999, 107).

The "public peace," however, is simply one aspect of, if not synonymous with, the public's police. It therefore only made sense that Thomas went on to quote approvingly from a leading nineteenth-century treatise on the *police power*, "The vagrant has been very appropriately described as the chrysalis of every species of criminal. A wanderer through the land, without home ties, idle, and without apparent means of support, what but criminality is to be expected from such a person?" (*Chicago v. Morales* 1999, 104, n. 4 [quoting Tiedeman 1886, 116–17]).

The point of this chapter, however, is not to explore the relationship between police power and *the* police power (on this point see Neocleous 2000; and see chapter 5), but to illustrate those features of the criminal process as a whole that reflect its foundation in the power to police. It has long been black-letter law in the United States that the power to punish, and therefore the entire enterprise of state coercion through criminal law, is grounded in the police power (*Foucha v. Louisiana* 1992, 80; LaFave and Scott 1986, § 2.10; Laylin and Tuttle 1922, 622; *Sutton v. New Jersey* 1917). This doctrinal fact, however, is treated as though it were of no consequence whatsoever, if it is noted at all. It is odd, to say the least, that the foundation of criminal law, the basis for the right to punish, has attracted so little attention. Despite an ever-expanding literature on the theory of punishment, however, the nature of the legal or political authority underlying the state's criminal process has been left unexplored. How can this be?

Police Power as Patria Potestas

The answer lies in the concept of the police power itself. The police power is constructed as inevitable, self-evident. The power to police, it is said, is incident to the very idea of government. To govern is always also to police. Sovereignty without the power to police is no sovereignty at all. At the same time, the police power is defined as indefinable, limitless. To identify a state action as grounded in the police power is to insulate it from analysis and critique. The police power is but an "idiom of apologetics" (Hamilton and Rodee 1933, 190 [quoted in Novak 1994, 1082, n. 58]).

Merely to recognize the label "police power" as inoculation against principled critique, however, is not enough. The potency of the police concept makes sense only if we see it within its genealogical context. As I have argued elsewhere in some detail, the inevitability and limitlessness, even the often-asserted naturalness, of the police power reflects its origins in the patriarchal power of the householder over his household (Dubber 2005b). The householder's patriarchy, in other words, is more than a convenient metaphor used by eighteenth-century writers (Rousseau 1755; Blackstone 1769, 162) to capture the nature of domestic government in the purported service of the public welfare, i.e., "the police." It is, rather, a basic mode of governance that can be traced throughout the history of Western politics, beginning at least with the pre-Aristotelian *Oikonomikos*, "a work of practical advice to the gentleman landowner about the sound management of an estate, its slaves, household, and land" (Meikle 1995, 5). Today's "public peace" is grounded in the ancient "householder's peace," and the power to police is a modern manifestation of the householder's authority to maintain his peace, expanded and transferred onto the state-as-household.

To consider the criminal process—as with any other governmental practice or institution—in light of the police power thus means to explore the extent to which its functioning can be illuminated by regarding it as an instance of patriarchal household governance.

Historically, the householder's patriarchal power over his household was unlimited *except insofar as he proved himself unfit for his post.* Unfitness was a character—or personality—flaw that prevented the householder from functioning as the maximizer, or at least the sustainer, of the household's welfare. So in medieval law the lord was prohibited from depriving his serf of life or limb (Pollock and Maitland 1896, 1:415–16, 437; Hyams 1968, 127). It is important to understand, however, that this limitation—doubtless of greater theoretical than practical significance—did not derive from anything like the serf's "right" to physical integrity or even to life, never mind to treatment consistent with "human dignity." It was of evidentiary significance: certain punishments were so brutal (later on, the "rule of thumb" performed a similar function) that they were indicative of the punisher's inability to run the household or lack of interest in discharging the function of maximizing the household's welfare, since a life- or limbless serf was at least presumptively useless as a household resource. A patriarch not in control of his emotions was incapable of policing himself. And someone incapable of internal police—of himself—also was incapable of external police—of others.

This apparent limitation on patriarchal power, however, itself implies the existence of a superior and limitless patriarchal power. Each familial patriarch ultimately was subject to the authority of the royal patriarch, who claimed the power to police over his subjects considered as members of his macro household. The king himself was not subject to patriarchal power (except, in premodern times, to the patriarchal power of the Christian god, who regarded all of *his* creatures as members of his household, and whose patriarchal fitness was beyond scrutiny—unlike that of the [chief!] gods of the Greeks or the early Germans, whose follies are the stuff of mythology).

Police power then is primarily concerned with status. The patriarch's power derives from his status as householder. That status is defined in relation to the status of the members of his household. The householder governs, and the household is governed. Discipline is used against household members who act in a manner inconsistent with their status (on sumptuary police regulations, see Hunt 1996). The most obvious and blatant form of acting up is to defy the authority—and thereby to deny the status—of the householder. The most extreme manifestation of defiance is the destruction of the householder—*treason* (grand or petit, depending on whether the victim is the head of the macro or a micro household) or, in its original sense, *felony* as the breach of the duty of loyalty owed the householder (Pollock and Maitland 1896, 1:303).

At the same time, if the householder "acts down" by behaving in a manner characteristic of the mean or base who constitute the household, then he is demoted—or rather demotes himself—to the status of the governed. Where he was once the whipper, he now becomes the whipped (*Foote v. State* 1883 ["An Act to inflict corporal punishment upon persons found guilty of wife-beating"]). Reduced to the status of those incapable of self-policing (self-restraint, "politeness"), he is now subject to the police power of another who is capable of externalizing his internal capacity to self-police and whose self is expanded to include the entirety of his household.

Threats—and open challenges—to the authority of the policer are threats to the household itself. As the embodiment—*not* the representative—of the household, the householder's welfare is also the household's. So important is the welfare of the householder that the remotest threat to his well-being must be eliminated. Already imagining the death of the macro householder is treason. (By contrast, only the actual killing of the micro householder amounts to—petit—treason [Treason Act of 1351, 25 Edw. 3 stat. 5 c. 2].)

The policer-householder will not hesitate to interfere as soon as a threat to his authority manifests itself. The greater the threat, the earlier he is likely to interfere. The police power thus is often associated with preventive—as opposed to remedial—measures (Bentham 1789, 102; *Commonwealth v. Alger* 1851). Prevention, however, is neither essential nor unique to police. It may be empirically true that the policer will often interfere earlier rather than later. Ex post intervention, however, is not necessarily incompatible with the police power, although it may provide evidence of unfitness to govern insofar as it indicates vindictiveness (or tardiness), which in turn would represent a failure of self-police on the part of the policer. Nor is ex ante intervention necessarily *compatible* with the police power as it may indicate paranoia or fearfulness. To regard police as characterized by prevention thus is to miss its discretionary essence: the policer will choose whatever measures he considers to be best suited to accomplish his end of maintaining the police of the household, which is coextensive with his peace, or *mund* (Herlihy 1985, 48; see also Hyams 1968, 96), be they preventive or not. The policer certainly is not precluded from taking preventive measures, but that is not to say that he will not turn to retrospective measures if necessary.

In a patriarchal regime the victim of every offense is the householder. The paradigmatic offense is the breach of the householder's peace. Offenses against members of the household are significant insofar as they are offenses against the household, including its head. Offenses against members of the household challenge the householder's ability to maintain the peace and therefore his authority. They also deprive him of a resource. Mayhem, for instance, was punished as "an atrocious breach of the king's peace, and an offense tending to deprive him of the aid and assistance of his subjects" (Blackstone 1769, chap. 15). Most dramatic was the elimination of a royal human resource through homicide; the circumstances surrounding the homicide were beside the point as the king-householder lost a human resource either way—even killings in self-defense required a royal pardon, i.e., the macro householder's exercise of his discretion *not* to punish (Baker 1990, 601).

If an outsider inflicts the injury, the medieval householder must be made whole, either through the payment of wergild or through the delivery of an equivalent resource (the offending sword, servant, tree, dog; Brunner 1894b). Injuries inflicted by one household member upon another are dealt with at the discretion of the householder, to be exercised in the interest of the household's welfare.

Gustav Radbruch saw in intrahousehold discipline of household members by the householder the origin of criminal law (Radbruch 1950). Intrahousehold offenses are different in quality from external ones; besides diminishing household resources and challenging the householder's *mund*, they reflect disloyalty. Disciplining the offender serves to reassert the householder's superior status and to prevent future resource deprivation, at the lowest possible present cost. That is why physical discipline, such as whipping, is a more popular disciplinary sanction than the other traditional householder sanction, incarceration—it indicates superiority without incapacitating the offender from contributing to the household's welfare for extended periods of time. Injuries to life and limb are suspect—and cast suspicion on the householder's ability to police the household—because, and insofar as, they are liable to have a long-term incapacitative effect.

Interhousehold offenses, by contrast, are resolved through arrangements among the heads of household. Radbruch regarded the resolution of interhousehold disputes as the origin of modern international law (Radbruch 1950). The head of the offending household is responsible for the delivery of the wergild or other compensation to the head of the offended household. If attempts at interhousehold settlement failed, the offended householder could turn to violence, often resulting in a cycle of vengeance that could be broken only with the disappearance of one of the households, through either destruction or subjugation, i.e., the integration of its members into the surviving household. This alternative dispute resolution through violence (in case compensation could not be arranged) can be seen as the origin of the modern law of war, insofar as it too was subject to rules of proportionality and did not amount simply to an acting out of hostilities.

Those offenders who belong to no household—or at least are treated as such—do not fit into this household-centered regime. They are subject to the patriarchal power of no one. They are the unpoliced. They are the "lordless men" of Anglo-Saxon dooms who must either be integrated into a household, and thereby subjected to the police of another, or become not only lordless, but "peaceless" as well (Pollock and Maitland 1896, 1:31). As outlaws, vagabonds, rogues they roam the countryside and can be destroyed with impunity or subjected to whatever lesser harm seems fitting (cf. Brunner 1894a; Agamben 1998).

Unlike the policed, their treatment is not even subject to theoretical limitation. Visiting boundless cruelty upon them does not reflect a deficit of self-police; they no longer contribute to the police of any household, micro or macro, so that their well-being, their productivity (their human resource), and even their existence is of no import. They are treated like wolves, except that even wild animals are under the protection of the king—as members of the king's macro household, any harm to the life or limb of a wild animal is also an offense against the king's *mund*. This is the origin of game laws, which—as Blackstone pointed out—were eventually mistaken for protections of the authority of local lords, who were, however, no more than caretakers, or custodians, for the king's animal resources (Blackstone 1769, 174).

Carceral Police: Wars on Crime and Other Police Actions

Modern equivalents of the lordless man can still be found in national and international affairs, long after the label "outlaw" has disappeared from the official vocabulary of the criminal process (though in English law the term remained in use well into the nineteenth century). In the international realm, the lordless man is the "irregular" or "enemy" combatant, or "partisan" (cf. Schmitt 1963). Prisoners of war (POWs) are subject to the laws of war. They belong both to another macro household (they are citizens, or at least permanent residents, of another nation) and, just as important, to a micro household (that country's armed forces) that is under the police control of various intermediate householders (from the commander in chief down to the leaders of smaller units). As such, POWs are entitled to treatment analogous to the treatment they would receive within their own micro (military) household, down to the retention of internal status—i.e., rank—differentiation within POW camps. In fact, their treatment is to be comparable to that of members of the armed forces that are holding them in custody (Department of the Army 1956, §§ 101, 158).

Partisans, by contrast, as unpoliced human threats are entitled to no protections of any kind. They may be shot on the spot (Department of the Army 1956, §§ 80–82). Should they be taken prisoner for one purpose or another (e.g., clarification of status [Liptak 2004], interrogation), their guards do not (and could not) act as placeholders for their nonexistent heads of household. Guards are free to treat them as they see fit, without regard to their welfare; at the same time, their welfare does not affect the welfare of the guards' household. Absent the disobedience of specific orders (which always constitutes a police offense), their treatment does not reflect upon their guards' ability to police themselves, because their treatment is not meant to police.

The "war on terror" detainees at Guantánamo Bay's Camp X-Ray were classified as "unlawful enemy combatants" precisely because this classification removed them beyond the reach of the law of war and the domestic law of the United States (Cole 2002). Instead they are subject only to whatever constraints their captors (and interrogators) choose to impose upon themselves. As a facility, Camp X-Ray therefore differs from a POW camp and, perhaps more significant, an ordinary prison for criminal suspects and convicts. By contrast, POW camps and convict prisons are organized as quasi households and, in that sense, as police institutions. The POW has not violated any norms, nor has he acted beyond (or beneath) his station. The captive regular soldier has performed his household function, which turns out to be inconsistent with the police of the captor household. He is constructively governed according to rules analogous to those of his own

household until he can be reintegrated into that household (through a prisoner exchange or at the end of the war).

The prison inmate, unlike the POW, has violated a household norm—or,
in the case of pretrial detainees, at least has been suspected of having violated
one. As such, he requires not only sustenance, but also correction. For that
reason, the law of war prohibits housing POWs in ordinary convict prisons,
or "penitentiaries," even for disciplinary purposes (Department of the Army
1956, §§ 98, 173).

Traditionally, prisons—*houses* of *correction*—have been organized under
a quasi-familial model, be it as a family, a factory, a military unit, or a slave
plantation, with the warden occupying the position of head of household
and the guards acting as overseers. Even when prisoners were officially designated "slaves of the state" (*Ruffin v. Commonwealth* 1871, 796), they were,
as slaves, treated as household members, i.e., not as mere detainees but as
inmates, a term also used for members of a Germanic household (Vinogradoff 1913).

Focusing on the exceptional treatment of the unpoliced highlights the
similarities between law and war and suggests that even waging a "war on
crime" does not necessarily imply a complete paradigm shift from "tradi
tional" law enforcement. The U.S. war on crime began in the 1960s in large
part as a war on *organized* crime. The war on organized crime, however, was
a distinctly *inter*familial dispute in that the micro household of the police was
pitted against the micro household of the Mafia. In a different interfamilial
scenario, the Kennedy family—with Robert Kennedy as Attorney General
leading the charge—waged war on various "crime families" (see Goldfarb
1995). Mafiosi were subject to the police of their superiors who enforced
certain codes of conduct, much as police officers on the beat were policed by
their higher-ups in addition to being subject to the laws of the macro household, the nation. In this sense, the war on crime began as a civil war.

The crime war metaphor threatens to break down, however, as soon as
one tries to apply it to the eradication of so-called street crime. The disturbances of the late 1960s that gave rise to Nixon's declaration of a war on
crime unmodified were not attributed to organized crime (Nixon 1968).
Instead, the phenomenon of street crime was from the beginning highly racialized, so that the only group to which enemies in the war on crime might
be seen to belong was a racial group: African Americans. In fact, much of

the fear of street crime arose from its apparent randomness; it was radically disorganized, unpoliced by crime families or syndicates. The war on crime unmodified was no longer a struggle among households within the confines of the macro household. Instead of a civil war, it was a domestic police action against a racial group that mirrored the external "police actions" against North Vietnam (as well as previously against North Korea and subsequently against Iraq) (Corn 1999; Agamben 2000, 102; see also chapter 7).

The enemies of the second, broader stage of the war on crime were more analogous to partisans, or enemy combatants, than to military enemies in war. Even when attention was turned to criminal gangs, these clusters of criminal threats tended to be conceptualized differently than the organized crime families of the original war on crime, as their structure was often assumed to be less complex and more fluid, with insufficient oversight and continuity to qualify for the title of a criminal organization. Unlike a low-level mafioso, enemy combatants in the war on crime were not subject to the police authority of a micro householder. As lordless men, as unpoliced threats, they were beyond the scope of the police of the macro household. As alien combatants, they were not subject to correction but to incapacitation through various means, ranging from execution to prolonged warehousing to continued postrelease supervision (see Garland 2001; Dubber 2002b; see also Bastian 2004).

Prisons for domestic enemy combatants in the war on crime unmodified are not run on a police power model. They are not so much households as they are *camps*, in the sense described by Giorgio Agamben (Agamben 1998; see chapter 7). The warden is not the father, nor the factory owner, nor the military superior. The *familial* model that best fits a carceral warehouse for enemy combatants is the slave plantation, not only because of its racialized hierarchy, with nonwhites predominating among the "inmates" and whites predominating among the guards (Dubber 1995, 720–22), but also because the distinction between lordless men, on the one hand, and nonhuman members of the plantation household, on the other, may be difficult to draw. Even the slave, however, remained subject to the police power of the householder, which meant that—at least in theory—his ill-treatment could expose the householder to discipline at the hands of the macro householder, provided it reflected the householder's unfitness to police (Dubber 2005b). Not even these theoretical, or aspirational, limitations apply to the treatment of prisoners as domestic enemy combatants.

In practice, of course, the treatment of prisoner-inmates as nonhuman members of the prison's quasi household may closely resemble that of prisoner-outlaws as unpoliced (and unpoliceable) nonmembers of that, or any other, household. The very fact that even the rightless slave could be conceptualized as a member of the household illustrates that, at bottom, the object of internal household governance (the policed) is essentially *ahuman*. He, she, or it is a resource in the hands of the householder (the policer)—the power to police is the "power to govern men and things" (*License Cases* 1847, 583). While the competent householder will adjust his governance according to the nature of his object, differential and object-specific treatment is determined by considerations of expediency and the maximally efficient use of available resources, as opposed to the object's entitlements or "rights." It may be prudent to give household members notice of what constitutes proper behavior since it is easier to obey explicit rules than implicit ones, but they are not *entitled* to receive notice, nor would they have standing to complain about the absence of notice in the event of a reprimand for the violation of an unannounced—and presumably unknown—rule. The household includes, after all, not only humans, but also animals, inanimate objects, and real property, not all of which could receive notice, never mind act accordingly. At best, to the extent that humans, for instance, operate more efficiently with notice—and perhaps, in some sense, animals as well—a householder may decide to give notice, even as a rule, whenever he seeks to manage (certain) humans (or animals), on certain days, in certain situations (Fuller 1969, 207–17; rule of law principles as prudential guidelines of "managerial direction").

The point is that police governance is driven by the policer-householder's analysis of the exigencies of a given threat scenario. The householder decides what is best for the household at any given moment and therefore also determines what requires his disciplinary attention. He may decide to use his disciplinary power, or he may decide not to use it. He may decide that a household governed by consistent rules operates more efficiently than one without such rules. He is the ultimate arbiter of threats—a particular act may constitute a challenge to his authority (or a threat to the household's police), or a certain thought, even a glare, or a less than expeditious carrying out of an order, or tardiness, or improper dress (either too fancy—an assumption of higher status—or not fancy enough—a sign of disrespect;

Hunt 1996), or impolite language, or an insufficiently bent knee, and so on (the list is by necessity endless). Since different household members may manifest disrespect in different ways, there is no reason to think that they are subject to identical rules of behavior, other than the one rule that they must not cause or threaten harm to the commonwealth of the household and or to the authority of its head.

Criminal Police: Protecting the Peace of Macro and Micro Households

Justice Thomas's reference to peace officers in *Morales* was meant to remind us that police officers do more than enforce the law; they also keep the peace. Vagrancy, the offense at issue in *Morales*, is the peacekeeping offense par excellence (cf. Neocleous 2005). As lordless men loitered about the English countryside in the fourteenth century, the royal household sought to control them by reintegrating them into various households in various ways, by forcing them to accept job offers rather than pursuing more lucrative employment opportunities, by delivering them to a householder who claimed them as his own, and eventually by committing them to the quasi household of the prison (23 Edw. 3, New Statute, c. 1 [1349]; 25 Edw. 3, Stat. 1, c. 1 [1350]). Vagrancy statutes thus served to protect, not any peace, but the *king's* peace—i.e., the king's *mund* over his newly claimed macro household of the realm—through various means, including, at the beginning, the use of micro households as local peacekeeping institutions.

But focusing on vagrancy threatens to obscure the true scope of criminal police. For *every* offense in the end is a police offense, and not just those traditionally categorized as such. Ultimately, there is no distinction between the two functions of the police officer. She is not *also* a keeper of the peace; she is nothing else. Being a peace officer is not part of a police officer's function; it is her only function. Criminal law in its entirety derives from the state's power to police; a crime is a crime insofar as it breaches the peace (*Foucha v. Louisiana* 1992, 80; LaFave and Scott 1986, § 2.10; Laylin and Tuttle 1922, 622; *Sutton v. New Jersey* 1917). But "the peace" is simply the householder's *mund*, and its "breach" represents an offense against the householder's authority to maintain the *mund* of his household. A crime is an "offense" precisely because it offends the sovereignty of the state. The "victim" of murder is not the person whose life has been extinguished or his relatives or any other person who suffers indirectly as a result of his death—it is the sovereign whose authority has been challenged (see *Heath v. Alabama* 1985; Dubber 2002b).

Hausfriedensbruch and *Landfriedensbruch*—breach of the house peace and of the land peace—are one and the same insofar as the peace of the land (the public peace) is also the peace of the sovereign's house (the private peace). Breaking the peace of a micro householder constitutes two offenses, then, one against the micro householder and one against the macro householder who long ago has incorporated all micro householders into his macro household, reducing former householders to household members. The offense of treason illustrates the point. Originally, there was only treason, the ultimate act of *felonia*, i.e., the breaking of the bond of loyalty between any man and his lord. Then, with the Treason Act of 1351, petit treason was distinguished from treason unmodified: petit treason was directed at the micro householders, and treason unmodified at the macro householder (Treason Act of 1351, 25 Edw. 3 stat. 5 c. 2).

Petit treason could be committed only against the *head* of a micro household, the local lord. Treason unmodified, by contrast, could be committed against any member of the king's *micro* household (Treason Act of 1351, 25 Edw. 3 stat. 5 c. 2). Furthermore, the king's micro household included not only his immediate relatives (his family in the narrow sense) but also his officials. An offense against a royal justice, for instance, was an offense against the king himself and therefore constituted treason. (In fact, it was this expansive definition of the king's personal household, and the concomitant broad reading of treason, that prompted the definition of treason in the Treason Act in the first place and, much later, would become a bone of contention in the lead-up to the American Revolution [Dubber 2005b].) Still, while merely imagining the king's death was enough to be treason, one would actually have to kill a royal official to commit treason. The scope of petit treason was likewise limited to actual killings of local lords, reflecting once more the integration of the micro householder into the king's macro household. The local lord deserved no more, and no less, protection through the criminal law than did a royal official.

Eventually, petit treason disappeared entirely, along with—in Anglo American law, but not in German law (see German Penal Code §§ 123 [breach of house peace], 125 [breach of land peace])—breach of the house peace. Only treason unmodified remains, where it is understood to mean treason against the sovereign. The integration of the micro householder and his household into the macro household is complete: Initially, there were only offenses against the micro householder. Then offenses against the macro householder were differentiated from, and considered more serious than, offenses against the micro householder. Eventually, there were only offenses against the macro householder.

Today petit treason is classified as ordinary murder.[2] As with any other homicide, the murder of a micro householder constitutes a crime only insofar as it offends the dignity of the sovereign. Killing a micro householder is no longer offensive to the micro householder himself but to the macro householder. As with any other homicide, murdering a micro householder defies the macro householder's authority, and breaches his *mund*, all the while depriving him of a human resource.

In the United States, the rationale of petit treason survives, however, even if the crime did not. The offenses of breaking and entering, and of trespass, are at bottom offenses against the householder's peace. The move away from a territorial or physical approach to the law of trespass—and, by extension, the law of burglary, which is defined as trespass plus an intent to commit a crime while inside—represents not so much an abandonment of anachronistic formalism as it does a more direct manifestation of the nature of trespass as a breach of the peace, as opposed to the penetration of a physical barrier: trespass was always about breaking a peace, not a window. Similarly, the householder's discretionary authority to use deadly force to protect his household against burglary, even if none of its human constituents is endangered in any way, survives in many U.S. jurisdictions (N.Y. Penal Law § 35.20(3); see Dubber and Kelman 2005, chap. 7).

Most interesting, perhaps, is the significant role the peace of the micro household continues to play in the federalist system of U.S. government and, more specifically, in the conceptualization and development of federal criminal law in relation to state criminal law. The theory of U.S. federalism attempts to integrate micro households—states—into a macro household while maintaining their household identity (sovereignty). The states must retain their police power, for without that power they would no longer exist as political households. The American revolutionaries went so far as to deny the national government the power to police, framing the federal government instead as a coordinator, arbitrator, and representative of a group of sovereign households (contrast chapter 3, which explores the evolutionary dispersion of central police power in Canadian federalism). Having thrown off the policer-king, the American Founding Fathers were understandably leery of subjecting the newly independent states to the police power of another householder. And so they arranged for an apersonal national government that facilitated the exercise of the states' internal police power (Dubber 2005b).

This arrangement persists on paper to this day. In fact, however, the federal government soon began exercising a police power, all the while insisting that its power was limited to the regulation of interstate and international commerce and the like (see, already, Freund 1904, 63; see also Novak 2002, 269–70). The Founding Fathers did not go so far as to deny the national government the sovereignty that they thought essential to the very notion of government. The concept of sovereignty, however, was not radically reconceptualized, but remained rooted in the concept of the householder's authority. As a householder, any sovereign also possessed the power to police. And so setting up a national government necessarily also meant granting that government the power to police. The history of the federal police power in the United States—and with it of federal criminal law as a manifestation of that power—thus has been the history of its denial. Most recently, in *United States v. Lopez*, the U.S. Supreme Court struck down a federal criminal statute because it amounted to a de facto exercise of the police power, a power the federal government does not have de jure (*United States v. Lopez* 1995). And yet federal criminal law continues to expand, while courts continue to intone the familiar refrain that criminal law remains "the business of the States" (*Patterson v. New York* 1977, 201).

The classification of a *state* statute as an exercise of the police power has the exact opposite effect: it virtually insulates the statute from scrutiny. (When it comes to federal statutes, the commerce clause—which gives the federal government the power to regulate interstate commerce—performs very much the same function, *pace Lopez*.) The one notable exception to this general rule is the infamous case of *Lochner v. New York*, where the U.S. Supreme Court invalidated a state maximum-hours statute backed up by criminal sanctions as an improper exercise of the police power (*Lochner v. New*

York 1905). (The Court reasoned that there was an insufficient connection between the means—limiting the number of hours bakers could work—and the purported end—the police, i.e., the public welfare, as opposed to the welfare of bakers or the interests of unions.) This opinion, however, was soon repudiated by the Court—most notably in a series of cases upholding New Deal legislation—and has for decades been the subject of virtually unanimous criticism, if not outright derision, among judges and academic commentators, to the point where "Lochnerization" became synonymous with judicial usurpation of power.

The coexistence of federal de facto police power and state de jure police power is most vividly illustrated by the so-called dual sovereignty exception to the prohibition against double jeopardy. Since a crime is a crime insofar as it gives the state offense, a single act can be subject to punishment by several offended sovereigns. If the fatal blow is inflicted in one state and the victim dies in another, both states can take offense and punitively respond to the assault on their sovereignty in the form of a violation of one of its criminal norms and the deprivation of one of its human resources. This double punishment for a single act does not technically violate the federal constitutional prohibition against twice putting someone's life or liberty in jeopardy "for the same offense" (U.S. const. amend. V) because there were in fact two offenses—one against the first state, and another against the second (*Heath v. Alabama* 1985). More significant for our purposes, the dual sovereignty exception also applies to acts that offend both a state and the federal government. The nation, in other words, also enjoys sovereignty and therefore also possesses the police power incidental to it.

The distinction between petit treason and treason highlights not only the distinction between the macro household of the state and micro households within it, but also that between the king's macro household and his own micro household. While it is true that the expansion of royal power was also the expansion of the royal household—by means of the expansion of royal "common" law applied and enforced by the royal courts—the distinction between the king's micro household and the macro household (the kingdom) remained significant. This distinction underlies that between bureaucracy and population, between state and civil society (cf. Neocleous 2005), between officials and the public. In England the household origins of today's state institutions were better preserved than in the United States, as illustrated by such institutions as chancery (headed by the chancellor, the king's chaplain, also referred to as "the king's conscience"), exchequer, chamber, and wardrobe ("Household" 2004).

Even as the macro householder expanded his household to encompass every resource—human and otherwise—within his realm, he also maintained the distinction between his micro and macro households. While, within his micro household, every member owes deference to him as the householder, every member of the macro household also owes deference to members of the sovereign's micro household, who are under his immediate *mund*. Members of the sovereign's micro household perform the function analogous to that of the slave overseer in the plantation household—they enforce and protect the authority of the master while personifying it. The head of household is constructively present in its deputies and any offense against them is ultimately an offense against him. Disobedience of a police officer's orders thus is also disobedience of the sovereign, an offense against the authority of the state (see, e.g., N.Y. Penal Law § 195.10; refusing to aid police officer classified as offense against "public administration"). Even injuring a police animal "while in the performance of its duties" is criminalized (N.Y. Penal Law § 195.06). The German Penal Code devotes an entire chapter to offenses constituting "resistance to state authority" (German Penal Code chap. 6).

Offenses against a state official represent two offenses against the state: like all other offenses, they offend the public peace; but they also constitute a form of treason in that they specifically offend the private peace of the sovereign's micro household (see, already, Treason Act of 1351, 25 Edw. 3 stat. 5 c. 2; killing of royal justice constitutes treason unmodified). For that reason they are subject to enhanced punishment; the offender has manifested an exceptional level of disrespect for state authority and therefore requires exceptional correction.

While the distinction between the sovereign's micro household and his macro household continues to be vigilantly policed—also in the criminal prohibition of impersonating state officials (see, e.g., N.Y. Penal Law §§ 190.25 and 190.26)—it is at the same time obscured and denied in various ways. Note, for instance, state officials' self-characterization as "public servants." The servant status of public officials is taken quite literally. U.S. federal criminal law, for instance, sanctions breaches of a duty of loyalty owed by public servants to the public. It constitutes federal criminal fraud to deprive the public of its "right to honest services" (18 U.S.C. § 1346). This federal criminal provision mirrors—and increasingly serves to supplement—private law, which places upon employees the same duty of loyalty toward their employers (see Dubber and Kelman 2005, chap. 11). It is not difficult to conceptualize a business as a quasi household; by contrast, thinking of clerks at the local Department of Motor Vehicles office as members of a household governed by the public-as-householder is not so easy. Public servants are servants of the public only—and at best—in the sense that they are servants of the sovereign who in turn *represents* the public.

Representation should not be confused with identity, however, no matter how strenuously the ideology of the modern democratic state might deny the existence of a sovereign apart from the public it is said to represent. "The public," after all, is also the sovereign's macro household. To declare the identity of public and sovereign cannot alter the fact that the sovereign continues to exercise the power to police over the public considered as members of his household. That is what the police power is, after all—the expansion of patriarchal power over one's micro household to the macro household of the state (Rousseau 1755).

Now, it is of course true that, at least in the United States, members of the public, or to a lesser degree even members of the sovereign's micro household (though members of the President's "cabinet" continue to "serve at his discretion," as do his cadre of "White House" advisors, counsels, deputies, etc.) no longer owe personal allegiance to an individual householder. The personal head of the household has been removed, but the mode of household governance has been retained. Allegiance is still required—and its absence sanctioned—but the allegiance now pledged, in the United States, is to apersonal lords and, eventually, to a god: "the Flag of the United States of America, and to the Republic for which it stands: one Nation under God, indivisible, with Liberty and Justice for all." Alternatively, the head of the republican household is said to be "the law" (in Thomas Paine's words, "in America THE LAW IS KING" [Paine 1776]). In this view, the head of household to whom loyalty is owed is not an abstract symbol of a political community but an abstract idea, or perhaps a set of abstract norms. (The U.S. Pledge of Allegiance captures one central aspiration of the idea of law—"liberty and justice for all.") The republican sovereign then is the public, a flag, a nation, a deity, an idea, or an aspiration. Whatever the sovereign is, it is emphatically *not* a person. This credo was treated as true by definition; for if the sovereign were a person, the United States would no longer be a republic, and the American Revolution would have been for naught.

But what is true by definition is not necessarily true in fact. In fact, sovereignty is always also personal as persons wield the power to police over the very public whose identity with sovereignty is postulated. Since their sovereign power is not acknowledged, however, it also is not subject to scrutiny or critique. In fact, since the state itself does not exist according to the prevailing ideology, and as the public polices itself in the position of both policer and policed, householder and household, state power becomes invisible. From the perspective of the stateless United States, the problem of the legitimacy of police power is limited to those countries—"continental Europe"—that acknowledge the existence of the state and recognize the administration of the state and its relationship with the public, on one hand, and the government, on the other, as a central challenge of state governance.

A principle of legality (*Legalitätsprinzip*) that radically—if incompletely—restricts the discretion of state officials, say, by requiring them to pursue every violation of state norms, is therefore only appropriate in these countries (German Code of Criminal Procedure § 152; principle of compulsory prosecution). In the United States, state officials need no such constraints because whatever power they exercise, they exercise in the name of the public as householder. They are, at most, the public's deputies, mere instruments of the public's self-police.

Acting Up and Acting Down: White Collar Crime and the Case of Martha Stewart

Many members of the public do identify themselves with state officials in general, and police officers in particular, and thus view themselves as insiders, i.e., as members of the sovereign's micro household, or perhaps deny the existence of a distinction between the sovereign's micro and macro household altogether. This identification is particularly common, we may surmise, among those members of the public who rarely come in contact with state officials or, if they do come in contact with them, summon their assistance, rather than feel the sting of their nightstick. These individuals, we may further speculate, in private life also are more likely to wield householder power rather than be the object of another's householder power.

Collectively, as the law-abiding public, these individuals regard themselves as engaged in a common policing task with police officers, finding the distinction between themselves and the state obscured. That distinction, however, emerges all too clearly on those occasions when they feel state power brought to bear against them, rather than against those whom they regard as the proper objects of police power. So complete is the identification between the privileged and the police that even minor exercises of state power that would appear routine to the mass of the policed (see, for instance, the outcry about traffic arrests of suburbanites [cf. *Atwater v. City of Lago Vista* 2001]) are experienced as blatant overreaches of state power against the public by one of its servants.

Perhaps the most dramatic reminder of the vigilance with which the state polices the line between its micro household and the public's macro household, between the state and civil society, is the prosecution of white-collar crime. Consider, for instance, the much-publicized case against Martha Stewart, the self-made queen of domestic bliss and CEO of Martha Stewart Living Omnimedia, a company listed on the New York Stock Exchange and with over two hundred million dollars in annual revenue (in 2003). In April 2004, Stewart was convicted of lying to federal investigators about her reasons for selling stocks in another company. She was convicted of "obstructing justice" and making false statements to federal officials, both serious crimes under federal law, each punishable by up to five years in prison (18 U.S.C. §§ 371, 1001). The following month, Frank Quattrone, an investment banker, was convicted of obstruction of justice for forwarding an e-mail instructing subordinates to destroy documents related to an ongoing federal investigation (Glater 2004). In both cases, the defendants were not charged with the criminal conduct that was under investigation. The investigations with which Stewart and Quattrone were said to have interfered in fact turned up insufficient evidence of criminal conduct. The cover-up was not worse than the crime; it was the crime itself.

Stewart and Quattrone were put in their place. They were prosecuted for crimes against the state. In summation, the federal prosecutor in Stewart's trial urged the jury to contemplate the victim impact of her lies to federal investigators: "Don't think about the S.E.C. Don't think about the F.B.I., though they certainly were victimized. It's really our entire nation, our country, that is victimized" (Toobin 2004, 72).

Note that this plea not only labels state agencies as the victims of a criminal offense, but then glides from the victimhood of the Securities and Exchange Commission and the Federal Bureau of Investigation into that of the "entire nation." The implication here is that an offense against the authority of the state is an offense against civil society, much as an offense against the authority of the householder is an offense against the household. The welfare, if not the survival, of the macro household (civil society) depends on the householder's (the state's) ability to take measures as he (it) sees fit.

Identifying the interests of civil society with those of the state allows one to deny the possibility of difference between the two. When the operation of the state is obstructed, when a police officer's orders are disobeyed, when evidence is destroyed, when criminal liability is denied under oath or to a federal investigator's face, the victim is not just the state but "really" the entire macro household policed by the state.

Martha Stewart's case in particular illustrates the macro householder's age-old struggle of integrating micro householders into the macro household. As the head of a corporation, Stewart policed the members of her corporate household. This did not entitle her, however, to disrespect the authority of the macro householder over her. And so the state reminded her of her inferior status. In fact, the prosecution went farther; it implied that Stewart was unfit even for her status as micro householder, by exposing her gratuitously abusive behavior toward members of her micro household which—much like the medieval lord's inflicting harm on his man's life or limb—suggested that she was incapable of policing herself and therefore of policing her household. She was literally "demeaned," i.e., exposed as "mean" in the traditional sense of "low" or "base" (Strachan-Davidson 1912, 170), and her correction may be seen as reflecting her failure to act her part as a member of the macro household and, at the same time, as the head of her micro household. (It is no accident that frequent comparisons were drawn between Stewart and another businesswoman who was the target of a federal white-collar prosecution some ten years earlier, hotelier Leona Helmsley, dubbed the "Queen of Mean" [see Hales 2004].) In the end, her case was not about reminding Stewart that she was not above the law; it was about reminding her that she was below the state.

At this point, it should be noted that the criminal conduct under investigation in Stewart's and Quattrone's cases bore no obvious relation to harm suffered by particular individuals (i.e., by victims other than the state and its agencies). Securities fraud is a regulatory offense that is said to threaten the "integrity" of financial markets (*United States v. O'Hagan* 1997, 654). Under this view, the point of punishing securities fraud is not so much to prevent financial losses to individuals as it is to encourage—or at least to remove a disincentive for—individuals to invest in the market, on the theory that fewer people would invest less money in a market that does not give them a fair shake, say, because insiders trade on the basis of nonpublic information.[3]

The criminal offense of securities fraud, in other words, itself is a policing tool in the hands of the regulatory state, even if the institution being policed is the market (which is supposed to do best without policing). Securities fraud interferes with the state's regulatory framework and threatens its police authority (see, already, Blackstone 1765, 264; policing of "public marts"). For that reason alone, and wholly apart from any impact on individual victims, it entitles the state to use its police power to criminalize it.

Securities fraud, along with obstruction of justice and false statements, illustrates a type of offense that is central to the police power model of the criminal process: the victimless obedience offense (Dubber 2002b). In its focus on victimless obedience offenses, the police power model of the criminal process differs significantly from Herbert Packer's well-known crime control model of the criminal process (Packer 1968). Packer drew a distinction between what he termed the due process and the crime control models of the criminal process. Whereas the due process model sought fairness and truth, the crime control model was concerned with the efficient suppression of crime. Packer's crime control model, however, still assumed that the paradigmatic victim of a criminal offense is a person. The paradigmatic offenses were homicide, rape, robbery, and burglary, each conceptualized as an (intentional) act of interference with the rights or interests of another person. To prevent this interference, or at least to minimize its occurrence, the crime control model sought to put in place an efficient system of case disposition. The due process model operated with the same notion of crime, even though it emphasized bringing the perpetrators of these crimes to justice, rather than eradicating crime.

The police power model abandons this shared individualist foundation. Its paradigmatic crime is the offense against the state. Put another way, crimes that would appear victimless under the due process or crime control model now do have a victim, the state. Under the police power model of the criminal process, the state as householder disciplines individuals as members of the household for threats to its authority. The police power model thus is, at bottom, a familial model.

A rather different familial model has been proposed as an alternative to Packer's two models. In 1970 John Griffiths criticized Packer for drawing a false distinction between the due process and crime control models. In Griffiths's view, both models could be reduced to a "battle model" of the criminal process, one that "assumes disharmony, fundamentally irreconcilable interests, a state of war" (Griffiths 1970, 371). Instead, Griffiths argued, we should proceed from "an assumption of reconcilable—even mutually supportive—interests, a state of love."

The police power model proceeds from an altogether different assumption of identity—between the interests of the state and the interests of society, and by implication of every one of its members, including the offender herself. Punishment is no longer punishment, but correction. Offenders are subjected to "peno correctional treatment," which may include capital punishment (Dubber 2000). The state as patriarch metes out correction as it sees fit, rather than meting out justice for what is deserved. Where there is no conflict, there is also need for constraint.

The rationale for punishment under the police power model is treatmentism, which upon closer inspection turns out to be no rationale at all but rather the denial of the need for one (nor is it, strictly speaking, about punishment, which might be taken to imply constraints of desert and blame): once redefined as treatment, punishment needs no justification (or its justification is self-evident; Dubber 2002a). While Griffiths—and many others with him, including the drafters of the Model Penal Code, which has set the tone for U.S. criminal law scholarship and reform since the 1950s—held a benign view of treatmentism as rehabilitation, the police power model of the criminal process has shifted emphasis onto the repressive side of the treatmentist coin, incapacitation. Incapacitation is rehabilitation without the hope—or pretense—of reform.

The paradigmatic offender of incapacitative treatmentism is the incorrigible lordless man, who is literally beyond correction. The paradigmatic sanctions of incapacitative treatmentism thus are (physical or civil) death through execution; fatal imprisonment (which is fatal either because the sentence is life imprisonment without the possibility of parole or because prison conditions are such that death is likely before expiration of a sentence short of life)[4]; postprison supervision under strictly enforced and highly intrusive conditions; and a host of collateral disabilities (including ineligibility for state support and, most important, mass disenfranchisement—now four million persons [Allard and Mauer 2000]), which incapacitate by themselves in addition to increasing the likelihood of carceral incapacitation in the future. Heinrich Brunner long ago postulated outlawry as the *ur*penalty, which deprived its object of all rights (Brunner 1894a). Other, lesser, penalties—including afflictive penalties against the body—represented merely sticks in the bundle of deprivations that is outlawry. Today, physical and civil death are modern forms of outlawry, from which all lesser incapacitative police sanctions derive.

Rules of Law in the Police Power Model of the Criminal Process

In the remainder of this chapter, we will explore how some representative doctrines of U.S. criminal law fare in a police power model of the criminal process. Not surprisingly, traditional rules of criminal law—some of the most cherished among them—will turn out to interfere little with the operation of the treatmentist police regime in action. They survive mainly as the object of theoretical investigation and the subject of university instruction, in a parallel principled universe largely untouched by the reality of the criminal process.

LEGALITY PRINCIPLE

Let us begin with the principle that comes closest to an explicit attempt to place the state's police power within rules of law, the principle of *legality* (see Dubber and Kelman 2005, chap. 2). While U.S. law is occasionally said to recognize a principle by that name, a look at its various components suggests that it does not in fact place significant constraints on the discretionary power of state officials in the criminal process.

As we have already noted, there is no requirement that prosecutors or police officers pursue every provable violation of a state criminal norm (principle of compulsory prosecution), leaving charging and investigatory decisions to the discretion of individual officials, without meaningful guidance or review of any kind.

Moreover, the requirement of notice is entirely fictional. Good-faith reliance on a misinterpretation of a state criminal norm does not constitute a defense (see, e.g., *People v. Marrero* 1987). Publication of state criminal norms is required, but the publicity of legislative deliberations preceding the adoption of the norm satisfies the requirement (*United States v. Casson* 1970).

Retroactive criminal norms are prohibited, but here too courts have turned a blind eye to the retroactivity of judicially created—as opposed to statutory—norms (*Rogers v. Tennessee* 2001). In addition, they have refused to apply the prohibition to modern punitive measures such as registration and notification requirements for sex offenders (*Smith v. Doe* 2003) and even the indefinite incarceration of so-called sexually violent predators beyond their legally imposed sentence (*Kansas v. Hendricks* 1997).

Another aspect of the legality principle, specificity, is sporadically enforced and often treated less as a constitutional requirement than as a rule of statutory construction. Federal criminal law in particular abounds with vague criminal prohibitions that are regularly upheld on the ground that their vagueness was intended by the legislature. The federal racketeering statute (the Racketeer Influenced and Corrupt Organizations Act [better known as RICO]), for instance, explicitly provides that it "seek the eradication of organized crime," and to that end directs that "the provisions of this title shall be liberally construed to effectuate its remedial purposes" (Pub. L. 91–452, §§ 1, 904, 84 Stat. 922 [1970]). Another prominent example is federal mail fraud and "honest services" fraud in particular (18 U.S.C. § 1346), as the following exchange between a legal advisor to a congressional subcommittee considering the proposed adoption of the honest-services fraud statute (Ronald Stroman) and a justice department official testifying in support of its adoption (John C. Keeney) illustrates:

Mr. Stroman: Well, honest services of [a] public official, do you think that is . . . specific? I mean what does "honest services" mean? Certainly if I am a public official—

Mr. Keeney: Well, it means that—it means what the circuit courts of appeals have been saying for years that when a [public official] corruptly uses his office he is depriving the citizens of that State of his honest services.

Mr. Stroman: . . . If I am an official in the Government and I see the term "honest government," that certainly does not alert me . . . as to what you are trying to cover. I do not know what that means. . . . I would have to read the cases to specifically understand what the statute is attempting to get at. (Mail Fraud 1988, 48–49)

The vagueness of the federal mail fraud has been lauded as a breakthrough in the war on crime because it places discretion in the hands of state officials (prosecutors and, to a lesser extent, judges) to determine its proper scope: "When a 'new' fraud develops—as constantly happens—the mail fraud statute becomes a stopgap device to deal on a temporary basis with the new phenomenon, until particularized legislation can be developed and passed to deal directly with the evil" (*United States v. Maze* 1974, 405 [Burger, C. J., dissenting]; see also Kahan 1997). Displaying great appreciation for the difficulty of precisely defining prohibited conduct in advance in the pursuit of criminal elements, federal courts in particular have largely abandoned the traditional canon of strictly construing ambiguous criminal statutes according to the "rule of lenity" (*in dubio pro reo*; Kahan 1994).

Actus Reus

Traditional ("common law") principles of criminal liability likewise fit uneasily into the police power model of the criminal process. The presumptive limitation of criminal liability to affirmative acts, for instance, is beside the point in a system that seeks to identify threats to state authority. An attitude of disobedience can manifest itself in affirmative acts as well as in omissions. Any time the state commands action, the failure to act challenges its authority.

In some respects, omission liability has become the norm, rather than the exception. Take possession offenses, which account for a significant proportion of arrests and prison sentences in U.S. criminal law[5] and range from misdemeanors to first-degree felonies punishable by life imprisonment without the possibility of parole (e.g., *Harmelin v. Michigan* 1991). Possession offenses cannot be reconciled with the traditional act requirement in criminal law for the simple reason that possession is not an act, but a status, or a relationship between an individual and an object (see generally Dubber 2002a). So they are recast as omission offenses: possession of an item is criminal insofar as it implies the failure to separate oneself from the object, based on a general—but implicit—duty to *dis*possess oneself of contraband (see, e.g., Model Penal Code § 2.01; Texas Penal Code § 6.01[b]).

White-collar offenses provide another example.[6] Omission offenses are widespread in white-collar criminal law. A prime example is the crime of failing to file a tax return. Omission is also a common offense modus in corporate criminal law; the notion of a corporation not engaging in a voluntary act it ought to (and therefore must have been able to) commit is apparently less problematic than that of a corporation engaging in a voluntary act it ought not to commit (e.g., Model Penal Code § 2.07[1][b]). Moreover, officers within the corporation tend to be held individually liable for failures of supervision, rather than for affirmative acts. The omission may even consist of a failure to prevent or to end another omission, as in the seminal case of *United States v. Park*, where the CEO of a supermarket chain was held criminally liable for failing to keep a subordinate from failing to keep one of the chain's warehouses sufficiently rat free (*United States v. Park* 1975).

Mens Rea

The traditional *mens rea* requirement fits no more comfortably into the police power model of the criminal process than does the *actus reus* requirement. Strict liability crimes are proliferating in U.S. criminal law. Simple possession offenses, which criminalize mere possession of an item without the need to prove an intent to use it in some way (for instance, through consumption or distribution in the case of controlled substances and through operation or threatened operation in the case of firearms), are popular policing tools (Dubber 2002a). Felony murder, which imposes strict murder liability on anyone who causes—even accidentally—another's death in the course of a felony, remains a central feature of U.S. criminal law doctrine, despite decades of academic criticism (see Dubber and Kelman 2005, chap. 10). Statutory rape, i.e., sexual intercourse with an underage female, continues to be treated as a strict liability felony. As a New York appellate court put it, a statute that "forbids 21-year-old males from having intercourse with females under 17, regardless of whether the accused is aware of the female's age" falls under "what is called the police power where the emphasis of the statute is evidently upon achievement of some social betterment rather than the punishment of the crimes" (*People v. Dozier* 1980).

In the case of white-collar crime, strict liability is the rule, rather than the exception. Individual criminal liability in a corporate setting frequently requires no proof of *mens rea*—the mere failure to discharge one's supervisory duty is often enough, without the need even to prove negligence (*United States v. Dotterweich* 1943).

In the case of *corporate* criminal liability, strict liability is the paradigmatic offense form, as traditionally the concept of a corporate *mens rea* was considered too fanciful a construct (or at least yet more fanciful than that of a corporate *actus reus*). Here the trend has been toward the recognition of corporate criminal liability for intentional crimes (*State v. Chapman Dodge* 1983), just as individual criminal liability has moved in the opposite direction, away from a presumed limitation to intentional crimes to the recognition of criminal liability for strict liability offenses.

In either case the police power model has increased the scope of criminal liability and thereby the authority of state officials who wield the unconstrained discretion to seek criminal sanctions against a particular object. From the standpoint of the discretionary police power model, the presence or absence of *mens rea* (or, for that matter, *actus reus*) is simply of no moment—the decision whether a particular threat source requires elimination, or at least containment, rests with the sovereign and his deputies, largely unconstrained by cumbersome doctrinal rules (see Kahan 1997).

Offenderless Offenses

In an important sense, the police power model of the criminal process operates with offenses that are not only victimless, but offenderless as well. The *actus reus* and *mens rea* requirements are compromised to such an extent that the humanness, or the personhood, of the offender is no longer a prerequisite for criminal liability. To the extent that the police power model of the criminal process focuses on the identification and elimination of threats to the state, rather than the definition and punishment of wrongs to persons, and reflects the sovereign's "power to govern men and things" (*License Cases* 1847, 583), the distinction between human and nonhuman threats has no principled basis. As threats to the police, persons are no more entitled to certain treatment than are other types of threat. It may well be, of course, that a wise policer will in fact differentiate between human and nonhuman threats, just as a wise householder might decide to treat his wife differently from his sons, his daughters from his horses, and his slaves from his olive trees. But, from the perspective of police, all threats are rightless, including human ones. At bottom, the object of police governance through the criminal process is the threat, not the offender.

Not traditional conduct offenses but status offenses and character offenses characterize the police power model. Explicit status offenses like loitering have been revived in the war on gangs (*Chicago v. Morales* 1999). Implicit status offenses like possession dominate the business of police, prosecutors, and courts (occasionally combining one status with another, as in the popular felon-in-possession statutes [Dubber 2002b, 73–74]). Character offenses like honest-services fraud criminalize disloyalty in any form. Endangerment offenses of all shapes and sizes—reckless endangerment (Model Penal Code § 211.2) is only the most explicit among them—that authorize the state to interfere before the infliction of harm, in many cases before the creation of risk in a particular case, flourish (Dubber 2005a).

So-called inchoate (or preliminary) offenses, like attempt, conspiracy, facilitation, and solicitation, similarly authorize state officials to interfere at ever-earlier points in the spectrum from criminal character to criminal thought to criminal act. Criminal solicitation, for instance, is complete once one person writes a letter asking another to commit a crime, even if the letter is not delivered, never mind read by its intended recipient (*People v. Lubow* 1971). An attempt has been committed as soon as the person has taken a "substantial step" in the direction of consummating the offense, no matter how far she is from actual consummation (*Commonwealth v. Donton* 1995); the defense of impossibility has been abandoned so that anyone manifesting abnormal dangerousness is punishable even if her attempt had no chance of succeeding, say, because the police officer she thought she was disobeying was in fact an actor on a TV show or because the cocaine she thought she was buying from an undercover agent was actually powdered sugar (*People v. Dlugash* 1977). A criminal conspiracy today is complete once one person *thinks* she is agreeing with another to commit a crime, even if her supposed coconspirator has no intention of ever committing it, so that there is no chance of the conspiracy bearing fruit (*People v. Berkowitz* 1980). Criminal facilitation has been committed as soon as a person does anything that she believes may help another to commit a crime; criminal intent on the part of facilitator is no longer required (*People v. Gordon* 1973). And, of course, even conduct that falls well short of an attempt, or for that matter of traditionally nonpunishable "preparation," is criminalized under the host of possession statutes that populate modern U.S. criminal law—including those criminalizing the possession of instruments of crime or weapons (Dubber 2002a).

In general, the creation and interpretation of criminal law is driven by a deeply felt need to facilitate the elimination of criminal threats. Ease of enforcement accounts for the popularity of possession offenses in the war on crime: they are easy to detect (through everyday pat downs or searches incident to arrest) and easy to prove (thanks to the elimination of *actus reus* and *mens rea*) (Dubber 2002a). Any residual complications are removed through the liberal use of presumptions (from presence to possession, from possession to knowing possession, from knowing possession to the intent to use; on "Anti-Social Behaviour Orders" in the United Kingdom as police facilitators, see chapter 5).

Criminal Procedure

The absence of constraint through traditional doctrinal rules of law permeates the entire criminal process; it characterizes not only the substantive law of crimes, but the law of criminal procedure (i.e., the criminal process in the narrow sense) as well, not to mention the practice of penal enforcement, which—as we have already noted—occurs primarily in carceral warehouses, where inmates are at best policed and at worst detained as lordless men.

Criminal procedure under the police power model is dominated not by the traditional criminal trial, but by plea bargaining, which brings to bear the full power of the householder-state upon the suspect in that it is dominated by the essentially unreviewable discretion of state officials—including not only prosecutors and judges, but also court-appointed defense counsel and public defenders (Dubber 1997). Appellate review of plea agreements is virtually nonexistent. Except for a small minority of cases (less than 10 percent), all criminal cases are resolved through a guilty plea, not counting cases that are resolved through a bench trial, a juryless streamlined proceeding before a judge. While plea bargaining in theory is not necessarily inconsistent with a different model of the criminal process (Dubber 2004), plea bargaining in practice fits the police power model well, and does so by design: it is marked by the steeply hierarchical relationship between state officials and suspects, manifested in part by sentence discounts for acts of self-degradation and self-incrimination ("acceptance of responsibility" and "substantial assistance"; U.S. Sentencing Guidelines §§ 3E1.1, 5K1.1).

The process of the state's reasserting its authority through degradation and humiliation, of course, is not complete with the entry of a guilty plea (or, in those rarest of cases, a guilty verdict). It continues, and intensifies, with the imposition and infliction of the criminal sanction, which publicly communicates and then inscribes onto the convict a message of degradation. The paradigmatic sanction in U.S. criminal law is incarceration in warehouses for criminal threats, supplemented with intrusive noncarceral state supervision that treats offenders as incapable of self-police and frequently results in the resubmission to carceral supervision for technical violations of parole or probation conditions. (In 2001 the U.S. carceral population reached two million, at the world's highest incarceration rate of seven hundred per hundred thousand, with another four million persons on various types of "supervised release" [Bureau of Justice Statistics 2002a and 2002b; Walmsley 2002].)

Despite the obvious degradation implicit in the imposition and infliction of such police sanctions, U.S. criminal law recently has sought to sharpen the message of degradation and humiliation. Although corporal sanctions (with the important exception of capital punishment) have yet to resurface (but see Blecker 1990; Newman 1995), shaming sanctions have found enthusiastic supporters among the judiciary and even academic commentators. The degradation of white-collar offenders has attracted particular attention (see Kahan and Posner 1999). Not only does their elevated social status leave greater room for degradation, but—as illustrated in the Martha Stewart case previously discussed—their offensive behavior may be taken as evidence of an overestimation of their status vis-à-vis the state and its norms.

Public shaming, however, has been advocated for and applied in other cases as well. In *United States v. Gementera*, for instance, a 24-year-old convicted of "pilfer[ing] letters from several mailboxes along San Francisco's Fulton Street on May 21, 2001" was sentenced by a federal trial judge to "spend a day standing outside a post office wearing a signboard stating, 'I stole mail. This is my punishment.'" (*United States v. Gementera* 2004; with additional examples). The sanction was upheld on appeal against the charge that it constituted "cruel and unusual punishment" in violation of the Eighth Amendment to the U.S. Constitution on the ground that shaming sanctions are "hardly unusual" given their "proliferation" in U.S. courts. Persons convicted of driving while intoxicated, committing sexual offenses, and soliciting prostitution find themselves frequently among the targets of degradation sanctions (for instance, by being forced to wear special bracelets or to display bumper stickers identifying their crime of conviction, or having their picture, personal information, and crime of conviction published in newspapers, on billboards, on local TV stations, on the Internet, and distributed to neighbors and local schools).

Conclusion

To say that the criminal process can profitably be analyzed from the perspective of the police power is not to say that it cannot be viewed from other perspectives as well. In fact, I have argued elsewhere that the criminal process can be seen as manifesting the principle of autonomy, the basic principle of legitimacy in political theory since the enlightenment (Dubber 1998, 2004a). In the autonomy model, central features of state punishment—including the legality principle, the conduct and intent requirements in the substantive law of crimes, the jury trial before representatives of the offender's community, even plea negotiation as a participatory process of self-punishment in the law of criminal procedure, and inmates' participation in prison governance along with the retention of inmates' minimal rights as persons—are (re)conceptualized as attempts to legitimate the practice of punishment by rendering it consistent with the idea of self-government (Dubber 2004b).

One way of thinking about the police and autonomy models of the criminal process is as radicalizations of Packer's crime control and due process models.[7] Since the publication of Packer's *Limits of the Criminal Sanction* in 1968, the war on crime has transformed the comparatively quaint crime control model, which centered on the protection of individual rights through preventive interference, into the police power model, which instead seeks to eliminate threats to state authority. This development has thrown the due process model into sharper relief and exposed it as an essentially groundless historical construct ill suited to prevent the emergence and eventual dominance of the exigency-driven police power model. Today, the police power model better captures the reality of the criminal process, while the autonomy model must content itself with shaping its ideology.

Notes

1. See, for instance, the "principal objective" of the *International Journal of Police Science and Management*: "to facilitate . . . research into the criminal justice system and the practicalities of its day-to-day management of criminal justice organisations including, but not necessarily confined to, the police. Topics such as police operational techniques, crime pattern analysis, crime investigation management, accountability, performance measurement, interagency cooperation and public attitude surveys are welcome" (*International Journal of Police Science and Management* 2004).

2. Note, however, that originally the concept of murder too was intimately bound up with the notion of a betrayal of one's lord and was therefore treason (O'Brien 1999, 79; 1996).

3. Consider, once again, the Stewart case. Initially, Stewart also was charged with *securities fraud*—and not merely with making a false statement to state officials— for having denied any insider trading with the intent to artificially inflate her company's stock price by dissuading investors from selling shares. (This count eventually was dismissed by the trial judge on the facts, not on the law.) Here, securities fraud and false statements work hand-in-hand to enforce state authority (see Moohr 2004).

4. As of 2003, almost one in every ten prison inmates in the U.S. was serving a life sentence. In some states, including California and New York, that proportion approximates one in five (Mauer, King, and Young 2004).

5. For instance, in 1998, possession offenses accounted for 17.9 percent of arrests in New York State and 20 percent of jail or prison sentences (Dubber 2002a, 834, 857).

6. Note also that the concept of a white-collar offense itself is based not on conduct but on status.

7. Another way is to regard the distinction between the two models as reflecting that between the realms of "police" (patriarchal apersonal order maintenance according to maxims of expedience) and of "law" (self-government of persons by persons under principles of justice). The latter distinction is explored in Dubber 2005b and problematized in Farmer 2005.

References

Agamben, Giorgio. 1998. Homo sacer: *Sovereign power and bare life*, trans. D. Heller-Roazen. Stanford, CA: Stanford University Press.

———. 2000. *Means without ends: Notes on politics*, trans. V. Binetti and C. Casarino. Minneapolis: University of Minnesota Press.

Allard, Patricia, and Marc Mauer. 2000. *Regaining the vote: An assessment of activity relating to felon disenfranchisement laws*. Washington, DC: The Sentencing Project.

Atwater v. City of Lago Vista 2001. 532 U.S. 318.

Baker, J. H. 1990. *An introduction to English legal history*. 3d ed. London: Butterworths.

Bastian, Robert L. 2004. Exporting America's shame. *Los Angeles Times*, May 6.

Bentham, Jeremy. 1789. An introduction to the principles of morals and legislation. In *The works of Jeremy Bentham*. Vol. 1, ed. J. Bowring. Reprint. New York: Russell & Russell, 1962.

Blackstone, William. 1765. *Commentaries on the laws of England*. Vol. 1. Oxford: Oxford University Press.

———. 1769. *Commentaries on the laws of England*. Vol. 1. Oxford: Oxford University Press.

Blecker, Robert. 1990. Haven or hell? Inside Lorton Central Prison: Experiences of punishment justified. *Stanford Law Review* 42:1149–249.

Brunner, Heinrich. 1894a. Abspaltungen der Friedlosigkeit. In *Forschungen zur Geschichte des deutschen und französischen Rechtes*, 444–81. Stuttgart: J. G. Cotta.

———. 1894b. Ueber absichtslose Missethat im altdeutschen Strafrechte. In *Forschungen zur Geschichte des deutschen und französischen Rechtes*, 487–523. Stuttgart: J. G. Cotta.

Bureau of Justice Statistics. 2002a. *Prisoners in 2001*. Washington, DC: U.S. Department of Justice, Office of Justice Programs, July.

———. 2002b. *Probation and parole in the United States*. Washington, DC: U.S. Department of Justice, Office of Justice Programs, August.

Chicago v. Morales 1999. 527 U.S. 41.

Cole, David. 2002. Enemy aliens. *Stanford Law Review* 54:953–1005.

Commonwealth v. Alger 1851. 61 Mass. 53.

Commonwealth v. Donton 1995. 439 Pa. Super. 406.

Corn, Geoffrey S. 1999. "To be or not to be, that is the question": Contemporary military operations and the status of captured personnel. *Army Lawyer*, June, 1–18.

Department of the Army. 1956. *Field manual, the law of land warfare*. Washington, DC: Headquarters, Department of the Army.

Dubber, Markus Dirk. 1995. Recidivist statutes as arational punishment. *Buffalo Law Review* 43:689–724.

———. 1997. American plea bargains, German lay judges, and the crisis of criminal procedure. *Stanford Law Review* 49:547–605.

———. 1998. The right to be punished: Autonomy and its demise in modern penal thought, *Law & History Review* 16:113–46.

———. 2000. Penal panopticon: The idea of a modern model penal code. *Buffalo Criminal Law Review* 4: 53–100.

———. 2002a. Policing possession: The war on crime and the end of criminal law. *Journal of Criminal Law and Criminology* 91:829–996.

———. 2002b. *Victims in the war on crime: The use and abuse of victims' rights.* New York: New York University Press.

———. 2004a. Toward a constitutional law of crime and punishment, *Hastings Law Journal* 55:509–72.

———. 2004b. The criminal trial and the legitimation of punishment. In *The trial on trial*, ed. R. A. Duff et al., 85–100. Oxford: Hart Publishing.

———. 2005a. The possession paradigm: The special part and the police model of the criminal process. In *Defining crimes*, ed. R. A. Duff and S. Green, 91–118. Oxford: Oxford University Press.

———. 2005b. *The police power: Patriarchy and the foundations of American government.* New York: Columbia University Press.

Dubber, Markus D., and Mark G. Kelman. 2005. *American criminal law: Cases, statutes, comments.* New York: Foundation Press.

Foote v. State 1883. 59 Md. 264.

Foucha v. Louisiana 1992. 504 U.S. 71.

Freund, Ernst. 1904. *The police power: Public policy and constitutional rights.* Chicago: Callaghan.

Fuller, Lon L. 1969. *The morality of law.* Rev. ed. New Haven: Yale University Press.

Garland, David. 2001. *The culture of control: Crime and social order in contemporary society.* Chicago: University of Chicago Press.

Glater, Jonathan D. 2004. On Wall Street today: A break from the past. *New York Times*, May 4, 2004.

Goldfarb, Ronald L. 1995. *Perfect villains, imperfect heroes: Robert Kennedy's war against organized crime.* New York: Random House.

Griffiths, John. 1970. Ideology in criminal procedure or a third "model" of the criminal process. *Yale Law Journal* 79:359–417.

Hales, Linda. 2004. In the court of public opinion, Martha merits a split decision. *Washington Post*, July 17, 2004.

Hamilton, Walton H., and Carlton C. Rodee. 1933. Police power. In *Encyclopedia of the Social Sciences*. Vol. 12, ed. E. R. A. Seligman, 190–93. New York: Macmillan.

Harmelin v. Michigan 1991. 501 U.S. 957.

Heath v. Alabama 1985. 474 U.S. 82.

Herlihy, David. 1985. *Medieval households*. Cambridge, MA: Harvard University Press.

"Household." 2004. In *Guide to Medieval Terms*, ed. J. J. Arkenberg. http://orb.rhodes.edu/Medieval_Terms.html.

Hunt, Alan. 1996. *Governance of the consuming passions: A history of sumptuary law*. New York: St. Martin's Press.

Hyams, Paul R. 1968. *King, lords and peasants in medieval England: The common law of villeinage in the twelfth and thirteenth centuries*. Oxford: Clarendon Press.

International Journal of Police Science and Management. 2004. *Aims and scope*. http://www.vathek.com/ijpsm/aims.shtml.

John Jay College of Criminal Justice. 2004. Department of Law, Police Science, and Criminal Justice Administration. http://web.jjay.cuny.edu/~law-pol/lpcj_home.html.

Kahan, Dan M. 1994. Lenity and federal common law crimes. *Supreme Court Review*, pp. 345–428.

———. 1997. Three conceptions of federal criminal-lawmaking. *Buffalo Criminal Law Review* 1:5–22.

Kahan, Dan M., and Eric A. Posner. 1999. Shaming white-collar criminals: A proposal for reform of the federal sentencing guidelines. *Journal of Law and Economics* 42:365–88.

Kansas v. Hendricks 1997. 521 U.S. 346.

LaFave, Wayne R., and Austin W. Scott, Jr. 1986. *Substantive criminal law*, 2d ed. St. Paul, MN: West Publishing.

Laylin, Clarence E., and Alonzo H. Tuttle. 1922. Due process and punishment. *Michigan Law Review* 20:614–45.

License Cases 1847. 5 How. 504.

Liptak, Adam. 2004. In first rulings, military tribunals uphold detentions of four. *New York Times*, August 14, 2004.

Lochner v. New York 1905. 198 U.S. 45.

Mail Fraud 1988. Hearing before the subcomm. on criminal justice of the house comm. on the judiciary, 100th Cong., 2d Sess. 7.

Mauer, Marc, Ryan S. King, and Malcolm C. Young. 2004. *The meaning of "life": long prison sentences in context*. Washington, DC: The Sentencing Project.

Meikle, Scott. 1995. *Aristotle's economic thought*. Oxford: Clarendon Press.

Moohr, Geraldine Szott. 2004. White collar crime, prosecutorial power, and the adversarial system. *Buffalo Criminal Law Review* 8:165–220.

Neocleous, Mark. 2000. *The fabrication of social order: A critical theory of police power*. Sterling, VA: Pluto Press.

Newman, Graeme. 1995. *Just and painful: A case for the corporal punishment of criminals*, 2d ed. Monsey, NY: Willow Tree Press.

Nixon, Richard. 1968. *Toward freedom from fear (position paper on crime)* (presented in New York, May 8, 1968. Reprinted in Cong. Rec. 114: 12936, 12936 [May 13, 1968]).

Novak, William J. 1994. Common regulation: Legal origins of state power in America. *Hastings Law Journal* 45 : 1061–97.

———. 2002. The legal origins of the modern American state. In *Looking Back at Law's Century*, ed. A. Sarat, B. Garth, and R. A. Kagan, 249–83. Ithaca, NY: Cornell University Press.

O'Brien, Bruce R. 1996. From *morðor* to *murdrum*: The preconquest origin and Norman revival of the murder fine. *Speculum* 71 : 321–57.

———. 1999. *God's peace and king's peace: The laws of Edward the Confessor.* Philadelphia: University of Pennsylvania Press.

Packer, Herbert L. 1968. *The limits of the criminal sanction.* Stanford, CA: Stanford University Press.

Paine, Thomas. 1776. *Common sense.* In *Rights of man, common sense, and other political writings.* Reprint. Oxford: Oxford University Press, 1995.

Patterson v. New York 1977. 432 U.S. 197.

People v. Berkowitz 1980. 50 N.Y.2d 333.

People v. Dlugash 1977. 41 N.Y.2d 725.

People v. Dozier 1980. 72 A.D.2d 478, 424 N.Y.S.2d 1010.

People v. Gordon 1973. 32 N.Y.2d 62.

People v. Lubow 1971. 29 N.Y.2d 58.

People v. Marrero 1987. 69 N.Y.2d 382.

Pollock, Frederick, and Frederic William Maitland. 1896. *The history of English law before the time of Edward I.* 2d ed. Reprint. Cambridge, UK: Cambridge University Press, 1968.

Radbruch, Gustav. 1950. Der Ursprung des Strafrechts aus dem Stande der Unfreien. In *Elegantiae juris criminalis: Vierzehn Studien zur Geschichte des Strafrechts.* 2d ed., 1–12. Basel: Verlag für Recht und Gesellschaft.

Rogers v. Tennessee 2001. 532 U.S. 451.

Rousseau, Jean Jacques. 1755. *Discourse on political economy.* Reprint. Oxford: Oxford University Press, 1994.

Ruffin v. Commonwealth 1871. 62 Va. 790.

Schmitt, Carl. 1963. *Theorie des Partisanen: Zwischenbemerkung zum Begriff des Politischen.* Berlin: Duncker & Humblot.

Smith v. Doe 2003. 538 U.S. 84.

State v. Chapman Dodge 1983. 428 So. 2d 413 (La.).

Strachan-Davidson, James Leigh. 1912. *Problems of the Roman criminal law.* Vol. 1. Oxford: Clarendon Press.

Sutton v. New Jersey 1917. 244 U.S. 258.

Tiedeman, Christopher G. 1886. *A treatise on the limitations of police power in the United States considered from both a civil and criminal standpoint.* St. Louis, MO: F. H. Thomas.

Toobin, Jeffrey. 2004. A bad thing. *The New Yorker*, March 22, 2004.

Treason Act of 1351, 25 Edw. 3 stat. 5 c. 2.

United States v. Casson 1970. 434 F.2d 415 (D.C. Cir.).

United States v. Dotterweich 1943. 320 U.S. 277.

United States v. Gementera 2004. 379 F.3d 596.

United States v. Lopez 1995. 514 U.S. 549.

United States v. Maze 1974. 414 U.S. 395.

United States v. O'Hagan 1997. 521 U.S. 642.

United States v. Park 1975. 421 U.S. 658.

Valverde, Mariana. 2004. The production of urban moral order: Appellate courts and their knowledge games. www.law.berkeley.edu/institutes/csls/valverdepaper .pdf.

Vinogradoff, Paul. 1913. Foundations of society: Origins of feudalism. *Cambridge Medieval History* 2:630–54.

Walmsley, Roy. 2002. *World prison population list.* 3d ed. London: Home Office Research, Development and Statistics Directorate.

CHAPTER FIVE

The Jurisprudence of Security

The Police Power and the Criminal Law

LINDSAY FARMER

In a series of lectures delivered at the University of Glasgow between 1762 and 1763, Adam Smith, the Professor of Moral Philosophy, delineated the province of jurisprudence. He defined it in general terms as "the theory of the rules by which civil governments ought to be directed" or, otherwise, "the theory of the general principles of law and government" (Smith 1978, 5, 398). This he saw as comprising four main objects: the maintenance of justice, the provision of police, the raising of revenue, and the establishment of arms. Police in turn comprised three objects: cleanliness, security, and cheapness or plenty (331). Security was understood as the object of "preventing all crimes and disturbances which may interrupt the intercourse or destroy the peace of the society by any violent attacks," and it required the rigorous and severe execution of properly formed laws as well as street patrols to deter or intimidate villains. He went on to comment that security was not only to be achieved through the provision of laws or numbers of town constables but also depended on the spread of commerce and prosperity. That law was no guarantee of security was demonstrated by two examples. First, he compared London and Paris, arguing that though London was larger and had but few police statutes there was less crime than in Paris, where the police was a "very burthensome part of the law" (332). He then pointed out that in Glasgow, "where each one seldom has but one man servant, there are few or no capitall [*sic*] crimes committed, and those that are, most commonly by strangers; whereas at Edinburgh, where the resort of the nobility and gentry draws together a vast number of servants who are frequently set adrift by their masters, there are severall [*sic*] every year" (333).[1] The control of crime thus depended as much on the management of the economy and the production of social wealth, which would reduce the number of servants and dependents, as on creating new laws or placing greater numbers of constables on the streets.

This passage is well-known, having frequently been cited by those concerned to recover the broad European police tradition referred to by Smith from its more narrow modern meaning. "Police" was to be understood as the science of government in a broad sense, which for Smith linked it to the nascent science of political economy and explained his disinclination to investigate further the principles of either cleanliness or security as distinct topics (at least as far as these related to penal laws or institutions; Neocleous 2000a, chap. 2). My interest here, however, is less in the differences or historical shifts between the two senses of police than in the tensions in the relationship between jurisprudence and police. It is clear that for Smith the science of police was understood to fall within the province of jurisprudence, and that this was broadly consistent with contemporary understandings of the subject (Hume 1981, chap. 2). However, although the lectures undertake a broad historical survey of the connections between principles of justice and historical forms of government, the bulk of the subject matter of "police" is dismissed here as being of only inferior importance. Yet Smith's broad understanding of jurisprudence was itself later to be excluded from the province of Anglo American jurisprudence, pushing the concept of police even further toward the peripheries of legal thought. Police, in the broad sense, remains firmly within the sphere of government but outside the sphere of law or justice.

There is a further tension between justice, seen as the principles governing the public and private relations between persons (particularly with respect to the security of property), and criminal law, seen as security. Smith saw the sphere of private law as including rules protecting personal rights (person, reputation, and estate) against the delinquency of others (Smith 1978, 103–40), with the justification for the infliction of punishment arising from the private resentment of the victim moderated through the sentiments of the impartial spectator (104). At the same time, he refers to the importance of considerations of public good or utility as factors in the creation of penal law and the justification of punishment, though the precise relationship between the individual and collective interest is not explored.[2] Justice is a matter of private right, and more particularly private law, rather than being a principle governing the relation between state and individual. Indeed, though the tension between security of property and person and a more general security has pervaded academic discussion, in practice, Anglo American law has long found it convenient to favor this latter view of the criminal law as the guardian of an ill-defined collective interest (see chapter 4). The question of justice, except perhaps in the systemic and managerial sense of criminal justice, is frequently marginal to the exercise of criminal law.

These tensions that we find in Smith, between police, law, justice, and security, continue to stalk the modern debate about the police power. One of my aims in this chapter is to begin to distinguish between some of the senses in which these terms are used in contemporary theoretical, historical, and comparative debates to clarify the issues at stake. In so doing I want also to express an unease with the way that certain broad categories such as police power are used in the literature, for the term "police power" has acquired a number of different meanings that are not always consistent with one another. My other main aim can be described more positively, and ambitiously, as the attempt to recover a sense of jurisprudence that is broad enough to include study of the police power. If questions of police and security have been excluded from the province of jurisprudence, then it is surely important to ask how our understanding of that field can be changed so as to reincorporate these issues. And in doing this I shall argue that it is useful to recover the sense from Smith of the study of jurisprudence as a historical inquiry into the theory of the rules by which civil government ought to be directed.

The chapter is in three sections. First, I shall draw on the historical and theoretical literature on police science to make a series of critical remarks about the relation between police power and criminal law from a theoretical and comparative perspective. In the second section I will discuss the relationship between police power and the criminal law in relation to the introduction of the Anti-Social Behaviour Order in the United Kingdom, a recent instrument introduced for the control of public order and security. And in the final section I shall make some broader remarks about criminal jurisprudence understood as a jurisprudence of security.

Police Power and Criminal Law

Recent historical research has revitalized interest in police and police power in two important respects. On the one hand, social historians have challenged histories of the police that saw the development of a professional, uniformed force, on the model of the London Metropolitan Police, as a natural response to the growth of disorderly and criminogenic industrial cities. These revisionist accounts have drawn a strong distinction between the "old" and the "new" police, stressing three particular elements of the development. The new police did not act in a vacuum, usually replacing older established mechanisms for the production of social order; they focused solely on the prevention and management of crime, rather than social order (security) more broadly conceived; and there was frequently a great deal of resistance to the new police and the bourgeois values that they sought to impose (for a survey of this work, see Emsley 1996; Gatrell 1990; Storch 1975; Hay and Snyder 1989). The revisionist accounts have shown how this idea and practice of policing as professional crime control, organized in the form of a centralized bureaucracy, comes to dominate thinking about police and their powers, marginalizing continuities with and older understandings of the police function. There has developed, as a consequence, a separation between the institution and the idea of police (Neocleous 2000a, xi).

The second major development in police research has focused on the place of the police power and police science in the development of modern governmental institutions. It is common ground among historians that police power (in a broad sense) with its origins in the management of the family or household (*oeconomy*) was fundamental to the operation of the early-modern state. Recent research has pointed not only to the well-known history of police science in Germany and France (Pasquino 1991; Raeff 1983) but also to the more neglected place of police science within the Anglo American political tradition (Dubber 2004a, pt. 1; Neocleous 2000a; Tomlins 1993; Novak 1996). This police power was primarily directed at the development and promotion of the public good and comprised a vast and heterogeneous range of objects, from the maintenance of sewers and streetlighting to the regulation of trade and commerce and public peace and order. However, what has been distinctive about recent work in this area is the argument, influenced by the work of Foucault, that the traditional police power did not disappear with the rise of the modern state but was transformed through the rise of, among other factors, the science of statistics and the development of political economy to become part of a new rationality of government, so-called governmentality (Foucault 2000, 214–22; Dean 1999, chaps. 1, 2, and 4). This, Foucault argued, was a specific and complex form of power (institutions, procedures, analyses, tactics) that "has as its target population, as its principal form of knowledge political economy, and as its essential technical means apparatuses of security" (Foucault 2000, 220). While this form of analysis of power does not take the state and state institutions as its starting point, it is also important to note that Foucault sees the state as having been "governmentalized" in the sense that problems of sovereignty, such as the competences of the state, come to be thought of within the matrix of powers and knowledges that have been produced by governmentality (221). In a more specific sense, governmentality goes hand in hand with the modern liberal state and capitalist economy as the means by which population and individuals are managed so that individuals can become the self-governing subjects of the liberal legal order.

The concept of police thus plays a number of crucial roles in analyses of governmentality: as the foundational administrative science, as a term used to denote a range of administrative practices, as a technique of surveillance and intervention, or as a term to describe the way that social behavior is structured by relations of power. This can include the modern idea of policing, but importantly, also goes far beyond it.[3] While we might be inclined as a result to see police as what Frégier called "the most solid basis of civilization" (Pasquino 1991, 108), the fact that the term is often used in diverse ways by different writers, and the resultant slippage between the different uses, has an impact on the analytic power of the category. I want to consider three important areas of slippage and ambiguity.

The first slippage is between talking about police and talking about the police power, which I shall pass over briefly at this point, though we shall return to it later. In many revisionist accounts the development of the "new" police sees a displacement of the "traditional" positive idea of police as administration by the idea of policing as concerned solely with the control or prevention of crime. These accounts stress the role of the new police in shaping the developing capitalist order by the rigorous policing of certain public spaces and groups of the population or traditional customary practices that were seen to be inconsistent with the exclusive ownership of property (Gatrell 1990; Carson and Idzikowska 1989). The new field of policing is narrower in scope than the traditional police power, though police powers for the control and detection of crime are themselves greatly expanded. While the role of the police in the shaping of social order is acknowledged, it is mainly in a negative sense—for their role in eradicating or stamping out certain practices rather than something more positive. This view of police as prevention stresses the developments of techniques of surveillance and social control, or more generally the panoptical elements of policing, particularly in the control of urban space, which is in turn linked to the centralization of policing as a mechanism of state power (McMullan 1998; Tomlins 2005). And in analyses of late-modern society this stresses the links between policing, risk, and the governance of security (Shearing 2001; O'Malley 1999).

While there is clearly a danger here of overstating the effectiveness of policing, it is also important to consider the positive aspects of the police role and the continuities with exercise of the older police power (e.g., Valverde 2003; Novak 1996). Equally, while it is usually implied that police are part of a range of mechanisms of security, the specificity of criminal police (whether public or private) as an institution or technique or its relation to the wider sense of police power is not examined.[4] Just as the exercise of police power cannot be reduced to institutionalized policing, the modern police must be viewed as operating within a range of institutions and practices that can be understood as police power in its broadest sense. It might also be remarked that the criminal police has developed a new police science—forensic science and criminal detection—that is completely discontinuous with older ideas of police science, and there is a tendency to neglect this (Valier 2001; Cole 2002). The important point here is that there are several senses of the idea of police in play and that the relation between these different senses is not clear. There is a basic distinction between the idea of police as an institution and of police as a form of governance. However, this latter sense breaks down between those who see it as unsystematic and continuous with the "traditional" police power and those who see it as evolving into a more systematic, risk-based form of governance, and while these two positions are not necessarily inconsistent with each other, the relationship needs to be much more clearly articulated. In either case it is necessary to examine specific practices in their institutional and social context to be clear what is to be understood by the term police.[5]

This is linked to a second slippage, which is one of periodization. The bulk of the literature on governmentality and crime focuses on changes in the policing of society with the development of neoliberalism. The attraction is obvious, as commentators on neoliberalism have persistently drawn attention to the dismantling of the welfare state, the deregulation or privatization of traditional areas of state activity and, in the sphere of crime, the development of new risk-based techniques of crime management and new forms of responsibility (Garland 1996, 2001; Garland and Sparks 2000; Feeley and Simon 1992, 1994; Shearing 2001). These analyses seek to answer the question of how social order and security can be guaranteed if the state is not to act in its traditional role as sovereign guarantor of order. However, it is worth noting that implicit in this kind of question is an assumption of the (traditional) centrality of the state that may not be warranted. Indeed, if techniques of governmentality have their origins in the late eighteenth and nineteenth centuries, as Foucault argues, we would expect to see the development of risk-based policing and responsibilization at a much earlier stage. There may be a qualitative change in late-modern society, but in this case the concepts of either police or governmentality may be too broad to be of much use in analyzing the developments. In fact, some writers go further to claim that in certain areas, such as licensing, there is a continuity with premodern ideas and techniques of police (Valverde 2003). To the extent that this is the case, however, it becomes unclear what is specific about governmentality as a form of power and raises, for me at least, the question of whether it is worth analyzing these forms of power as police power at all.

This leads to the third area of slippage, which is the one that is of greatest interest to me in this chapter, that between police and law, specifically criminal law, because here we see how the vagueness in the usage of the term "police" and in periodization have an impact on analyses of the police power and hence on how we might think about a jurisprudence of security. Mariana Valverde's analysis of police power is characteristic of many when she argues that police is "analytically separate from both the illiberal logic of sovereign punishment and the coercive logic of disciplinary normalization" (2003, 239). This is a claim that has two elements. On the one hand, it suggests that police power is a distinct field of intervention, characterized by the heterogeneity of its objects, the discretion with which it is exercised, and the fact that it has no clear or systematic knowledge format. To this Dubber adds that there is a strict hierarchy between the governors and the governed, that it is preventive, and that it is animated by considerations of efficiency rather than justice (2004a, introduction). On the other hand, it is a claim that there is a distinction between sovereign, or juridical, power and police power. Valverde says little explicitly about the former, but her analysis rests on Foucault's claim that juridical power is a sovereign power exercised by the state as a form of coercive power, based on prohibition (Foucault 1979, pt. 5).[6] Dubber goes somewhat further in presenting a compelling normative argument. For him, law is the "autonomous government of citizens by citizens" and is always based on consent, and thus carries a different understanding of the subject and object of governance (2004a, 91). This argument implies that law is grounded in a normative understanding of justice that is distinct from sovereign power. He also argues, however, that criminal law is a central manifestation of police power, thus reversing our normal assumption that it is the police who are applying the criminal law (Dubber 2004a, chap. 8; and see chapter 4). Thus, in addition to the three senses of police (the institution, police as heterogeneity, police as risk), there are three (overlapping) ideas of law in circulation: law (the juridical) as a means of characterizing a form of political order, law as a normative claim about the mode of government appropriate to certain subjects,[7] and law as a mode through which police power is exercised. Each of these is important but, equally, each raises different issues depending on the concept of police under discussion.

The first sense raises some broad theoretical issues about the relationship between law and political order, which need be only outlined at this point. Traditional political theory has interpreted sovereignty in juridical terms: founded on a contract and structured by rights. The analysis of governmentality, by contrast, argues that political and social relations cannot be reduced to the legal relation and that we should additionally focus on the governmental practices that shape the subject as the self-governing, rational actor presumed by political theory (Dean 1999, chap. 6).[8] Law remains important but is transformed into a normalizing power, alongside a range of other apparatuses (Ewald 1991). Thus, rather than viewing the modern period as one in which the juridical increased in importance, with the rise of freedom of contract and in the constitutions and codes of the nation-state, Foucault argues that it is a "phase of juridical regression" (1979, 144). The term "juridical" should thus be taken as a way of describing a particular historical form of sovereignty, which has also shaped our theoretical understanding of the concept.

More important for my argument are the relationships between police and law raised by the other two claims. I want to consider two aspects of these relationships. The first is the question of whether criminal law is a mode of exercise of police power, an autonomous form of power, or indeed both. This raises the crucial issue of how we would distinguish between the two. The literature suggests a number of possible bases for this distinction: the end pursued by each, the form of intervention, the subjects of regulation, and the forms of accountability. However, in each case, it is not clear to me that the grounds are adequate to support the distinction. Police power aims at the production and provision of security, but so too does the criminal law, where the power to punish is characteristically justified in the utilitarian terms of its role in preventing or deterring crime (Hart 1968). Police is heterogeneous, but anyone who has looked at a criminal code or studied the workings of the criminal courts will be able to tell you that so too is the law. Academic analyses focus on general justificatory principles and their role in structuring and justifying the use of state power, but this is hardly reflected in practice. The criminal law is applied to autonomous subjects, but this is a claim that is of greater rhetorical than practical impact (Norrie 2003; Lacey et al. 2003). The criminal law has historically also been a means of regulating or controlling risky conduct, with many central legal categories (e.g., recklessness) being formulated explicitly in terms of risk (Farmer 1997, chaps. 4, 5). The problem here seems to be less that of overstating the formality of law than of contrasting a normative claim about the proper realm of law with a descriptive claim about the nature of police (which is not unconnected to the tendency to see police as a residual category).[9] This further underlines the point, made by several authors, that "police" is seen as a descriptive category—and might lead us to ask the question of what a normative theory of police might look like.

This leads into the second issue, that of what would hang on the distinction. This goes beyond arguments about the proper spheres of police and law into arguments about the control of police—though here it will be necessary to introduce yet another understanding of police power. The conventional legal understanding of police powers in the United States and United Kingdom refers to the control and accountability of individual officers and the institution of police more generally (Loader 2000; Walker 2000). Police powers thus generally concern issues of how police officers deal with individual suspects and questions of how police forces should be managed by, and be made accountable to, political institutions. However, if we accept the argument of Neocleous (2000a, 117) and Dubber (2004a) that police power is independent of, not derivative from, the rule of law, this conventional focus is not only too narrow but is fundamentally misconceived. If, on the one hand, the criminal law is a mode of exercise of police power, the law can be seen as only one way the application and use of police power is structured. Law may limit the *use* of the power in particular situations because it is the preferred mode of application but cannot be expected to limit the *scope* of the police power more generally. This, as Dubber argues, remains fundamentally without limits. If, alternatively, we accept the argument that the criminal law is an independent form of power, we are implicitly also accepting the argument that the police power cannot be governed by law alone. It may show the external limits of that power (i.e., it does not extend to the government of autonomous subjects), but there remains a pressing need both to chart the power and to subject its exercise to "principled scrutiny" (Dubber 2004a, 197).

The control of police power thus requires thought not only about the form of law but also the institutional and political context within which the power is exercised, and this is where we must introduce a fourth understanding of the term that refers precisely to this context. In the United States the development of the police power has played out in a particular way with respect to the distinctions between federal and state powers, as the police power has been viewed as an executive power primarily linked to state government and thus as distinct from those public legislative (i.e., "political" in the modern sense) powers held by the federal government (Dubber 2004a, pt. 2). This introduces an important comparative aspect to any consideration of the police power, since in the context of the constitutional arrangements of the United States or Canada the debate about the control of police power is always also a political question resting on the distinction between federal and state powers, the former being subject (at least in theory) to the limits laid down by the constitution, while the latter is not. This broader context is crucial to any examination of the relationship between police and law, and one important function of the "new police science" would be precisely that of mapping this in greater detail.

However, this comparative context might also mean that the concept of the police power might be of limited use in the analysis of other social and political contexts. If debate about the police power in the United States has been conducted largely in terms of these questions of constitutional competences at the expense of consideration of the scope or guiding principles of the power, it is striking that in the British context even this element is missing. As I previously noted, the legal consideration of police power has been reduced to issues of criminal procedure and police-force management, reflecting the dominance of the modern institutionalized definition of policing.[10] The broader police function (in the traditional sense) has been taken over by local government, which possesses extensive powers to regulate the local environment. This, however, is rarely understood as an aspect of the police power, while policing is not normally understood as raising issues of governance beyond those of restraint and accountability. Equally, while police powers have come to be seen as raising issues of public law, and latterly human rights, they are strangely divorced from criminal law—which doctrinally, at least, continues to be viewed as a species of private law aimed at the protection of individual "rights," notwithstanding the widespread use of the criminal law for the protection of public values and institutions.

In the United Kingdom, then, a clarification of the relationship between criminal law and police power depends on the need to develop a much clearer understanding of the institutional and political context in which they interact—in Smith's terms, inquiring into the rules of civil government. While some recent work on police and crime has paid attention to community and local governance (see Crawford 1997), this has not been linked to local government or an understanding of the police power more generally. It is this relationship between local community standards, centralized managerial concerns, and the criminal law that must be opened out if we are to attempt to develop a jurisprudence of security. We can begin to study this relation through an examination of the recent introduction in the United Kingdom of the Anti-Social Behaviour Order.

The Anti-Social Behaviour Order

One of the most striking developments in British criminal justice over the last few years has been the introduction of the Anti-Social Behaviour Order (ASBO). This instrument was created in 1998 as part of a strategy adopted by the new Labour government for dealing with disorder, and its use was extended in England and Wales, and Scotland in 2003.[11] Aimed at a diverse range of persistent and low-level social disorder—noisy neighbors, truant youth, persistent drunks, drug dealing, graffiti, intimidating behavior, and so on—the ASBO seeks to give police, local authorities, and communities themselves new powers of control. The order, which might be obtained by the police, local authorities, or social landlords, can exclude named individuals from certain areas and prevent them from associating with each other for specified periods of time. The recent legislation gives police additional powers to disperse groups of people who are disturbing the public and to close premises (such as illegal drinking dens or places where drug dealing or consumption is taking place) that are regarded as the source of disorderly behavior, as well as extending powers to issue fixed-penalty notices. Parents can be made responsible for the control of their children through the issue of parenting orders (Padfield 2004). Local authorities, moreover, are now required to develop a strategy for the control of antisocial behavior, in consultation with police, landlords, and community groups (Scottish Executive 2004; Home Office 2003). The obtaining of an order does not require proof that there has been a breach of the criminal law, but breach of an order is a criminal offense. With its focus on the manifestations of persistent disorderliness the ASBO seems to bring together the themes (the control of urban space, alcohol abuse, juvenile offending, and petty violence) that have dominated the history of modern policing. It does so, moreover, in a way that links it up with a broader police power, as it is local authorities, rather than the police alone, who have been given a range of powers and responsibilities to prevent disorderly behavior.

Looked at in these terms, the ASBO would appear to be an excellent example of the traditional police power. As I have already pointed out, the behaviors targeted by the ASBO are heterogeneous, ranging from actions that are no more than nuisances to others that would fall clearly within the scope of existing criminal offenses.[12] Little links them other than that all can conveniently be lumped together under the label of their antisocial quality. Some of the concerns identified relate to the management of the environment or of housing, while others are a matter of crime reduction or prevention. They do not even seem to share a common idea of order or disorder. Some of the listed concerns relate to the control of individual behavior in public or private spaces, a sense of order or peace that might be opposed to that of disorder or disruption. Other concerns, however, such as those relating to the communal environment, suggest a sense of disorderliness as untidiness or visual disruption, as relating to graffiti or litter. These have little in common, unless it is to be found in the concept of community, a term that does a lot of work as it describes both the source of the concerns and the institutions of enforcement and is also performative in the sense that it seeks to enact the type of social interaction or space that will be the outcome of the strategy.[13] The power itself, then, in its definition appears to be disorderly, unlimited, and coercive.

Yet it is clear that the development of the ASBO also suggests changes in the government and production of social order, and in analyzing this we can be more specific about the content of the police power and the manner of its exercise. I would like to draw attention to four particular aspects of this development. First, the very emptiness of the category "antisocial behavior" means that particular localities and agencies will shape the content according to their own special concerns. Already there is clear evidence of conflict between the targets of government and community concerns (Flint 2002, 624)—even were we to assume that any community had consistent and established norms and values. What is significant here then is the particular network of responsibilities that is being drawn, linking central and local government, the police, social landlords, and community groups (Brown 2004; Vaughan 2000). This points to the long-standing, if neglected, link between police and local government and the way that responsibilities in this area have been redrawn in recent neoliberal initiatives around community crime prevention (Crawford 1997, 34–44). Second, the form of the ASBO suggests government at a distance and the creation of new kinds of responsibilities for the actions of others, making landlords take responsibility for the behavior of their tenants, parents for the actions of their children. Yet, in the privatization of certain duties, in the new networks and allegiances that are being actively fostered, and in the heavy-handed distribution of responsibilities, distinctive patterns of control are emerging that cannot be reduced to either the traditional police power or newer forms of actuarial justice. Third, while we can note the absence of a clear "knowledge format" in the self-evidence of the category, and that this would seem to differentiate the ASBO from more scientific techniques based on risk management, we should also note that there seems to be clear overlap with the actuarial justice of the "new penology."[14] The use of exclusion zones and curfews, the active management or monitoring of individuals and space by security agencies implies not only a coming together of these different types of techniques but also, to the extent that certain groups are excluded, evidences a radical departure in social policing. Finally, it is important to note here that the ASBO is not unique in the British context. Ashworth points out that its form parallels other types of order being created by statute that "deliberately move away from conventional criminal law approaches" (2004, 272),[15] and this would suggest that we are seeing changes in both the form of the criminal law and the police power. Security is being sought through the avoidance of what are perceived as burdensome due process protections and the development of innovative legal instruments, a new "civil-criminal" law (Zedner 2003a, 2003b). Where for Adam Smith the civil law was the realm of justice and a limit to the police power, we see here conversely that the blurring of the boundary between civil and criminal law does not increase the prospects for justice but potentially erodes them.

This brings us, then, to the question of the place of the criminal law and the possibility that law might limit or control the operation of the police power. The legal form of the ASBO has been the subject of a great deal of critical comment, largely because it explicitly seeks to avoid many of the procedural protections provided by the criminal law and under the Human Rights Act 1998 (Ashworth 2000, 2004). In fact, it appears that one of the principal purposes of the creation of the ASBO was to make possible the regulation of behavior that was difficult to prove in a criminal court either for reasons of sufficiency of evidence (where witnesses did not want to testify or where proof was simply unavailable) or where it was hard to prove the persistence of the conduct. As a civil order, the conduct is subject to lower standards of proof and certain evidential restrictions (such as the restriction on hearsay evidence) do not apply. The criminal offense is breach of the order, which does not require an investigation of intention or context or indeed of the grounds on which the original order was granted. This may lead to criminal punishment and, just as importantly, may be grounds for eviction where the person is in social housing. Criminal lawyers have thus been arguing that the ASBO is in fact criminal in character, because of the penal form of the sanctions, the nature of the proceedings, the nature of the acts penalized, and so on—a move that has given new life to a very old debate about the nature of the criminal law (Farmer 1996)—so as to ensure greater procedural protection for the defendant. However, it is unlikely that this line of argument, relying as it does upon claims about the fundamental nature of crime, the sanction or criminal proceedings, will be fruitful since it is directed principally at redescribing the form of the proceedings on the breach of the ASBO and not at the scope or manner of definition of the police power.[16] Indeed, even if the European Court of Human Rights were to declare that these were really criminal proceedings, and thus subject to protections under article 6 of the European Convention on Human Rights, the decision would scarcely affect the scope of the police power, merely its mode of enforcement in the particular context of the ASBO. If the criminal law has security as its object, then the argument in favor of constitutional or human rights protections can be only very partial unless perhaps more attention is paid to the constitutionalization of the substantive criminal law. Only by this means might it be possible to establish the grounds for a normative critique of the exercise of the police power.

Two alternative, and potentially more fruitful, lines of criticism have been advanced by Peter Ramsay (2004), focusing on the definition of antisocial behavior in the Crime and Disorder Act. His first argument goes beyond the criticisms of the lack of procedural protection to address the idea of legal subjectivity implied by the ASBO. He draws attention to the fact that antisocial behavior is defined in such a way that the courts are required by the Act to focus on the attitudes and character of defendants (rather than their behavior) when imposing an order, and that the order creates a positive duty rather than a prohibition (2004, 911–16). He points out that the basis of fault here is not the defendants' state of mind but their character or disposition toward their fellow citizens—that they have not acted as good citizens, neighbors, tenants, and so on. He contrasts this idea of "relational" citizenship with the idea of citizenship as a legal status, the formal equality that is recognized in the criminal law. Citizenship is not assumed as the formal basis of legal order but is assessed in the context of the evidence of antisocial behavior. The law relating to ASBOs does not proceed through a series of formal prohibitions of interference with objectively defined interests, but through an evaluation of continuing relationships. Thus, persons who are subject to an order are not entitled to full citizenship rights because of their prior failure in their duties toward their fellow citizens. This argument is potentially significant because, rather than simply trying to redescribe the police power so as to render it subject to due process protection,[17] it seeks to develop a normative conception of citizenship as the basis for the operation, and critique, of the police power. The police power is not seen as a residual category, or as bad criminal law, but as one that may be defined—and limited—in terms of a legal conception of citizenship and the duties to which it gives rise.

The second argument, also derived from the definition of antisocial behavior in the Act, focuses instead on the prospects for judicial scrutiny of the process through which behavior subject to the Act is defined. Acknowledging, as many critics have pointed out, that the Act creates a vast potential for the operation of discretionary power, Ramsay suggests that the defense provided in § 1(5) of the Crime and Disorder Act of 1998, that the behavior complained of was "reasonable in the circumstances," might create the potential for judicial scrutiny of the exercise of the power (2004, 918–20). A judgment of reasonableness is a political judgment, and the criteria for making this kind of judgment could be provided by the formulations of policy in the local-authority antisocial behavior strategy. He thus concludes that this section could be characterized as "defining the criteria for the exercise of a discretionary administrative power" (919). Once again the significance of the argument lies in the fact that, rather than stopping at the pessimistic conclusion of most lawyers that the Act creates an unlimited discretion, it seeks to explore how the Act provides legal resources for the regulation of that discretion. Importantly, the basis for scrutiny in this case is not normative but political, as it seeks to subject the actions of the network of administrative agencies that formulate antisocial behavior (including the police) to principled scrutiny.

The Jurisprudence of Security

In the quotation with which this chapter began, Adam Smith argued that the subject matter of jurisprudence was the "general principles of law and government." Anglo American jurisprudence has for a long time been more interested in law than government, has focused more on abstract rules rather than institutions, and has paid too little attention to the historical or sociological context within which law and legal institutions develop. In conclusion I want to argue that our understanding of the police power would benefit from a reinstatement within this older and broader tradition of jurisprudence, and I suggest that this is what I have been trying to work toward in this chapter.

Modern jurisprudence has focused almost exclusively on the question of sovereignty, whether of institutions of the state or of the individual. This leads to a viewing of issues in terms of the definition and control of juridical power, with certain fields (security, police) being seen as executive powers that are beyond control. This establishes the classical liberal problematic of government (Dean 1999) centered on the question of how to maximize individual liberty (or sovereignty or autonomy) against the state. If we can learn anything from the debate about police power here, it would be that these questions of sovereignty should be understood from within the context of the institutions and practices of government that have formulated them. Police power appears as a residual category when viewed from within this liberal problematic of government precisely because it is marginal to the juridical concept of sovereignty—notwithstanding that the practices of police have been central to the construction of the responsible, autonomous individual. By reversing our perspective we can see not only that the operation of the police power is a central institution of modern society, but also that we must seek to conceptualize it in terms that do not describe it as a lesser or subordinate form of sovereignty. This does not mean that this power cannot be exercised by and through law—and is not therefore the proper subject of jurisprudence—but that we should not begin to conceptualize it in terms of the sovereign state or individual. The significance of Smith's formulation thus lies in the fact that he not only captures the moment at which study of the police power is beginning to be marginalized within Western legal thought but also offers a juridical framework, focused on interpersonal relations rather than sovereignty exclusively, within which we began to reconceptualize the normative bases of police power. Rethinking the police power within this framework can offer ways of thinking about how it has been fundamental to the liberal project in ways that cannot be reduced to the purely juridical. Central to such an approach is the need to produce a theory of the police power that is historical and contextual and gives as much weight to the institutions of government as to the system of law (Dubber 2004b), but if we are to produce a normative, rather than merely descriptive, account of the police power, it is necessary also to think about concepts such as security that have been fundamental to the operation of that power.

It is clear that the concept of security is something that is both ever present and neglected in political theory, a feature that might be related to its obviously vague and indefinable quality.[18] Security is something that is desired, but at the same time can perhaps never be achieved. Security is a foundation of justice and liberty, even if its position as such has not been properly recognized (Neocleous 2000b). However, a recognition of this fact can take us only so far, for the crucial issue here concerns the changing content of the concept of security and the role of legal norms in the shaping and defining of the concept. For Adam Smith, security was closely related to security of property, both because security of property holding was seen as the foundation of social order and because the growth of prosperity—that is, the distribution of property—was seen as the principal means of securing a continuing social order against criminal activity. It is clear that our own understanding of security both includes and reaches beyond this, at least if we take seriously the manifold analyses of insecurity and risk in modern or late-modern society, where we are said to be faced by a range of global, national, and local threats. We are threatened by the environment and by terrorism, as well as a range of more conventional economic, social, and psychological threats, and the function of government (or more properly, of governmental institutions) is to produce security through the management of those risks. Security in this sense must be understood as a relational concept—both spatially and temporally—and one that is produced and defined through particular institutions and networks of government. Law cannot then be seen as having an independent normative basis, or as standing in opposition to the demand for security, for it has been central to the production of security in modern society. A jurisprudence of security, then, requires attention to certain points: what is being secured by law and how? What kind of threats is it being secured against? And in the context of crime and police we must ask how criminal law stabilizes or secures expectations, in relation to the conduct of both social life and government and state power.

We can conclude, then, with two more specific observations about the relationship between criminal law and police power. First of all, it is important to note that while the scope of the police power is extensive, it is frequently exercised through legal norms, and to the extent that this is the case this creates certain formal obligations on the mode of the exercise of power. Laws may create areas of discretion, but this discretion is usually subject to limits. Legal action is never purely arbitrary action. Thus, while the law may not in this way limit the scope of the police power, it can in important ways impose limits on the exercise of that power. Second, the police power is above all concerned with interpersonal relations and their management within particular localities and over certain periods of time. In securing these social relations the police power will draw upon existing social concepts such as property or citizenship that may both describe the practices and offer a normative basis for that practice. These justifications of police power are not fixed, and, as we have seen, with respect to the concept of citizenship, may offer the prospect for the critique and limiting of police power. The proper aim of a jurisprudence of security must be that of mapping the networks of institutions and practices, and underlying justifications for the exercise of that power. In this way, as Adam Smith recognized, security and police can be regarded as proper objects of the study of jurisprudence.

Notes

Thanks to Sarah Armstrong, Beverley Brown, and the participants in the Buffalo workshop.

1. Note that implicit in his account here is a recognition that there need be no causal relation between crime and punishment, something that ran counter to most contemporary thinking about penal law.

2. The feelings of resentment (or their absence) might provide an upper limit to the amount of punishment that could be justified, but nothing is said about its role in the definition or punishment of crime.

3. See the critical remarks of Neocleous (2000a, preface), bemoaning the loss of the sense of violence or state power.

4. I.e., how the idea of police becomes focused on a particular institution. Neocleous (2000a) goes furthest in attempting to develop this kind of analysis. See also Boyne (2000) for a critical analysis of "panopticism."

5. There is a clear parallel here with the way that the term "social control" was used in writings about crime and punishment in the 1980s. For a critical review of this, see Cohen (1989).

6. This seems to be the basis of the claim that the logic of punishment should be seen as "illiberal," though other parts of the argument suggest that she sees law as providing a framework of rights that interacts with disciplinary and police powers.

7. Which is also a claim about certain types of criminal law (Dubber 2004a, pt. 3).

8. This is not so much the claim that police is the disciplinary "underside" of law (McMullan 1998, 122) than that police and law are complementary.

9. Typically, this might also be an argument about overcriminalization or over-regulation in the modern law and the need to retrench and respect the proper spheres of police and law (e.g., Dubber 2002; 2004a, pt. 3; Ashworth 2000).

10. This is also reflected in some of the critical writing about policing informed by the literature on governmentality. This looks at the fragmentation of the policing function through the lens of governmentality and risk, without considering how the police power has been and continues to be exercised through traditional institutions of government. See, e.g., Loader (2000, 324) who looks through, above, beyond, and below government in his analysis of plural policing.

11. Crime and Disorder Act 1998 § 1. Extended in England and Wales by the Anti-Social Behaviour Act 2003, and in Scotland by the Anti-Social Behaviour etc. (S.) Act 2004.

12. For example, the Anti-Social Behaviour etc. (S.) Act 2004 § 143 defines antisocial behavior as actions, or a course of conduct, that causes or is likely to cause alarm or distress to at least one person not of the same household, a definition that is more or less identical to the definition of the common-law crime of breach of the peace (see Christie 1990).

13. In Scotland it is worth noting that antisocial behavior is within the remit of the Minister for Communities rather than the Minister for Justice. In England and Wales it falls within the traditional remit of the Home Office.

14. Ramsay (2004) analyzes the legal definition and concludes that decisions are likely to be made on the basis of common sense and general knowledge rather than actuarial tables. Although, at the same time, the trends in crime in control collected by Feeley and Simon (1992, 1994) under the rubric the "new penology" are themselves heterogeneous.

15. He identifies four different types of technique (Ashworth 2004, 266–72): new forms of preventive order (sex offenders, harassment, ASBO, etc.); civil orders backed by criminal sanctions; compelling social landlords to take responsibility for behavior on their premises; and restorative justice orders.

16. This point has now been considered by the House of Lords in the case of *R (McCann and others) v. Crown Court for Manchester and another; Clingham v.*

Kensington and Chelsea Royal London Borough Council, (2003) 1 AC 787. The court dismissed the appeal on the grounds that these were civil proceedings, but it held that before making such an order, given the seriousness of the matter involved, the court should be satisfied to the criminal standard of proof that the defendant had acted in an antisocial manner. This seems to create a new hybrid procedure, while the strength of any protection offered is unclear.

17. See n. 9.

18. Although it is worth noting that security is of increasing importance in discussions of global policing, e.g., Deflem 2002.

References

Ashworth, Andrew. 2000. Is the criminal law a lost cause? *Law Quarterly Review* 116:225–56.

———. 2004. Social control and "anti-social behaviour": The subversion of human rights? *Law Quarterly Review* 120:263–91.

Boyne, Roy. 2000. Post-panopticism. *Economy and Society* 29(2): 285–307.

Brown, Alison P. 2004. Anti-social behaviour, crime control and social control. *Howard Journal* 43(2): 203–11.

Carson, K., and H. Idzikowska. 1989. The social production of Scottish policing, 1795–1900. In *Policing and prosecution in Britain 1750–1850*, ed. D. Hay and F. Snyder. Oxford: Clarendon.

Christie, Michael G. A. 1990. *Breach of the peace*. Edinburgh: Butterworths.

Cohen, S. 1989. The critical discourse on "social control": Notes on the concept as a hammer. *International Journal of the Sociology of Law* 17(3): 347–57.

Cole, Simon. 2002. *Suspect identities: A history of fingerprinting and criminal identification*. Cambridge, MA: Harvard University Press.

Crawford, Adam. 1997. *The local governance of crime: Appeals to community and partnerships*. Oxford: Clarendon Press.

Dean, Mitchell M. 1999. *Governmentality: Power and rule in modern society*. London: Sage.

Deflem, Mathieu. 2002. *Policing world society: Historical foundations of international police cooperation*. Oxford: Oxford University Press.

Dubber, Markus Dirk. 2002. *Victims in the war on crime: The use and abuse of victims' rights*. New York: New York University Press.

———. 2004a. *The police power: Patriarchy and the foundations of American government*. New York: Columbia University Press.

———. 2004b. The criminal trial and the legitimation of punishment. In *The trial on trial: Truth and due process*, ed. A. Duff, L. Farmer, S. E. Marshall, and V. Tadros. Oxford: Hart Publishing.

Emsley, C. 1996. *The English police: a political and social history*. London: Longman.

Ewald, F. 1991. Norms, discipline and the law. In *Law and the order of culture*, ed. R. Post. Berkeley: University of California Press.

Farmer, Lindsay. 1996. The obsession with definition: The nature of crime and critical legal theory. *Social and Legal Studies* 5:57–73.

———. 1997. *Criminal law, tradition and legal order: Crime and the genius of Scots law, 1747 to the present*. Cambridge, UK: Cambridge University Press.

Feeley, M., and J. Simon 1992. The new penology: Notes on the emerging strategy of corrections and its implications. *Criminology* 30:449–74.

———. 1994. Actuarial justice: The emerging new criminal law. In *Futures of Criminology*, ed. D. Nelken. London: Sage.

Flint, J. 2002. Social housing agencies and the governance of anti-social behaviour. *Housing Studies* 17(4): 619–37.

Foucault, Michel. 1979. *The history of sexuality*. Vol. 1: *The will to knowledge*. Harmondsworth, UK: Penguin.

———. 2000. Governmentality. In *Power*, ed. J. D. Faubion. New York: The Free Press.

Garland, David. 1996. The limits of the sovereign state: Strategies of crime control in contemporary society. *British Journal of Criminology* 36(4): 445–71.

———. 2001. *The culture of control: Crime and social order in contemporary society*. Oxford: Oxford University Press.

Garland, David, and R. Sparks, eds. 2000. *Criminology and social theory*. Oxford: Oxford University Press.

Gatrell, V. A. C. 1990. Crime, authority and the policeman-state. *The Cambridge social history of Britain, 1750–1950*. Vol. 3: *Social agencies and institutions*, ed. F. M. L. Thompson. Cambridge, UK: Cambridge University Press.

Hart, H. L. A. 1968. *Punishment and responsibility*. Oxford: Clarendon Press.

Hay, Douglas, and Francis Snyder. 1989. Using the criminal law, 1750–1850: Policing, private prosecution, and the state. In *Policing and prosecution in Britain, 1750–1850*, ed. D. Hay and F. Snyder. Oxford: Clarendon.

Home Office. 2003. *Respect and responsibility: Taking a stand against anti-social behaviour*. London.

Hume, L. J. 1981. *Bentham and bureaucracy*. Cambridge, UK: Cambridge University Press.

Lacey, Nicola, et al. 2003. *Reconstructing criminal law: Text and materials*. London: Butterworths.

Loader, I. 2000. Plural policing and democratic governance. *Social and Legal Studies* 9(3): 323–45.

McMullan, J. L. 1998. The arresting eye: Discourse, surveillance and disciplinary administration in early English police thinking. *Social and Legal Studies* 7:97–128.

Neocleous, Mark. 2000a. *The fabrication of social order: A critical theory of police power*. London: Pluto Press.

———. 2000b. Against security. *Radical Philosophy*. March–April, 7–15.

Norrie, A. 2003. *Crime, reason and history: A critical introduction to criminal law*. London: Butterworths.

Novak, William J. 1996. *The people's welfare: Law and regulation in nineteenth-century America*. Chapel Hill: University of North Carolina Press.

O'Malley, P. 1999. Governmentality and the risk society. *Economy and Society* 28:138–48.

Padfield, N. 2004. The Anti-social Behaviour Act 2003: the Ultimate Nanny-state Act? *Criminal Law Review* 712–27.

Pasquino, Pasquale. 1991. Theatrum politicum: The genealogy of capital—police and the state of prosperity. *The Foucault effect: Studies in governmentality*, ed. G. Burchell, C. Gordon, and P. Miller. London: Harvester Wheatsheaf.

Raeff, M. 1983. *The well-ordered police state. Social and institutional change through law in the Germanies and Russia, 1600–1800*. New Haven: Yale University Press.

Ramsay, P. 2004. What is anti-social behaviour? *Criminal Law Review*, 908–25.

Scottish Executive, 2004. Guide to the anti-social behaviour etc. (Scotland) Act 2004. Edinburgh.

Shearing, C. 2001. Punishment and the changing face of governance. *Punishment and Society* 3(2): 203–20.

Smith, Adam. 1978. *Lectures on jurisprudence*. Oxford: Oxford University Press.

Storch, R. 1975. The plague of blue locusts: Police reform and popular resistance in northern England, 1840–1857. *International Review of Social History* 20:61–90.

Tomlins, Christopher L. 1993. *Law, labor and ideology in the early American republic*. Cambridge, UK: Cambridge University Press.

Valier, C. 2001. Criminal detection and the weight of the past. *Theoretical Criminology* 5(4): 425–43.

Valverde, Mariana. 2003. Police science, British style: Pub licensing and knowledges of urban disorder. *Economy and Society* 32(3): 234–52.

Vaughan, B. 2000. The government of youth: Disorder and dependence? *Social and Legal Studies* 9(3): 347–66.

Walker, N. 2000. *Policing in a changing constitutional order*. London: Sweet & Maxwell.

Zedner, L. 2003a. The concept of security: An agenda for comparative analysis. *Legal Studies* 23(1): 153–76.

———. 2003b. Too much security? *International Journal of the Sociology of Law* 31: 155–84.

CHAPTER SIX

Police and the Regulation of Traffic

Policing as a Civilizing Process?

ALAN HUNT

Toward a Renewed Police Science

Approaches to the study of police and policing seem forever doomed to struggle to escape from under either the criminological equation of police and crime or the sociology of occupations focus on what the police do rather than on what policing does. The attempt to find a different space for the study of policing has been given impetus by the rise of a greater historical sensitivity in the social sciences. This has made it possible to escape the restrictions inherent in the view that the police were invented by Robert Peel in 1829. Not only has the history of policing been stretched, but it has also been expanded by attention being paid to early modern policing with its attention to the link between police and urbanism (Raeff 1983; Lofland 1973) and to the police science of the eighteenth century.

This expanded conception of policing involved a range of interventions in governance during the advent of capitalism and the modern state. The core concerns were with the augmentation of the population, its wealth and the size of the coffers of the city or state, and more generally with public happiness. For example, Bentham recommended eight police departments, including prevention, calamities, charity, and collecting statistics. The police science, *Polizeiwissenschaft*, that emerged after the Thirty Years' War during the first half of the seventeenth century was directed toward ideas of "prosperity" and "happiness"; aims that were significant because they identified the state with its subjects. Police government did not limit itself to general laws, but used specific, detailed regulation and decrees. This conception of policing was articulated most clearly by Blackstone as being

> the due regulation and domestic order of the kingdom, whereby the individuals of the state, like members of a well governed family, are bound to conform their general behavior to the rules of propriety, good neighborhood and good manners, and to be decent, industrious and inoffensive in their respective stations. (Blackstone 1809, 4:162)

Foucault suggests that during the epoch of police science the "police's true object is man" (1981, 248). The aims of policing were twofold: first, to provide the city with adornment, form, and splendor and, second, to foster working and trading relations between citizens. Policing was a form of rational intervention wielding political power over citizens by controlling "communication" (work, production, exchange, and accommodation).

This chapter accepts that modern policing is no longer about the adornment of the city, but it suggests that thinking of motoring and, specifically, traffic regulation as a form of communication might be a productive line of inquiry. My major thesis is that the acquisition by police forces of road traffic jurisdiction involved a significant component of that earlier conception of "police" as revolving around the general management and social smoothing of movement as a central feature of community life. This change was profound, but it did not displace those activities that so crucially define the self-consciousness of both police and public of policing as a war on crime. I need to be explicit that I want to avoid the evident attractions of an argument that claims to discover a unilinear movement back toward some earlier form of policing. Such a position can be particularly attractive where it reverses a commonly held view. Rather, I want to argue that policing has always involved and continues to involve a combination of different forms of regulation. It is important to note that influential rationalities can both highlight one dimension and render others invisible; this is precisely what the dominant "police and the war on crime" vision does. I will argue that policing as a mixed mode of regulation can be brought back into focus through an exploration of the relationship between police and motor vehicles.[1]

What is brought into relief by an expanded historical orientation is not just that policing has a long lineage, but more significantly that it raises the question, What is policing about? To what problem is policing a response? However, it is not necessary to rewrite the history of policing to pursue this line of inquiry, rather it can be undertaken by renouncing the commonsense linkage of police and crime. And in important ways this is already widely acknowledged since many police studies have revealed that "fighting crime" plays a relatively small part in the daily activities of police. Similarly, it is also well-known that police time is much more heavily invested in the regulation of traffic than in the detection of crime. Thus to focus attention on police and the regulation of traffic offers an uncomplicated strategy for escaping from the police-crime box.

Not long after coming to the view that the policing of traffic might be a fruitful line of inquiry, my reflections were given direction by a radio news item that reported that local police would be out over a holiday weekend in what was described as an effort to "civilize the driver" directed against antisocial driving practices such as tailgating and overtaking by weaving between lanes. It was the suggestion of the police being involved in civilizing missions that caught my attention. So before exploring policing as a civilizing project some attention to the "civilizing process" is necessary.

Policing as a Civilizing Project

Norbert Elias provides the starting point and intellectual resource. His major work, *The Civilizing Process* (1978, 1982), identifies a long-run historical process of an intensification of "social constraint towards self-constraint," in which social sanctions are reproduced in the individual as self-controls (1978, 190). Elias explains this shift as resulting from two primary societal processes: first, "lengthening chains" of social interdependence and, second, the concentration and monopolization of the means of physical force that is the precondition for processes of state formation. A civilizing process is not a conscious or planned project, it is unplanned and unintended; rather it is the "structure of society that demands and generates a specific standard of emotional control" (1978, 201):

> The more complex and stable control of conduct is increasingly instilled in the individual from his earliest years as an automatism, a self-compulsion that he cannot resist even if he consciously wishes to. The web of actions grows so complex and extensive, the effort required to behave "correctly" within it becomes so great, that beside the individual's conscious self-control an automatic, blindly functioning apparatus of self-control is firmly established. (1982, 232–33)

The result is that the mental self-restraint of the "civilized" human being yields significant stability. Individuals from infancy onward get attuned to a highly regulated and differentiated pattern of self-restraint (1982, 235). One important consequence is the emergence of an increasing separation between a private and a public sphere, each exhibiting quite specific forms of self-control. One important implication with respect to driving is that the motor vehicle is at one and the same time both private and public space; I can sing along out of key and curse old ladies in slow-moving vehicles, but at the same time I am located within a complex web of communicative interdependencies with other motorists, cyclists, and pedestrians.

One important criticism of Elias's account of the civilizing process needs to be addressed. His claim that the civilizing process is unplanned and unintended leads him to ignore purposeful social strategies and projects. It seems incontrovertible that such projects that aim to transform aspects of social life in specific directions are consciously and deliberately pursued, whether it be medical crusades against spitting, a feminist campaign against domestic violence, or driver education programs. Such undertakings have been variously described as "civilizing offensives" (Van Krieken 1989), "reform of popular culture" (Burke 1978; Malcolmson 1973), and, as I have elsewhere used, the narrower concept of "moral regulation projects" (Hunt 1996, 1999a). It should be stressed that there is no necessary opposition between unintended civilizing processes and intentional civilizing offensives since history does not take place on a single temporal (or, for that matter, spatial) plane; historical processes move in such a manner that long-run trends interact with faster-moving and more deliberate processes.

I have in the past argued that many important projects emerge from a range of different social locations that can be captured, if slightly polemically, by the idea that reform projects, particularly from the nineteenth century onward, emerge "from the middle" (Hunt 1999b, 415). Here I will focus attention on those forms of civilizing offensives that involve agencies designated to take charge of specific projects. Agents given such responsibilities become more common in urban spaces where interpersonal links become attenuated and general social control less effective. Thus, for example, in the early modern city there was general concern about people throwing their night soil into the street, but enforcement depended on regular and persistent action. The crucial technique was that of surveillance, the regularized and unremitting gaze that the police came to perform, but in the first instance was a wide variety of specific roles (night watchmen, bailiff, constables, etc.).

With the acceleration of industrialization and urbanization, nineteenth-century civilizing offensives became more the direct product of political calculation.[2] The collective mentality of the early Victorian bourgeoisie was full of a deep sense of disgust, fear, and foreboding. The educational reformer Kay-Shuttleworth articulated the middle-class view of the lower orders. "They eat, drink, breed, work and die; and . . . the richer and more intelligent classes are obliged to guard them with police" (Kay-Shuttleworth 1832, 1:580–81).

The contemporary debate over the condition of the working class articulated a whole set of middle-class anxieties run together (improvidence, immorality, idleness, crime, etc.). Discipline was secured in the factory through what Marx described as "the dull compulsion of economic relations" (Marx 1976, 899). Thereafter other aspects of working-class life, in particular recreations, such as rough sports, drinking houses, and unruly festivities, became the target of a miscellaneous assortment of reform projects (Burke 1978). A proliferation of reform associations set middle-class missionaries, philanthropists, home visitors, and social observers about the task of civilizing the working classes. Schemes for reaching the masses had declined by the 1870s, foundering on an increasingly corporate working-class culture that resisted busybody intruders.

From that time onward the police functioned, in Robert Storch's telling phrase, as "domestic missionaries," as agents of civilizing offenses and moral reform effected through the detailed surveillance of everyday working-class life and recreation (Storch 1976, 481). At first the increasingly frequent presence of the police on the streets was resented and resisted, sometimes violently. The primary feature of nineteenth-century police was a battle to secure social order in the public spaces of urban society. It is not my present concern to sum up these complex and varied engagements; suffice it to say, first, that the nineteenth-century police did very little crime fighting but spent their time monitoring the closing hours of pubs, harassing street betting, and moving on noisy groups of young men from street corners (Harrison 1982; Laqueur 1976). Second, it would be wrong to say that the working classes were tamed, but rather the pattern of social relations did change significantly with greater external conformism within an enclosed popular culture. Third, socially and economically significant sections of the working class had become "respectable" such that there was a crucially important set of "dividing practices," processes of regulation through separation and segregation, that were put in place between the respectable and the rest of the working class that in turn served to reinforce the passification of everyday life (Foucault 1982, 208–9).

The Modalities of Policing

Different modes or styles of policing stimulate the production and stabilization of specific modalities of social order in the sense that there are very different configurations in which order can be realized. For present purposes social order involves securing the normalization and reproduction of specific patterns of stable social relations. Arditi seeks to grasp this fabrication of social stability by means of the concept of "infrastructure of social relations" to refer to patterns of association and differentiation and the practices through which they are reproduced (Arditi 1998). A similar idea is articulated by Neocleous, who focuses on the role of administration and regulation in the "fabrication of social order" (Neocleous 2000). For example, a policing style that is oriented toward the maintenance of hierarchical social relations focuses on whether people keep their social and spatial place and is epitomized by the presence of status offenses (vagrancy, begging, etc.).

How might the modality of contemporary policing, specifically applied to the regulation of traffic, be characterized? Such a modality can be described as a "fragmented social order" in public space use that is normalized, reserved for specific functions (shopping malls are for consuming, not for loitering); individuals keep to their cars, traveling in the right direction at roughly the correct speed and with no unnecessary contact with others. The rise of encapsulated individualism exemplifies the more general features of an individualism that Elias describes as constructing "the invisible wall of affects which seems now to rise between one human body and another, repelling and separating" (Elias 1978, 69).

By the end of the nineteenth century the police had become a familiar, if still not entirely accepted, presence in urban space. They were about to face a new challenge, which would radically change their relations with the public. The advent of the automobile as the increasingly significant mode of commercial and private transportation was to revolutionize in an unplanned and unintended way the relationship between the police and all classes of citizens. In the first phase some sections of the police strove to prohibit these new monsters. In Britain there transpired what has many of the features of a minor civil war fought out in the prosperous county of Surrey, which was on the route to that increasingly important destination of the early twentieth-century middle classes, the seaside on the south coast. Police laid hidden speed traps; a motorist's organization responded by employing cyclists to flag warnings to their members and paid the legal expenses incurred in contesting charges (Emsley 1993). Since the early motorists were drawn from among the affluent, they expected deference and respect from all functionaries, the police included, and typically expected their social equals sitting on the bench to believe the word of "a gentleman" over that of the self-evidently inferior policeman. It is probable that the different detailed configuration of relations between police and motorists in Europe and North America reflect the lesser importance of the socially superior motorist in the early years of the twentieth century.

Between the two world wars the number of motor vehicles increased, resulting in important changes in the relations between police and motorists. With much equivocation the police found themselves with a general jurisdiction over the wide-ranging implications of the motor vehicle; not only did they police an expanding array of "traffic offenses," but also they played a central part in traffic regulation, doing point duty at intersections. They also became increasingly involved in traffic management, regulating many aspects of the flows of people and vehicles in public spaces, and additionally assumed an educational role involving such activities as driver skidpans and school road-safety lessons.

The police came increasingly to deploy a very different discourse from the one that had arisen in the nineteenth century when their activities were directed almost exclusively to the social order of working-class communities and the occasional salute to their social superiors. This new discourse revolved around the promotion of an educational relationship between police and motorist. Miller McClintock, author of the first traffic engineering textbook, defined traffic police as educators: "Think of him as teacher of civic and community obligations" (McClintock 1927, 17). At the senior policy-making levels the police increasingly articulated projects to "educate the motorist" and more generally softened the stern face of enforcement by ensuring that police received some basic vehicle-repair training to be able to come to the aid of stranded motorists. Employing the dividing practice of distinguishing between the "ordinary motorist," who only inadvertently breached the growing list of traffic rules, and the "road hog," who drove recklessly with no concern for the safety of others and had to be "dealt with" for the good of the general public, bridged the tension between enforcement and education. The "ordinary motorist" was to become ever closer to the statistical norm of the ordinary citizen. The educational discourse was deployed within a pastoral logic. To protect all road users, the police must strive to ensure adherence to a pattern of norms of civilized conduct by all; the police had to act as the patient shepherd guiding the individualist road user.

The police increasingly found themselves entangled with the motor car. Without much reflection on the implications, the police found themselves standing on duty at intersections and developing standardized hand signals to direct vehicles and pedestrians. The consequence of the large demand on police resources consumed by directing traffic was to accelerate the technologies of traffic regulation. The next part of this story is one in which innovative technologies displaced or transformed the original acquisition of jurisdiction over traffic. The traffic light is, much as Bruno Latour's revolving door, a classic instance linking humans (police, motorists, pedestrians) and nonhumans (signals, signs, road painting; Latour 1988). Indeed the nonhuman traffic light has many advantages over humans in that it is cheaper and always on duty. It is significant to note that when first introduced between 1914 and 1920 the red-green (precursor to red-amber-green) traffic light was manually operated by the police because it was feared that without the human form of a police presence motorists would not obey the traffic lights (McShane 1990, 382). In the early stages many police forces were dubious that traffic lights and other visible signals, lacking as they did the power of arrest, could ever take the policeman's place. But in the longer run traffic lights and other sign systems would come to have a calming effect. The neutrality and impartiality of the nonhuman signal induces a high level of internalization and thus ensures fairly automatic compliance of the great majority of motorists, and this in turn results in a utilitarian improvement in the efficiency of traffic flow, especially after the invention of automatic timed lights (ca. 1924). Walter Benjamin was undoubtedly correct in his observation that traffic signals subjected the human subconscious to a complex training (Benjamin 1969, 175). It should also be noted that traffic lights had a major economic impact on policing, reducing costs and freeing up police time.[3] However, as we will see later, compliance and efficiency through traffic signs is not guaranteed.

An important consequence of technological regulation has been the increased separation of motorists and pedestrians. In the early stages, nonhuman traffic regulations favored the motorist, especially in North America, although less so in Europe, with widespread adoption of jaywalking ordinances. One of the consequences of the introduction of the octagonal stop sign at intersections was that it did not provide protection for pedestrians crossing the street. Although pedestrians have never been as well represented by special-interest organizations as have motorists, who came to have large and powerful motorist clubs, subsequent developments provided a variety of mechanisms for pedestrian crossings. Subsequently, jaywalking ordinances ceased to be enforced and in most instances have been repealed. However, there remain important conflicts of interests between motorists and pedestrians. In recent years this has generated widespread experimentation with technologies of "traffic calming" such as residential communities' speed bumps, which are popularly referred to as "sleeping policemen" in Britain. Such innovations are explicitly conceived as civilizing projects to promote the pacification of interactions between motorists, pedestrians, cyclists, and, more generally, residential communities.

Attention should also be given to the fertile productivity of the elaboration of signage (Hermer and Hunt 1996). The increasing standardization and internationalization of traffic signs makes the experience of driving subject to a governance-at-a-distance through a dispassionate bureaucratic system. This is particularly evident when idiosyncratic national eccentricities have been retained; for example, the roundabout or traffic circle, widely used in Europe but largely absent in North America, can cause erratic responses from drivers not familiar with its specific rules of usage. The roundabout came about because of the irregularity of European roads while the four-way stop is more appropriate to the U.S. grid pattern of roads. These regional variations are gradually disappearing as globalization in the form of tourism requires uniformity of the rules of the road.

While nonhuman regulatory devices and sign systems have removed the police from much direct contact with the motorist, increasing importance has come to be conferred on contact arising from traffic accidents. Not only has there been a proliferation of driving offenses, but some, such as those involving the consumption of alcohol, have acquired a further significance. The link between alcohol and motoring has been strongly moralized through the figure of the "drunk driver" and illustrates how relations that at first sight appear to be matters that connect issues of harm and imposition of liability often exhibit significant moral dimensions (Hunt 2003).

The routinization of cars as the ubiquitous form of transport involves social processes that are both individualizing and totalizing. Motorists are isolated inside their vehicles, cocooned and disassociated from others even though, at the same time, they are each part of a collective flow, or at times of gridlock, of collective frustration. Yet these same conditions, in which driving is a communicative activity dependent on knowing and predicting the behavior of others, bring about a separation from others that can lead to a disregard that escalates into road rage. As Foucault observes, "I think that the main characteristic of our political rationality is the fact that this integration of the individuals in a community or in a totality results from a constant correlation between an increasing individualization and the reinforcement of this totality" (Foucault 1988, 162).

The most significant change in relations between police and motorists arose from the increasing frequency of traffic accidents. The crucial factor is the enmeshment of the police and the insurance industry. Compulsory third-party motor insurance confers an essentially clerical-administrative role on the police, whose accident reports have become the most important condition for successful insurance claims. This relationship is confirmed by the near universality of a legal duty to report traffic accidents. This linkage between police and insurance has added a large and time-consuming clerical function to the police role. It may also be noted that motor insurance provides another distinctive instance of the interconnection between humans and nonhumans; motor insurance has two distinct dimensions, the human side involving the compensation for injury and loss of earnings, while the nonhuman aspect engages with the damage to vehicles and their repair and replacement.

The advent of the automobile generated diverse changes in the practices and technologies of policing. From the mid-twentieth century, traffic policing brought the police much more frequently into contact with an increasingly representative cross section of the population as car ownership spread. Those who are conventionally labeled "ordinary people," who had had little or no contact with the police, now encountered them, but generally in circumstances not of their own choosing, circumstances arising from vehicle accidents, breakdowns, or motoring infractions. It should be stressed that the unpredictable character of these police-public contacts imbued them with a certain tension in which both sides exhibit a certain wariness. The general social resolution of this tension has resulted in a marked formalism in which the police are polite and adopt the service discourse of "sir" and "madam," which lasts only so long as the motorist remains compliant. Any move toward arrogance or aggression allows the police to adopt the more familiar coercive stance of dealing with an "offender." This is one of the reasons the official discourse on driver education fades before the more familiar image of chasing "bad guys," with the result that a significant proportion of traffic work becomes transformed into chasing young males in fast cars or visible minorities in the wrong location or vehicle.

An important contemporary exemplification of police "civilizing projects" arises from the persistent popular discourses that call for greater police visibility by putting more police on the streets. This call needs to be understood in the context of policing becoming increasingly reliant on low-visibility technological practices. One of the most immediate ways to increase police visibility has been to have more police vehicles circulating at times and in places where commuting or consuming drivers are aware of their presence, although police cars parked by the side of the highway in high-visibility locations is an expensive way of affecting driver consciousness and producing the all-too-familiar temporary slowing of the flow of traffic. More evidently civilizing projects are conspicuous in the form of drunken-driving patrols, especially those that are announced in advance and associated with public holidays, festivities, or sporting events. The regulation of drunken-driving policing exhibits a mixture of civilizing and technological practices. The Breathalyzer replaced reliance on the older low-level police expertise in interpreting a driver's capacity to walk a straight line. More significantly, drunken-driving checks that stop large lines of drivers provide an opportunity for polite exchanges with "ordinary drivers" who, on confirming that they have not been drinking, are sent on their way with a cheery "Have a Happy Christmas."

Technological substitutes for human police such as traffic lights do not guarantee compliance. Some forms of traffic technology stimulate driver resistance. In the early period, as we have seen, drivers reacted strongly against speed-measuring devices, and this continues to generate controversy. Enforcement of speed regulations uses two forms of monitoring: the first is generalized speed zones, where notice is given of the presence of speed-measuring technology, and the second is the occasional use of unpublicized speed traps with human attendants. A particularly instructive case study is that of computer-linked photo-radar that can issue speeding tickets without human intervention. In many jurisdictions such technology has become a significant political issue. In the early 1990s the Ontario provincial government introduced this technology on the province's most important highway. The opposition Conservative Party took up the issue, and their promise to withdraw automatic speed ticketing played a not insignificant part in the subsequent Conservative electoral victory.

Why should some technological substitutions be more or less uncontroversially incorporated within the motorist's common sense while others induce significant distrust, hostility, and politically inflected resistance? With many technological innovations there is an initial resistance, but unless the sense of what is normal is significantly disturbed, the innovation becomes normalized. For example, the use of closed-circuit video cameras in public places and spaces, shopping malls, and the like, while arousing some initial concern, is now widely accepted. The difference in the case of photo-radar may well be that it is seen as shifting the balance of advantage too sharply against the motorist. There remain traces of early sentiments that viewed motoring as a game played out between motorists and police in which some techniques for imposing penalties are viewed as acceptable, but the latest round in the technological dance destabilizes the relationship between police and motorist, stacking the system against the motorist.

The legally available enforcement techniques are consistent with the trend toward bureaucratic administration that has resulted from the huge scale of the project of regulating driving. It is significant that such practices undermine the civilizing mission that I have argued is a component of the regulation of traffic. For such a project to remain vital, it requires a space for discretion.

The legal procedures associated with traffic regulation have been subject to a process of bureaucratic rationalization. Enforcement of traffic regulation increasingly acquired a distinctive relationship with the processes of the criminal law: on the one hand, there was a high level of formalism (justice without trial, absolute or strict liability, etc.) but, on the other, the retention of a significant discretionary field exemplified by informal or semiformal practices of warnings or cautions. But as Banton observes, the efficacy of verbal cautions declines with the decline in the general level of respect for the authority of the police (1964). These considerations suggest a persistent tension between calls for more positive and cooperative police-public interaction and objectives of efficiency in processing ever-expanding motoring infractions.

The expansion of road traffic offenses exemplifies the increasing importance of the monetary fine as the most common penalty. However, the fine came to take the form of "the ticket," which in important respects bypassed the formal criminal process in that, if paid, it circumvented court appearance and the more traditional features of contact with the criminal justice system. The consequence of this form of penalty was that parking tickets and speeding tickets became a familiar experience of law-abiding drivers and came to be viewed as part of the cost of motoring in the way that compulsory insurance and vehicle licensing were part of the economics of the motor car. This normalization of ticketed offenses became associated with the loss of any moral opprobrium such that drivers could even derive social status from the accumulation of tickets. The normalization of traffic infractions led to a search for more effective compliance techniques that used withdrawal of driving privileges through an increasingly complex range of graduated offenses for which demerit points could be imposed and whose accumulation would lead to the imposition of a driving ban. This complex array of fines and points provides a classic example of what, in a different context, Foucault called "micro-penalties" (Foucault 1977, 178).

The Hegemony of Safety as a Civilizing Practice

The social revolution effected by the rise of the motor car led inexorably toward the bureaucratization of the governance of traffic encompassing a range of techniques such as vehicle registration, vehicle classification, driver licensing, and driver testing. At the same time, and, most significantly, the bureaucratization of the enforcement of traffic regulation has become increasingly dependent on an array of technological devices used in speed assessment and accident analysis. At the same time there occurred a "governmentalization of policing" with standardized reporting, preoccupation with statistics, and the administrative wedding of police and insurance with regard to traffic accidents. These processes were closely linked to the rise of the police as experts, resulting from the technologizing of policing from fingerprinting to DNA testing, where courts increasingly rely on a variety of expert testimony in which the police still have a role but by no means a central one. As Foucault observed, "The juridical institution is increasingly incorporated into a continuum of apparatuses (medical, administrative, and so on) whose functions are for the most part regulatory" (1978, 144).

This governmentalization of both traffic and police is unified under the hegemony of discourses of safety. In the case of traffic regulation the inexorable rise of safety has seemed an entirely natural and self-evident process. From the earliest days of the motor, concern with the dangers associated with the new mode of transport produced an automatic reflex that resulted in inscribing rationalities of safety at the very heart of the regulatory process. One important result has been that, as the motorcar became the normal mode of transportation for an increasing proportion of the population, it resulted in the paradoxical refusal of the logic of the risk society theorists. Motorists enter their vehicles and drive with little or no apparent regard for driving as the most risky activity in their everyday lives; yet, despite this seeming refusal to recognize the dangers of motoring, discourses of safety are routinely invoked to legitimate proposed forms of regulatory intervention that enter into public debate. This centrality of the discourse of safety situates discussion of traffic regulation in a familiar utilitarian ethos that is especially evident in the texts of traffic safety and traffic management, which are preoccupied not only with safety but in varying and shifting combinations with concerns with efficiency. These predominantly utilitarian considerations do not erase regulation as a civilizing process, but they render it less visible such that today the policing of traffic involves a complex of forms of governance in which the core disciplinary practices are woven alongside civilizing practices.

Notes

1. There is a parallel between my thesis and the argument advanced by William Novak that the nineteenth-century United States exhibited a powerful tradition of governance, police, and regulation, the existence of which has been obscured by the preoccupation of neoliberal rationalities to impose a liberal vision of the United States' past (Novak 1996, ix).

2. This thumbnail sketch of the history of the link between policing and the civilizing process is based on England; while other countries experienced different modalities and patterns, the general pattern is sufficiently similar for present purposes.

3. While in the early years of the motor age police frequently had jurisdiction over parking, this important source of revenue was generally secured by municipal authorities and led to the separation of parking from other traffic regulation. Parking regulation was radically transformed by the technology of the parking meter.

References

Arditi, Jorge. 1998. *A genealogy of manners: Transformations of social relations in France and England from the fourteenth to the eighteenth century*. Chicago: University of Chicago Press.

Banton, Michael. 1964. *The policeman in the community*. London: Tavistock.

Benjamin, Walter. 1969. *Illuminations*, ed. H. Arendt. New York: Harcourt, Brace & World.

Blackstone, William. 1809. *Commentaries on the laws of England* [1765–1769], ed. E. Christian. London: Cadell & Davies.

Burke, Peter. 1978. *Popular culture in early modern Europe*. London: Temple Smith.

Elias, Norbert. 1978. *The civilizing process*. Vol. 1: *Changes in the behaviour of the secular upper classes in the west* [original title, *The history of manners* (1939)]. Oxford: Blackwell.

———. 1982. *The civilizing process*. Vol. 2: *State formation and civilization* [1939]. Oxford: Blackwell.

Emsley, Clive. 1993. Mother, what did the police do before there were cars? The law, the police and the regulation of motor transport in England, 1991–1939. *Historical Journal* 36(2): 357–81.

Foucault, Michel. 1977. *Discipline and punish: The birth of the prison*, trans. A. Sheridan. New York: Pantheon Books.

———. 1978. *The history of sexuality*. Vol. 1: *An introduction*. New York: Pantheon Books.

———. 1981. *Omnes et singulatim*: Towards a criticism of "political reason." In *The Tanner lectures on human values*. Vol. 2, ed. S. McMurrin, 223–54. Salt Lake City: University of Utah Press.

———. 1982. The subject and power. In *Michel Foucault: Beyond structuralism and hermeneutics*, ed. H. Dreyfus and P. Rabinow, 208–26. Chicago: University of Chicago Press.

———. 1988. The political technology of individuals. In *Technologies of the self*, ed. L. Martin, H. Gutman, and P. Hutton, 145–62. Amherst: University of Massachusetts Press.

Gordon, Colin. 1991. Governmental rationality: An introduction. In *The Foucault effect: Studies in governmentality*, ed. G. Burchell, C. Gordon, and P. Miller, 1–51 Hemel Hempstead, UK: Harvester Wheatsheaf.

Harrison, Brian. 1982. Traditions of respectability in British labour history. In *Peaceable kingdom: Stability and change in modern Britain*, 157–216. Oxford: Clarendon Press.

Hermer, Joe, and Alan Hunt. 1996. Official graffiti of the everyday. *Law and Society Review* 30(3): 501–26.

Hunt, Alan. 1996. *Governance of the consuming passions: A history of sumptuary regulation*. New York: St. Martins Press.

———. 1999a. *Governing morals: A social history of moral regulation*. Cambridge, UK: Cambridge University Press.

———. 1999b. The purity wars: Making sense of moral militancy. *Theoretical Criminology* 3(4): 409–36.

———. 2003. Risk and moralization in everyday life. In *Morality and risk*, ed. R. Ericson and A. Doyle, 165–92. Toronto: University of Toronto Press.

Kay-Shuttleworth, Sir James. 1832. *The moral and physical condition of the working classes employed in the cotton manufacture in Manchester*. London: James Ridgway.

Laqueur, Thomas W. 1976. *Religion and respectability: Sunday schools and working class culture, 1750–1850*. New Haven: Yale University Press.

Latour, Bruno. 1988. Mixing humans and nonhumans together: The sociology of a door-closer. *Social Problems* 35(3): 298–310.

Lofland, Lyn H. 1973. *The world of strangers: Order and action in urban public space.* New York: Basic Books.

McClintock, Miller. 1927. Police functions and street hazards. *National Safety News,* September.

McShane, Clay. 1999. The origins and globalization of traffic control signs. *Journal of Urban History* 25(3): 379–404.

Malcolmson, Robert W. 1973. *Popular recreations in English society, 1700–1850.* Cambridge, UK: Cambridge University Press.

Marx, Karl. 1976. *Capital: A critique of political economy.* Vol. 1, trans. B. Fowkes. Harmondsworth, UK: Penguin.

Neocleous, Mark. 2000. *The fabrication of social order: A critical theory of police powers.* London: Pluto Press.

Novak, William. 1996. *The people's welfare: Law and regulation in nineteenth century America.* Chapel Hill: University of North Carolina Press.

Raeff, Marc. 1983. *The well-ordered police state: Social and institutional change through law in the Germanies and Russia, 1600–1800.* New Haven: Yale University Press.

Storch, Robert D. 1976. The policeman as domestic missionary: Urban discipline and popular culture in northern England, 1850–1880. *Journal of Social History* 9:481–509.

Van Krieken, Robert. 1989. Violence, self-discipline and modernity: Beyond the "civilizing process." *Sociological Review* 37(2): 193–218.

CHAPTER SEVEN

Military Intervention as "Police" Action?

MITCHELL DEAN

In a small piece written in 1991, Giorgio Agamben (2000, 102) claimed, "One of the least ambiguous lessons learned from the [first] Gulf War is that the concept of sovereignty has been finally introduced into the figure of the police." He then proceeds to discuss the "nonchalance with which the exercise of a particularly devastating *jus belli* [just war] was disguised as a mere 'police operation.'" Far from eschewing such an idea, the rationales of police have in this situation "to be taken in a rigorous literal sense—particularly those concerning the idea of a new world order." Moreover, police operates within the "decision" on the "state of exception," which—following Carl Schmitt (1922)—defines the operation of sovereignty. None of this is particularly reassuring, concludes Agamben. He argues that the lack of public documentation of the Holocaust was because the extermination of the Jews was undertaken as a police operation. Further, "The investiture of the sovereign as policeman has another corollary: it makes it necessary to criminalize the adversary. . . . Such an operation is not obliged to respect any juridical rule and

185

can thus make no distinctions between the civilian population and soldiers, as well as between the people and their criminal sovereign, thereby returning to the most archaic conditions of belligerence" (Agamben 2000, 105).

For a small piece, Agamben's text on "sovereign police" covers a lot of ground. Many of these themes receive a much more extended reprise in *Empire* (Hardt and Negri 2000), where—despite whatever other differences—a very similar idea of military intervention as police is presented. Describing conflict within the new imperial power of empire, its authors suggest that "we have entered the era of minor and internal conflicts. Every imperial war is a civil war, a police action—from Los Angeles and Granada to Mogadishu and Sarajevo. In fact, the separation between the external and internal arms of power (between the army and the police, the CIA and the FBI) is increasingly vague and indeterminate" (Hardt and Negri 2000, 189).[1] The reason for this is that sovereignty and police have become linked: the new global ordering of imperial power "supports the exercise of police power, while at the same time the activity of global police force demonstrates the real effectiveness of the imperial ordering. The juridical power to rule over the exception and the capacity to deploy police force are thus two initial coordinates that define the imperial model of authority" (17). The right of police is backed by a right of intervention, which by way of "a permanent state of emergency and exception [is] justified by the appeal to essential values of justice. In other words, the right of the police is legitimated by universal values" (18).

Agamben and Hardt and Negri are readers of Michel Foucault. Foucault's discussion of police (e.g., 2001, 317–23) deals with a wide range of seventeenth- and eighteenth-century German, Italian, and French authors. *Empire* quotes a passage in which Foucault cites an early seventeenth-century tract by Louis Turquet de Mayerne called *Aristo-democratic Monarchy*. Foucault's analysis of this text shows that it demonstrates that while police appears only as a branch of administration, it in fact embraces everything, and that the object of police is people in their living, active existence. "As a form of rational intervention wielding political power over men," Foucault concluded (2001, 319), "the role of police is to supply them with a little extra life—and, by doing so, supply the state with a little extra strength." But how might this analysis be related to *Empire*'s use of the term to denote the form of exercise of imperial sovereign right? We are nowhere offered a discussion of the trajectory of the notion of police or an attempt to say how current police action is different from or similar to the police that existed across different European territories in former times. Hardt and Negri might wish to maintain that police still offers a power that supplements life—and is thus reconnected to their claims about "bio-power" and what they call, following Gilles Deleuze (1995), the "control society"—but this is undercut by its restriction of the term to "internationally sanctioned police action," meaning military action. Surely, if one wanted to talk of a global police today in the sense of Turquet or the German *Polizeiwissenschaft* (police science), it would need to go beyond military interventions and also include agencies of global economic intervention (the World Trade Organization [WTO], International Monetary Fund [IMF], World Bank) and humanitarian and moral agencies (nongovernmental organizations [NGOs]).

By contrast, Agamben's allusions (2000, 104–6) are unambiguously about the extralegal use of violence by sovereign authority. He cites the intimate relation between the Roman consul and the lictor, who carried the sacrificial ax used for capital punishment; the conquering Duke of Burgundy entering Paris in 1814 and greeting the executioner Coqueluche as his good friend; and, above all, the exercise of command within death camps. Police for Agamben could nowhere be better illustrated than in the pictures of U.S. treatment of prisoners in Abu Ghraib: a naked prisoner about to be set upon by military police dogs reveals barking sovereign power and cowering bare life.

The similarities between the two texts are not perhaps remarkable given their common context of debates and discussions within Italian Marxism. Agamben and Hardt and Negri move beyond the notion of police to characterize contemporary forms of global law and order—and this is where their fundamental differences begin. The former regards "the camp" as the institutional form of the permanent state of exception and as the new biopolitical paradigm or *nomos* of modernity; the latter claim to penetrate legal-constitutional forms to the processes of the material constitution of a new planetary order through the flows of biopolitical production. Questions of life and of death, of international law and order, or of what their other common reference, Carl Schmitt (1950), termed the "*nomos* of the Earth," it seems, are also glimpsed through these intuitions about contemporary military interventions as police.[2] Indeed, the thesis itself might be described as Schmittian rather than Foucauldian in that it places international police actions within the trajectory of the decline of a European-based system of international law rather than of the development of governmental techniques.

If we cool the theoretical temperature for a moment, it seems that the thesis common to these authors settles about five key ideas:

1.   Military operations have become police actions.
2.   Police actions are fundamental to the exercise of (imperial) sovereignty.
3.   Police actions are connected to notions of "just war" and justified by reference to human rights.
4.   Police actions entail the "criminalization" of the enemy.
5.   Most broadly, police actions have a fundamental role in contemporary world (dis)order.

Despite all this conceptual apparatus, it is rather difficult to have a clear understanding of what it means to say that military operations have become police actions. This is really the simple starting point of this investigation. Before we can begin to consider the thesis about contemporary military operations, we need to understand what they (and we) mean by the word "police." The more we understand the term and some of its older and more contemporary uses, the better able we are to consider the kind of argument just presented. Hence, before anything else, we need to work out whether this use of the term is legitimate and how it fits with other uses of the term.

What Is Meant by Police?

The view that recent military operations can be termed "police" actions is doubly perplexing. On the one hand, a cursory glance at the history of the term would show that police is a matter *internal* to states, as William Blackstone's canonical definition of police as the "due regulation and domestic order of the kingdom" announces (1830, 162). Police has thus typically been conceived of as a *domestic* rather than a foreign affair.

On the other hand, as the authors previously cited suggest, police is a sphere separate from law and includes the discretionary use of force, often in exceptional circumstances. Now while law and police have long coexisted *within* states, the relation *between* states has taken the image of a relationship of autonomous or sovereign political communities. This relationship is thus imagined as one in which to exist as a state is to have certain rights in international law, most particularly the right to noninterference in one's own internal affairs. As Tony Blair, Prime Minister of the United Kingdom, put it in regard to the existing international law he would contest, "A country's internal affairs are for it and you don't interfere unless it threatens you, breaches a treaty or triggers an obligation of alliance" (Byers 2004, 27). Police action as an action by an external agency (country, coalition, multilateral force, whatever) upon the domestic affairs of another state is simply not thinkable. Such action amounts to an act of offensive war, pure and simple, and we do not need to resort to the vocabulary of police to discuss it.

Those familiar with the conceptual history of the term "police" will know that the restriction of "police" to a constabulary force is a relatively recent addition to the core meanings of the term. There is a long history of rather different uses of the term or its linguistic variants from the thirteenth century in many parts of the European continent. German conceptual history tells us that "police" has meant a condition of order in a community, the regulations that seek to secure that order, and the civil administration that ensures that order (Knemeyer 1980, 172–81). For the Chancellor to the Elector of Saxony, Dr. Melchior von Osse, in the mid-sixteenth century, police "was identical both with the government and with the object and nature of the community as a whole" (Oestreich 1982, 155–56). In his landmark work, the U.S. sociologist Albion Small (1909) showed how the cameralist *Polizeiwissenschaft* encompassed the entire practical art of bureaucratic governing. Nor should we imagine that this broader use of the term has been excluded from the English language. In addition to its institutional and constabulary meanings, police has in various contexts meant policy, civil organization, civil administration, public order, and even civilization itself. Edmund Burke in 1791 (1808, 22) described the Turks as a "barbarous nation, with a barbarous neglect of police, fatal to the human race."

We can cite countless other examples of this broader understanding of police as a condition of good or even civilized order in a community and the means of acquiring and retaining it. Perhaps for now it is simply necessary to remind ourselves that "police" in this regard is far from designating a "repressive state apparatus." It can be a project to use admittedly hierarchical and regulatory means, including a calibrated deployment of violence, to produce the conditions of the good life or a condition of good police.

If we look to the *Oxford English Dictionary* (2004), we find the use of the term as an attributive noun in "police action" defined as "military intervention without formal declaration of war when a nation or group within a nation is considered to be violating international law and peace." It cites a number of uses of this phrase, the earliest of which is *Chambers's Encyclopedia* in 1959: "The Dutch started the first 'police action' and occupied large parts of the republic. After United Nations intervention a truce was signed." A similar attributive use of the noun "police" is found in the recent English translation of Schmitt's *The Nomos of the Earth*, written in Germany during World War II and published in 1950: "Bombing pilots use their weapons against the population of an enemy country as vertically as St. George used his lance against the dragon. Given the fact that war has been transformed into a police action against troublemakers, criminals, and pests, justification of the methods of this 'police-bombing' must be intensified" (Schmitt 1950, 321). This intensification for Schmitt is linked to the revival of doctrines of just war and the criminalization of the enemy.

Another attributive use of the term is found in "police power." I mention this because there is an earlier famous use of the term "police" in relation to military intervention. In December 1904, Theodore Roosevelt enunciated a Corollary to the Monroe Doctrine (quoted in Ferguson 2004, 52–53):

> Chronic wrongdoing, or an impotence which results in a general loosening of ties of civilized society, may in America, as elsewhere, ultimately require intervention by some civilized nation, and in the Western Hemisphere, the adherence of the United States to the Monroe Doctrine may force the United States, however reluctantly, in flagrant cases of wrongdoing or impotence, to the exercise of an international police power.

The notion of "police power" can also be found in the reports of the U.S. Supreme Court of 1827 (Oxford English Dictionary 2004) and is given definition in a *Dictionary of the Social Sciences* (Gould and Kolb 1964, 508):

> Police power may be defined as the broad and elastic power of government especially of one of the states of the United States, to restrict, control, regulate and restrain individuals and groups in the use of their liberty and property in order to protect and promote the health, safety, morals, convenience, peace, order and general welfare of other individuals and the public generally.

The doctrine proclaimed by President Monroe on December 2, 1823, codified existing ideas of the two hemispheres and the nonintervention of each into the realm of the other. Its innovation, however, was that the United States would fight to defend the southern republics of the Americas against European intervention (Ulmen 1987, 51). Roosevelt's Corollary takes this a step further: the United States could exercise "international police power" to "restrict, control, regulate and restrain" states or regimes where the peace, order, and welfare of individuals and nations were threatened by "wrong-doing or impotence." In other words, U.S. military intervention could be justified not only in terms of the defense of Latin American countries against the old colonial powers but also when and where their regimes present a threat to the peace and order of a specific group of nations—those that constitute the Western Hemisphere.

The use of the term in international relations to refer to certain types of military operations by nations or groups of nations would appear to have some important antecedents. If we turn to some contemporary concerns and practices, we find further and somewhat different instances of the use of the term in the context of international military activities.

It is the case, for example, that police forces, in our modern sense of the term as a body of officials for keeping the peace and maintaining law and order, are a component of many international interventions. For instance, a relatively small but significant percentage of UN armed personnel are termed "police" rather than "peacekeepers." As of July 31, 2005, the United Nations deployed, from a total of 67,468 individuals involved in peacekeeping operations, 5,991 civilian police officers (United Nations 2005). In June 2000, the European Union (EU) established a 5,000-member police force called the European Security and Intelligence Force that could be deployed in various locales (Bronson 2002, 130). In recent times, countries such as Australia and New Zealand have provided police to troubled countries—mostly in new or "failing states" in the current jargon—in their region, from East Timor to Papua New Guinea and the Solomon Islands (Squires 2003). Similarly, the North Atlantic Treaty Organization (NATO) dispatched police officers to Bosnia and Kosovo. A newspaper report on East Timor indicated a disagreement about the nature of the mission to continue in that country after the UN mandate finishes: the United Nations sought an extension of a diminished peacekeeping operation; Australia, with the United States and the

United Kingdom, wished to deploy a contingent of police (Dalton and Powell 2004). Police thus exists in some relation and tension with peacekeeping.

As followers of investigations into the torture in Iraqi prisons under the occupying forces will be reminded, a section of the U.S. military is called "military police." The brigadier general, Janis Karpinski, who was suspended and later demoted to colonel, was the commander of the 800th Military Police Brigade, and several of those who faced charges and were prosecuted as a result of these tortures were members of the 372nd Military Police company, which reported to her (Hersh 2004; Wikipedia 2005).

Moreover, there has been a wider discussion of the police capacities of the U.S. military in both recent Democratic and Republican administrations. The former Secretary of State Madeleine Albright argued that

> old modes of peacekeeping don't always meet current challenges. Peace operations today often require skills that are neither strictly military nor strictly police but, rather, a combination of the two. The international community needs to identify and train units that are able to control crowds, deter vigilante actions, prevent looting and disarm civilian agitators while, at the same time, winning the trust of the communities in which they are deployed. (quoted in Thomas 2001, 29)

The future National Security Adviser and Secretary of State Condoleezza Rice argued during the 2000 U.S. presidential campaign that "we need to think hard about the development of forces that are appropriate to police functions" (Bronson 2002, 127). These views were echoed by the future Secretary of State Colin Powell, who described the need in the Balkans to replace armed forces "with other kinds of organizations and perhaps police organizations to handle the remaining missions." Discussions of the obligation of the coalition in Iraq have used the term "policekeeping" as a key to rebuilding the internal security structure (Day and Freeman 2003). Policekeeping and information technology is also an object of analysis (Thomas 2001), and the issue of policing weak or failing states is now given consideration in policing journals (Goldsmith 2003).

If we take all these contexts, then, we find the kind of linkages we identified in the argument presented by our theorists. Police is linked to military operations. It is concerned with sovereignty insofar as it deals with the exercise of the powers of states and with the building and rebuilding of other states. It is framed by human rights issues. It addresses issues of crime. It operates in an international order. So in that sense, policy makers, statesmen, academics, and practitioners all use the term "police" in the kind of contexts we identified in the thesis of our critical theorists. Should we conclude, then, that all this stands in evidence of a thesis that military interventions have become police actions in a new international order?

To answer that, at least four meanings of the term should be distinguished:

1. Police as a constabulary force for instituting and maintaining public order and security
2. Police as a condition of good order within a community
3. Police as effective civil administration
4. Police as a form of action designed to deal with regimes and other actors who disrupt the international order in one way or another

I shall deal first with the relation of police to more classical conceptions of military operations, drawing mainly on the first three meanings, and then go on to this question of police and international order.

Police and Military

Where the more practical and technical discourses of police in international military settings would differ from our critical theorists, I think, is that they would want to make a clear distinction between military operations and police actions rather than accede to the thesis of the growing "indistinction" (as Agamben would perhaps put it[3]) between the two. But how would we begin to make that distinction?

As a preliminary attempt, we might say that the distinction can be summarized in the following ways:

1. *Police confronts a situation of disorder rather than an enemy.* In a situation or space of civil unrest and disturbance, such as an immediate postwar or postcombat zone, police initially finds itself at work in the elements of disorder from warlords, militia, and insurgents to looting mobs and protesting

crowds. Now, while some of these might be formally defined as the enemy in times of war and in combat zones, when the focus of the operations moves to peace enforcement, peacekeeping, and "stabilization," their status as enemy is pushed into the background. Police is concerned with the enemy as a source of disorder rather than the enemy as enemy. The U.S. Army *Field Manual on Stability Operations and Support Operations* (United States Department of the Army 2003, v) rather coyly recognizes the need for a shift of vocabulary in stabilization and peace operations when it defines "enemy" in this way:

> *Enemy* describes a hostile individual or group that US forces engage—or have the potential to engage—in combat. Within US doctrine, the term *enemy* is used as the object or focus of operations throughout the operations process. In the past, *enemy* was associated with opposing combat forces or individuals, whether the forces were military, paramilitary or civilians committing hostile acts. However, in some stability operations, especially peace operations, referring to one or more factions as "the enemy" damages the perception of US impartiality and hinders the ability to negotiate a peaceful settlement. Thus, the term is reserved for individuals and groups engaging Army forces or their partners in combat operations. In support operations conducted outside a combat zone, the term *enemy* is inappropriate.

The idea too that one might have to face adversaries in such action that could be either common criminals (in the prevention of robberies and looting), or nonstate political forces (terrorist networks, insurgents, militia), or somewhere between (drug cartels engaged in narco-business) suggests that police forces approach these adversaries in a somewhat different way to the traditional enemy in war—the armed forces of a nation. There is certainly a "criminalization" process going on here, but it is one that is far more subtle than, say, the simple redescription of partisans or movements of national liberation as terrorists. It might seek to follow the lines of connection and flows between various categories. For example, "Given the cooperative channels between criminal and terror networks, developing an effective policing and judicial capacity in failed and emerging states is coming to be recognized as an urgent priority for both domestic and global security" (Day and Freeman 2003, 305).

Another case of a shift away from classical military concepts of the enemy might be found in the U.S. Administration's refusal to regard many of those detained in its war on terrorism, including those who fought in the Taliban army of Afghanistan as well as al Qaeda suspects, as having the status of prisoner of war under the Geneva Conventions, that is, as having the status of captured enemy combatants protected by the laws of war. Following from the Presidential Military Order of November 13, 2001, the key terms are "illegal or unlawful enemy combatant," to describe their identity, and "detainee," to describe their current status.[4] A similar refusal appears to have been extended from Guantánamo Bay to many of those held in Iraq. Whatever the rationale of such a move, there is a clear denial of the classical military status of the enemy, and consequent rights as POWs when captured, to those detained. I would argue, however, that this shift of the status of the enemy is clearly different from that of contemporary policing operations. In the latter, the paradigm of the enemy is rejected altogether for one of social and political order. In the former, the notion of the enemy is not rejected but intensified and deprived of legitimacy to escape criminal legal liability.

2. *Police thus aims at defusing situations and restoring order rather than defeating the enemy and attaining victory.* At the heart of the distinction is the fundamentally different aim: "the constabulary officer will look to defuse the situation, rather than defeating his enemy" (Day and Freeman 2003, 305).

3. *The logic of police is preventive and developmental rather than one of victory and defeat.* In war, one party aims to defeat another. This classically leaves the victor in a situation of appropriation of land, territory, and resources or the right to demand tribute or reparations from the defeated nation. By contrast, a police action does not defeat and take away; it prevents, establishes, and constructs. A police action is designed to restore and maintain order and build civil administration. Further, police action must act in a way that is consistent with such administration. According to Day and Freeman (2003, 300), the role of what they call "policekeeping" in occupied Iraq is preventive. It is to "pre-empt and combat ethnic, religious and political violence, as well as economic crime and the establishment of shadow networks; also to police 'regular' crime, including that related to property and public order." It is also developmental. Policekeeping in Iraq seeks "the development of domestic

judicial and policing capacity, in order to provide an exit strategy for the international mission and the beginnings of a representative and regionally developed governance structure." The same preventive and developmental aspects are found in Madeleine Albright's preceding quotation. Police controls crowds, deters vigilantes, prevents looting, disarms agitators, protects innocents, wins trust, and builds communities.

4. *The use of force is more finely calibrated.* "Officers trained specifically for a constabulary role will not only conduct their threat assessments on the basis of 'when' they can use force but also have to make the more finely graded judgment of what is 'minimum reasonable force' given the situation" (Day and Freeman 2003, 305). Police exists as a kind of hybrid of force and consent, on a continuum between peacekeeping and peace enforcement (Thomas 2001, 29):

> Today, peace support operations are caught between these two extremes. Peace support personnel deal more often with crowds than armies. . . . Missions are increasingly intrastate with a police mission overtone. The missions do not fall neatly into either the peacekeeping or peace-enforcement category but approach "police-keeping" performed by "police-keepers."

Police thus is distinguished from peacekeeping. Peacekeeping is usually a neutral, impartial, third-party activity undertaken with the consent of belligerents. Police by contrast can be military or civilian, international or local, and deal with civil problems, from crowd control, looting, and vigilantes to the ownership of land, houses, and livestock. Classically, peacekeeping is deployed to provide a buffer between two opposing militaries and thus confirms the logic of war; by contrast, police is about establishing and maintaining order within a territory, with all the heterogeneous aims that entails.

5. *While police and military operations should be consistent with the rule of law and human rights, only police is dedicated to the spread and enforcement of both.* Consider how the U.S. Field Manual outlines the role of host-nation security forces in counter-insurgency operations:

> The first objective of the police is to destroy the illegal infrastructure of the insurgent organization. Police intelligence must identify and locate leaders,

penetration agencies, intelligence and PSYOP [psychological operations] agents, terrorists, and recruiters. The police arrest them using the minimum violence necessary. These arrests should be based on probable cause and executed on the warrant of a disinterested magistrate. To maintain government legitimacy, the police must follow the due process of law. Corruption and abuse of human rights by security forces and the judiciary can contribute significantly to society turmoil. (United States Department of the Army 2003, 3–15)

The same role of police in the building of the rule of law and respect for human rights is much more clearly spelled out in another document, the *Report of the Panel on United Nations Peace Operations* (United Nations 2000). The so-called Brahimi Report examines the implications of an integrated and preventive doctrine of peacekeeping. Here, the UN international civilian police do not simply monitor local police forces but "reform, train and restructure local police forces according to international standards for democratic policing and human rights, as well as having the capacity to respond effectively to civil disorder and for self-defence" (United Nations 2000, 7). Such an operation appears to have been carried out in East Timor. On May 20, 2004, the *Sydney Morning Herald* reported the handover to East Timor of its own policing and defense (Moore and Skehan 2004, 10). At the handover, it reports, "the UN police commissioner, Sandra Peisley, said 157 officers would remain behind, down from a peak of 1580" who came from 39 nations.

In Carl Schmitt's analysis of the system of international law that governed military combat between the seventeenth and early twentieth centuries, the *jus publicum Europaeum*, war is regarded as being conducted among equal European sovereign states, in which combatants recognized each other as *justi hostes* (just enemies) and in which what Schmitt calls a "non-discriminatory" war was possible. "Both belligerents had the same political character and the same rights; both recognized each other as states" (Schmitt 1950, 142). This system achieved a "bracketing" of war in that formally conducted war between legitimate sovereigns was not subject to moral-theological evaluation of just causes. "The right of war was based exclusively on the quality of the belligerent agents of *jus belli*, and this quality was based on the fact that equal sovereigns pursued war against each other" (Schmitt 1950, 143). We have seen that Schmitt was hostile to what he perceived as the degeneration of war into a police action. From our analysis we can see that police is intrastate rather than interstate, conducted against the elements of disorder, including criminals and those classed as security risks, rather than enemies, whether just or unjust, and deployed according to an at least nominal attachment to human rights and the establishment of the rule of law. Police is conducted on the basis of a fundamental moral discrimination.

Schmitt's image of the aerial bombardment, presumably of German cities, is that of St. George lancing the dragon. In most Renaissance paintings (such as those of Bellini, Raphael, and Tintoretto) of this famous scene, there is the presence of a third figure, the Princess Sabra, who was next to be sacrificed to the voracious beast. Often the dragon is surrounded by the skulls and bones of its previous victims as in the graphically violent image by Carpaccio.[5] In some versions of the story, St. George does not kill the dragon but tames it and puts it on a leash. Here at the very least we have another kind of image of police: not the moralization of war but the use of carefully calibrated force and minimum violence to protect suffering humanity so that it might begin to build a civil society.

Police and Empire

Central to the argument about military intervention taking the form of police actions is the idea that this is linked to a new form of imperial power, world (dis)order, or *nomos* of the earth.

When we turn to recent discussions of U.S. imperial power and military intervention, however, we find that a recurrent theme is the *lack* of police capabilities. Michael Mann (2004, 239–40) uses the failure of the United States to provide an effective constabulary force to stem the looting and mayhem that followed the fall of Baghdad to U.S. forces in April 2003 as evidence of his thesis of the incoherence of U.S. power. He suggests this stems from the "over-militarizing" of America's national security strategy and foreign policy. Figures of the second Bush administration have made it clear that they are not interested in military intervention that involves what they call "nation building," central to which would be both the narrow policing capacities (establishing and training police forces) and the wider police objectives of the establishment of an effective civil order and administration.

This has been clear in the President's criticisms of Bill Clinton's overseas adventures during the 2000 presidential campaign, comments by the Secretaries of Defense and State on the U.S. role in the Afghanistan war, and in the President's statements on Iraq. The latter is best summed up as, "We will remain in Iraq as long as necessary and not a day more" (Ferguson 2004, 149–50, 165, 203). In this regard we can say that far from exercising police powers in Roosevelt's sense, the second Bush administration eschews the idea that its interventions are there to build civil order for the population of those areas of now defeated rogue regimes and thus contribute to the good police of the international community. The question of whether this is about a reluctant imperial power whose national temperament is anti-imperial (Ferguson 2004), whether it is simply an "incoherent Empire" (Mann 2004), or whether it is consistent with a peculiarly U.S. dialectic of economic presence and political absence in international affairs (Schmitt 1950, 255–57) starts to indicate the wider ramifications of the problem of its continued and acknowledged lack of proper policing capacities.

As we can see, the idea of police is quite useful in a discussion of the capabilities of various forces and institutions and the objectives of those forces in a given situation. But, contrary to the thesis of our critical theorists, it is the ability to distinguish between military and police force and objectives that acts as a condition of possibility of such a discussion. However, it is also necessary to distinguish between the identification of certain kinds of operations that are conducted *inside* another state as police operations and the more general claim that international military operations per se have become police operations. The latter is at the core of the claim by Agamben and Hardt and Negri and implies a change in international law. While the British government has made representations to the United Nations to have a limited right of unilateral attack for humanitarian reasons recognized, this proposal has so far been rejected, specifically by the G77, the 135-member coalition of third world countries (Byers 2004, 27–28).

What is implied in such a right is the idea that there is a common set of standards that can be recognized in any given instance. The effect of such a claim would be to turn international law away from the image of autonomous self-governing sovereign states to one of a community with common values. In other words, military intervention itself is justified by the notion of keeping public order and security of a definite community, the community of the world's nations. In rejecting the first image of international affairs and adopting the latter, Tony Blair has put it that "the essence of a community is common rights and responsibilities. We have obligations in relation to each other. . . . And we do not accept in a community that others have a right to oppress and brutalize their people" (Byers 2004, 28). Once the idea of an international community is accepted in these terms, like the idea of a Western Hemisphere in Roosevelt's Corollary, then it follows that what is at stake is the good police of that community. This right of intervention is a right of civilization. Those regimes and forces that disrupt this situation are in fact criminals and should be treated as such. On this point, G. W. Bush and Tony Blair have sought a confirmation of Schmitt's thesis of a world without effective international law: one in which there is a remoralization of war and criminalization of the enemy.

This kind of international police is a long way from the problematics of UN peacekeeping or even the requirements of stabilization operations — however poorly met — in the postcombat zones occupied by the United States and its allies. One kind of police would find its objectives in the careful establishment of order within a territory, including the disarming of militia and the prevention of murder, rape, looting, and civil disturbance, and the slow and difficult tasks of establishing a legal and civil administrative framework. The other would find its objectives in the ousting of rogue regimes such as North Korea. The thesis of military intervention necessarily becoming police action, found in our contemporary critical theorists, Schmitt, and aspects of Anglo American policy, fails to make the key distinction between the two: that is to say, between intrastate police actions conducted by, or with the assistance of, possibly multinational police forces and the justification for what amounts to an internationally conducted aggressive war.

Conclusion

Beyond the simple hyperbole, the theoretical overreach, and obscurantism found in the critical thinkers with whom we began, it is clearly legitimate to discuss certain kinds and aspects of military interventions as police. Police defines the position of certain actors: military and civilian police act in combat or postcombat zones under the aegis of the United Nations, the EU, NATO, or other groups of nations or even single countries. Police is above all a specific kind of action, When we begin to talk about "policekeeping," the keeping of police, the term once again acquires the sense of a condition of order and security, not to mention civilization, of something to be achieved and kept. The polymorphous nature of the use of the term, its "defining indefinability" (Dubber 2005), is linked to its list-making features. Its objects are heterogeneous: unruly crowds, armed militia, terror networks, traffic flows, levels of trust, human rights, the ownership of livestock, etc. What is also clear, given the concern for police at the United Nations (the Brahimi Report) or the problem of the training of police forces in countries such as East Timor, is that this discussion is linked to the international order of sovereign states. Police is also linked to humanitarian concerns and the establishment of the conditions of civil order. This kind of police has more in common with the productive powers supplementing life by establishing the strength of the state, noted by Foucault, rather than a world of criminal enemies, the *justa causa*, and the doctrine of preemption.

What is problematic is the elision, first, between military and police and, second, between police as the intrastate building of civil order and police as international aggression. Unless we can maintain these distinctions, certain kinds of arguments become unintelligible, e.g., a debate on the failure of the United States to invest in police-style forces and operations, or a debate over the kinds of international forces needed for the future of East Timor. Agamben's purely pejorative use of the term "police" is especially problematic: police action may be preferable to military action in a given situation, e.g., controlling crowds, doing traffic duty, guarding prisoners, etc. Moreover, police action is often tied to developing civil administration and linked to the establishment of legal institutions and process. The civilian police in the UN missions are conceived as a part of a team:

> Where peace-building missions require it, penal experts and human rights specialists, as well as civilian police, must be available in sufficient numbers to strengthen the rule of law institutions. Where justice, reconciliation and the fight against impunity require it, the Security Council should authorize such experts, as well as relevant criminal investigators and forensic specialists, to further the work of apprehension and prosecution of persons indicted for war crimes in support of United Nations international criminal tribunals. (United Nations 2000, 7)

Police here is linked to law and the establishment of legal institutions rather than operating by extrajuridical command "within a state of exception."

One fears that our critical theorists and our media diet of digital images from Abu Ghraib during 2004 will conspire to make the argument I have just suggested more difficult to maintain given that the soldiers directly involved were army reservists deployed as military police.

These pictures seem to be grist to Agamben's mill: what could be more exemplary of the relation of sovereign power to bare life than a picture of two army dogs threatening a naked man who is shuddering in terror? And what would seem to confirm Agamben's understanding of the Holocaust more than this? Isn't Abu Ghraib yet another place where law has ceased to operate and a police action took place? Isn't this an example of the potential of the camp, maintained by police rather than law, to again produce atrocity? And further, doesn't this once again prove that the *nomos* of contemporary modernity is the camp—from Guantánamo Bay to Baghdad? Are not the prisons and camps under the control of the Americans places of permanent states of exception where police action rules? And even *Newsweek* (Barry, Hirsh, and Isikoff 2004) appears to confirm this when it states of the Guantánamo Bay (Gitmo) facility, "The appeal of Gitmo from the start was that, in the view of administration lawyers, the base existed in a legal twilight zone—or 'the legal equivalent of outer space,' as one former administration lawyer described it." Certainly, there were extremely heinous crimes committed in Abu Ghraib by U.S. military police personnel among others.

On the other hand, there is truly something anesthetic in the political effects of such a view. It leaves one in a position of opposition to any attempts at policing in international affairs and indifferent to its variety of political effects. It leaves one in a position of not being able to distinguish between the means, objectives, and rationality of such policing strategies and that of the operation of military force. That seems to me the cost of such a view. Rather than posing the problem of how policing occurs in particular contexts; of its potentials, dangers, and benefits; of how it is or is not subject to juridical review and scrutiny, this view elides police with military intervention and presents a dogmatic form of criticism of policing activities. Instead of regarding police as by its nature outside the law, the question would be to examine how it is linked to the project to establish the rule of law and to the rationality of human rights.

Further, rather than reducing contemporary modernity to the camp with its police command, it is important to analyze how the practices of the camp can be subject to review and scrutiny—as they have been by not only the liberal press in the United States but the recent decisions of the U.S. Supreme Court.[6] Law and life are bound not in the monotonous action of a *nomos* that is reproducing the camp and bare life everywhere but in a series of discontinuous, contestable mobilizations of different rationalities and practices. Even the sphere of law is a contested one, as we have seen. On the one hand, we have a series of U.S. Administration memos and reports constructing arguments defending conduct normally regarded as torture under conditions of a war on terror and preparing the way for coercive interrogation techniques usually forbidden under international law with the intent of protecting U.S. officials from legal punishment (Greenberg and Dratel 2005). On the other, the U.S. Supreme Court has affirmed the right of detainees to challenge the legality of their detention before an independent tribunal and to have access to counsel. In other words, the Court has ruled that these detainees and camps are not in a state of exception subject only to the arbitrary authority Agamben calls police but open to scrutiny and due process like any other prison. The capacity to look at such a discontinuous and contested series of arguments seems to me the cost of the view that military operations have become police actions. The rationalities and practices of police might seem rather mundane issues compared to the worthy and mighty topics of sovereignty and law, not to mention world order, or the *nomos* of the earth. Yet our examination of these mundane concerns calls into question the manner in which such topics have been addressed by our theorists.

No doubt questions of police operations in combat and postcombat zones say much about the new matrix of international politics. But when we start to think about questions of police in peacekeeping, stabilization operations, and nation building, we begin to glimpse a field of rationalities and techniques through which certain everyday problems are to be made governable. If we are to indict or to praise the United States for acting like the world's policeman, then we might also want to consider whether such a policeman has failed or succeeded to develop effective police capability, including the training of forces in policing and the development of appropriate police techniques, and whether it has failed or succeeded the fundamental police task of rebuilding a civil administration. If whatever *nomos* of the earth today is possible largely depends on the exercise of the powers of the United States, then these would not be small failures.

Notes

1. See n. 3 and compare this quotation with Agamben's thesis.

2. In his introduction to Schmitt (2003, 10) Gary Ulmen writes, "For Schmitt, the *nomos* of the earth is the community of political entities united by common rules. It is the spatial, political, and juridical system considered to be mutually binding in the conduct of international affairs—a system that has obtained over time and has become a matter of tradition and custom. Ultimately the *nomos* of the earth is the order of the earth." The *"nomos* of the earth" is thus an attempt to give a philosophically and legally consistent concept of what recent political figures and authors call world order.

3. Agamben (1998, 9) uses the term throughout his text to describe "the process by which the exception everywhere becomes the rule . . . and [by which] exclusion and inclusion, outside and inside, *bios* and *zoē*, right and fact, enter into a zone of irreducible indistinction." "Military" and "police" would appear to conform to this logic in Agamben's thesis.

4. President George W. Bush's Military Order of November 13, 2001: Detention, Treatment, and Trial of Certain Non-Citizens in the War Against Terrorism; 66 FR 57833.

5. The painting *St. George and the Dragon* by Carpaccio (1455–1526), dating from 1502–1508, is housed at the Scuola di San Giorgio degli Schiavoni, Venice. A gallery of images of the story of St. George can be found at http://www.ucc.ie/milmart/grgwstart.html.

6. *Hamdi v. Rumsfeld* 2004; *Rasul v. Bush* 2004.

References

Agamben, Giorgio. 1998. Homo sacer: *Sovereign power and bare life*, trans. D. Heller-Roazen. Stanford: Stanford University Press.

———. 2000. *Means without ends: Notes on politics*, trans. V. Binetti and C. Casarino. Minneapolis: University of Minnesota Press.

Barry, John, Michael Hirsh, and Michael Isikoff. 2004. The roots of torture. *Newsweek*, May 24. http://msnbc.msn.com/id/4989436/site/newsweek/.

Blackstone, William. 1830. *Commentaries on the laws of England*. Vol. 4, 17th ed. London: Dawsons of Pall Mall.

Bronson, Rachel. 2002. When soldiers become cops. *Foreign Affairs* 81(6): 122–32.

Burke, Edmund. 1808. *Works*. Vol. 6. London: F. C. and J. Rivington.

Byers, Michael. 2004. A new type of war. *London Review of Books* 26(9): 27–28.

Dalton, Rodney, and Sian Powell. 2004. UN, Dili fight Canberra push to replace peacekeepers with police. http://www.etan.org/et2004/february/15-21/20undili.htm.

Day, Graham, and Christopher Freeman. 2003. Policekeeping is the key: Rebuilding the internal security architecture of postwar Iraq. *International Affairs* 79(2): 299–311.

Deleuze, Gilles. 1995. Postscript on control societies. In *Negotiations*. New York: Columbia University Press.

Dubber, Markus Dirk. 2005. *The police power: Patriarchy and the foundations of American government*. New York: Columbia University Press.

Ferguson, Niall. 2004. *Colossus: The price of America's empire*. New York: Penguin Press.

Foucault, Michel. 2001. *Omnes et singulatum*: Towards a criticism of political reason. In *The essential works, 1954–1984*. Vol. 3: *Power*, ed. J. D. Faubion, 298–325. London: Allen Lane.

Goldsmith, Andrew. 2003. Policing weak states: Citizen safety and state responsibility. *Policing and Society* 13(1): 3–21.

Gould, Julius, and William L. Kolb. 1964. *A dictionary of the social sciences*. New York: Free Press.

Greenberg, Karen J., and Joshua L. Dratel, eds. 2005. *The torture papers: The road to Abu Ghraib*. New York: Cambridge University Press.

Hamdi v. Rumsfeld 2004. 542 U.S. 507.

Hardt, Michael, and Antonio Negri. 2000. *Empire*. Cambridge, MA: Harvard University Press.

Hersh, Seymour M. 2004. Torture at Abu Ghraib. *New Yorker*, May 5, 2004.

Knemeyer, F.-L. 1980. Polizei. *Economy and Society* 9(2): 172–96.

Mann, Michael. 2004. *Incoherent empire*. London: Verso.

Moore, Mathew, and Craig Skehan. 2004. East Timor takes over own policing and defence. *Sydney Morning Herald*, May 24.

Oestreich, Gerhard. 1982. *Neostoicism and the early modern state*. Cambridge, UK: Cambridge University Press.

Oxford English Dictionary. 2004. Police. http://dictionary.oed.com/cgi.

Rasul v. Bush 2004. 542 U.S. 466.

Schmitt, Carl. 1922. *Political theology: Four chapters on the concept of sovereignty*, trans. George Schwab. Reprinted 1985. Cambridge, MA: MIT Press.

———. 1950. *The nomos of the earth in the international law of the* jus publicum Europaeum, trans. G. Ulmen. Reprinted 2003. New York: Telos Press.

Small, Albion W. 1909. *The cameralists*. Chicago: Chicago University Press.

Squires, Nick. 2003. Australia enters island war zone. http://www.globalpolicy.org/
nations/sovereign/failed/2003/0702solomon.htm.

Thomas, Timothy L. 2001. IT requirements for "policekeeping." *Military Review*
81(5): 29–35.

Ulmen, Gary. 1987. American imperialism and international law: Carl Schmitt on
the US in world affairs. *Telos* 72:43–71.

———. 2003. Introduction. In *The* nomos *of the earth in the international law of the
jus publicum Europaeum*, ed. C. Schmitt, trans. G. Ulmen. New York: Telos
Press.

United Nations. 2000. *Report of the Panel on United Nations Peace Operations*.

———. 2005. Monthly Summary of Contributors. http://www.un.org/Depts/
dpko/dpko/contributors/.

United States Department of the Army. 2003. *Field manual on stability operations and
support operations*, FM 3-07. Headquarters, TRADOC.

Wikipedia, 2005. Abu Ghraib torture and prisoner abuse. http://en.wikipedia.org/
wiki/Abu_Ghraib_prisoner_abuse.

CHAPTER EIGHT

International Police

RON LEVI AND JOHN HAGAN

In the early years of the twentieth century, U.S. President Theodore Roosevelt—in an effort to maintain U.S. dominance in the Western Hemisphere—justified international U.S. intervention on the basis of a lack of an international police force that could otherwise promote order among states and the lack of effective legal regimes that could resolve international disputes. Within Roosevelt's model, a police of the international community must pursue two apparently distinct goals: ensure that foreign states are and remain "stable, orderly, and prosperous" (Roosevelt 1904), while also guaranteeing a constabulary that will "secur[e] by the exercise of force the observance of solemn international obligations" (Roosevelt 1915, 23). Since no international police existed through which to achieve either of these goals—although Roosevelt optimistically anticipated the future possibility of a permanent force—this opened the opportunity (and, indeed, the self-proclaimed duty) for the United States to take on the role of international police, through what has come to be known as the Roosevelt Corollary to the Monroe Doctrine.

Roosevelt was not, of course, the first to invoke the possibility of an international police. Specific plans for an international police force date from Jeremy Bentham's eighteenth-century *Plan for an Universal and Perpetual Peace* (1789; see generally Janis 1984), foreshadows of an international police stem from ancient times (Davies 1930), and pacifist writing on world peace had been extolling the need for an international police constabulary for centuries (cf. Davies 1930, appendix B). But Roosevelt was also not the last to do so: in the wake of world wars, the importance and possibility of an international police was invoked by others such as Canadian Prime Minister Lester B. Pearson and legal theorist Hans Kelsen, and a model of international policing has become a core referent of UN peacekeeping missions (cf. Dean 2005). And in early 2004, a model of international police to promote good governance—although not named as police—was promoted in a speech by Michael Ignatieff, Harvard's Carr Professor of Human Rights Practice.

In chapter 7, Mitchell Dean provides a close analysis of how logics of transnational police are increasingly taken up. As he describes, police provides an analytic lens that has been pursued most vigorously by Hardt and Negri, whose analyses of empire link contemporary ideas of international security to transnational police activity—rather than a reliance on conventional forms of military operation, what they call a thinning out of "war"—to shape the world (2004, 19–20). For Hardt and Negri, international interventions increasingly take the form of police actions to promote the internal order and good administration of states worldwide (2000, 22–41; and see chapter 7). The result is a "continuous police activity" that centers on actively shaping and constituting the transnational itself in the name of security (Hardt and Negri 2004, 20–21, 239).

The argument that Hardt and Negri invoke—that military action is being replaced with a logic of imperial police—is drawn on by Dean in chapter 7 to examine the elision between military and police and the implications of this elision for international law and the potentialities of the transnational. We follow Dean by focusing on international police but begin by turning back the clock to examine how models of international police—whether police is designed as an effort to secure the stability and prosperity of foreign states or instead as a constabulary that can enforce international obligations—coexist in tension with paradigms that focus instead on *law*. Although analytic divisions between law and police have not always been evident on the domestic front, particularly in the European "police states" of the seventeenth and eighteenth centuries (cf. Raeff 1983), we suggest that a tension between these relatively distinct paradigms is often at the core of international programs.

This international divide between "law" and "police," we argue, is often mobilized to produce ideas about the transnational itself. On the one hand, programs for international reform are often imagined as purely a question of police, so that questions of law (which might often produce obstacles to this police) are displaced in the process. And, on the other hand, programs to promote international law are often invested with a wide array of legal tools and juridical authority but are provided no powers of "police" through which this authority can be effectively mobilized. The result is a running tension between police and law as transnational modalities of rule.

By tracing this tension through a brief series of texts, this chapter seeks to draw out some of the implications that this delineation of "police" and "law" have had in constituting the scope of the international itself—implications that we then draw on as central to understanding the possibilities and limits of a presently emerging transnational legal field, that of international criminal law.

Law and Police

To draw out the idea of a normative competition between "law" and "police" requires that we briefly back away from international governmentalities, and turn instead to "law" and "police" in the early nineteenth-century United States. As Christopher Tomlins (1993) demonstrates in his analysis of *Law, Labor, and Ideology in the Early American Republic*, law had not enjoyed a pre-eminent social role in the eighteenth century: it is only through an elite project to contain democratic participation that legal discourse gained purchase on all aspects of social life in the early nineteenth century (1993, 19–97), becoming a democratic and authoritative discourse in the postcolonial U.S. state (cf. Horwitz 1977, 1–30; Nedelsky 1989). But if law successfully gained supreme authority as the United States' paradigmatic discourse (Tomlins 1993, 21), its rise to normative prominence was—to say the least—contested.

Much stood in the way of retooling nineteenth-century life under the rhetorical banner of the rule of law, even with an increased use of law in regulating disputes (Tomlins 1993, 27, n. 35). As an ideational structure, law sought to redefine the role of the state, and thereby threatened a new expertise to reinterpret foundational social categories such as citizenship and state sovereignty (28–33). And what most vociferously stood in the way of law was a parallel contender for the status of paradigmatic discourse—a governmentality that rejected law's emphasis on individual rights and a limited state in favor of unity between the state and popular sovereignty (57)—that was inscribed in the logic of "police."

To understand the tension between "law" and "police" that we describe in the international context requires abandoning a merely "negative" idea of police (Pasquino 1991, 109). Rather than being limited to constabulary police forces (cf. Johnston 1992; Shearing 1992), police *as a modality of rule* refers instead to a more "positive" (or "productive") role for the state (Neocleous 2004), through which it surveils, knows, and intervenes in the social body, to produce the "smooth running of society" (Elden 2003, 247; Gordon 1991, 11, 45). This emphasis on *good administration* (Pasquino 1991, 112) is a far cry from a state that is limited by individual rights. Premised instead on a Continental unity between the state and civil society (Neocleous 1998, 431–37), the "police state" instead charges itself with *producing* the safety, happiness, and welfare of the citizenry (Novak 1996; Tomlins 1993, 55). This implicates an entire set of ideas and technologies of social policy (Neocleous 2000) for producing order, health, wealth, and security (Foucault 1980, 170)—including the need to know and surveil the population at large and to achieve proper order under the most varied, and often minute, conditions and circumstances (Valverde 2003; cf. Foucault 1991; Pasquino 1991).[1]

Within the "police" state, then, a central concern is with good administration and securing the order of nearly everything (Raeff 1983). Yet this emphasis on good administration, though it persisted on the Continent and was a viable contender in the postcolonial United States, was increasingly eclipsed in the new U.S. Republic. In its place was a paradigm that emphasized a limited state, a distancing from politics, and the protection of individual property rights—a discourse that centered on law and legal authority (Tomlins 1990). This included, to be sure, vestiges of "police," including the institutionalizing of constabulary police forces (Neocleous 1998; Garland 1996), and doctrines such as the "police power" of U.S. municipalities, which legislate to "secure generally the comfort, safety, morals, health, and prosperity of its citizens by preserving the public order" (Black 1990; Barnett 2004; Novak 1996; Neocleous 2000).[2] Law thereby became the discursive and institutional context within which a logic of police had to function (Tomlins 1993, 39, 59; Novak 1996; Dubber 2005), with the scope of police itself now bounded and defined by common-law courts and restricted from an earlier effort to promote social happiness to emphasize the maintaining of security and order (Gordon 1991, 20; Neocleous 2004; Pasquino 1991, 113; Tomlins 1993).

Sorting out whether the logic of police underlies all of the criminal law (Dubber 2005), whether the focus on police as "security" takes us beyond "law" (Neocleous 2004), or whether the distinction is elusive (see chapter 5) is not our project in this chapter. Instead, we draw on Tomlins's research (1990, 1993), which draws out how police and law function as alternative discourses, to investigate the effects of this alternation. We focus on how ideas of international police and law are placed in a competitive relationship with each other, how each can be the preserve of a different form of politics, and how police and law are conceived of as different projects, symbolically invested in for different effects.

For the most part, analyses of police are developed within the context of the national state, focusing on the criminal law, the regulation of work and labor, and the surveillance powers of administrative officials. As Dean indicates in chapter 7, police as a normative paradigm that extends beyond the state is rarely acknowledged. It is important, however, to realize that this general absence of attention to the international dimensions of police may be as much due to the analytic lens that is often adopted. Take, for instance, Tomlins's account of the postcolonial U.S. Republic. In its ascendancy, law was closely tied to the development of a federal government to secure property rights (Tomlins 1993, 88). This was not, however, a purely domestic project: it was underwritten with the visible support of artisan tradesmen, investing in the creation of a federal government in the hopes (later dashed) of securing a legally based regulation of international trade. This obliquely signals, from an earlier period, the imbrication of the national and the transnational—and that the intersection of police, law, and ideas about "the international" might not be anything new or unique.[3]

Police between Big Sticks and Good Neighbors: Theodore Roosevelt and the International Police

On December 6, 1904, U.S. President Theodore Roosevelt delivered the Annual Message to Congress (1904). Roosevelt was facing a potential international crisis: European powers, responding to the financial indebtedness of Latin American countries, had begun military blockades in the region. For the Europeans to command a military presence in Latin America raised the specter—from the perspective of the White House, certainly—of weakening U.S. control in the Americas, just in the wake of the Spanish-American War (Mitchener and Weidenmier 2004).

In his Message, Roosevelt laments the lack of judicial enforcement in the international sphere. And in the place of *law*, or at least until the time came when courts could enforce legal sanctions, he asserts the need of an institution of *international police* to ensure security and stability (Roosevelt 1904):

> There is as yet no judicial way of enforcing a right in international law. When one nation wrongs another or wrongs many others, there is no tribunal before which the wrongdoer can be brought. . . .
>
> Until some method is devised by which there shall be a degree of international control over offending nations, it would be a wicked thing for the most civilized powers, for those with most sense of international obligations and with keenest and most generous appreciation of the difference between right and wrong, to disarm . . . *the result would mean an immediate recrudescence of barbarism in one form or another.* Under any circumstances a sufficient armament would have to be kept up to serve the purposes of international police; and until international cohesion and the sense of international duties and rights are far more advanced than at present, a nation desirous both of securing respect for itself and of doing good to others must have a force adequate for the work which it feels is allotted to it as its part of the general world duty. . . .

A self-respecting, just, and far-seeing nation should on the one hand endeavor by every means to aid in the development of the various movements which tend to provide substitutes for war . . . and on the other hand that it should keep prepared, while scrupulously avoiding wrongdoing itself, to repel any wrong, and in exceptional cases to take action *which in a more advanced stage of international relations would come under the head of the exercise of the international police*. (Emphases added)

Roosevelt goes on to describe, as a separate matter, the arbitration work of the legalist Hague conference and the involvement of the United States in formulating arbitration treaties. Nations should, in Roosevelt's framework, continue to seek alternatives to war—and Roosevelt goes on to make explicit reference to, and give support for, the pacifist movements of the period that were advocating a *legalist* view of international relations, based on forums for arbitration being developed in The Hague (Kirgis 1996; Caron 2000). But his paradigm for attaining security through *international police* is distinguishable from that of international law, and he contemplates the latter as generally ineffective. Roosevelt is clear that progress in international relations will be marked by a permanent institution of international police, precisely because *police* presents a more effective route to security than law and the peace movement can provide (see Zasloff 2003).

There is no doubt that Roosevelt's invocation of an international police authority was thoroughly expansionist. The next day, he was identified by the London *Daily Chronicle* as "Police Constable Roosevelt of the International Police" (*New York Times* 1904a) and by the *New York Times* (1904b) as "Policeman for the Hemisphere." But, as articulated, Roosevelt's international police was also designed as extending the Drago Doctrine: as defined by the Argentinian Foreign Minister Luis María Drago in 1902, the doctrine expressed that foreign states could not rely on armed intervention to secure compliance with foreign debts and that in particular European countries could not rely on foreign indebtedness to use military force against nations in the Americas (Drago 1902; Ramsey 1998; Nagan and Hammer 2004).

Although often referred to as ushering in gunboat diplomacy, as a matter of police it is important to examine Roosevelt's proposal, which turns out not to be merely a repressive constabulary to enforce U.S. interests (cf. Holmes 2003). Instead, this international police represented a duty of nations to produce *order*, to avoid "barbarism," and to ensure civilization *tout court.* Through what has become known as the Roosevelt Corollary to the Monroe Doctrine, Roosevelt identifies precisely what this duty of international police entails, and he proposes that it is a duty of civilized nations to secure the welfare of foreign states *by ensuring that they are orderly and well administered in their domestic affairs.* Although lengthy, the following quotation provides the foundation for understanding the role and scope conditions of this turn-of-the-century international police and the role Roosevelt (1904) contemplated for the United States in the process:

> It is not true that the United States feels any land hunger or entertains any projects as regards the other nations of the Western Hemisphere save such as are for their welfare. All that this country desires is to see the neighboring countries *stable, orderly, and prosperous.* If a nation shows that it knows how to act with *reasonable efficiency and decency in social and political matters,* if it *keeps order and pays its obligations,* it need fear no interference from the United States.
>
> *Chronic wrongdoing, or an impotence which results in a general loosening of the ties of civilized society, may in America, as elsewhere, ultimately require intervention by some civilized nation,* and in the Western Hemisphere the adherence of the United States to the Monroe Doctrine may force the United States, however reluctantly, *in flagrant cases of such wrongdoing or impotence, to the exercise of an international police power.*
>
> If within [the borders of our southern neighbors] the reign of law and justice obtains, prosperity is sure to come to them. While they thus obey the primary laws of civilized society they may rest assured that they would be treated by us in a spirit of cordial and helpful sympathy. We would interfere with them only in the last resort, and then only if it became evident that their inability or unwillingness to do justice at home and abroad had violated the rights of the United States or had invited foreign aggression to the detriment of the entire body of American nations. (Emphases added)

Articulated in this way, international police provided the basis for an all-out U.S. expansionism in Latin America, and a mechanism for preventing a European naval threat (see Holmes 2005). And in the process, Roosevelt turns the 1823 Monroe Doctrine on its head: suggesting that adherence to the Monroe Doctrine, which had been regarded as preventing a new (European) colonialism in the Americas, might "force" the United States to intervene in Latin American affairs provided the basis for increased control over these newly independent countries, rather than a respect for their sovereignty (see Chayes 1985; Moore 1986).

That the United States should discharge this international police duty was thereby part and parcel of U.S. foreign policy regarding Latin America in the decades following the Spanish-American War and the strategic broadening of U.S. control over new foreign territories (cf. Cleveland 2002; Holmes 2005; Veeser 2002). This 1904 articulation of an international police power was subsumed under Roosevelt's "Big Stick" policy regarding Panama, the incorporation of the Platt Amendment into Cuba's constitution, and the entering into, in 1903, treaties between the newly independent Cuba and the United States (see U.S. Treaty Series 1903a, 1903b, 1903c). Among other obligations imposed on Cuba, these arrangements allowed the United States to lease or buy lands for naval purposes, such as leasing of the current base at Guantánamo Bay transacted at a time of nascent and circumscribed Cuban sovereignty (Hughes 1999; De Zayas 2004; Neuman 2004). It is perhaps fitting that Guantánamo Bay—the leasing of which was part of a broad design in which the international police power would fit—has now reemerged as the focal site for analyses that an international logic of "police" has blurred the line of conventionally military actions (see chapter 7; Agamben 2005), raising questions over how the treatment of detainees is to be governed and Guantánamo Bay imagined (see, e.g., Roach 2002; Gathii 2003; Scheffer 2003).

Yet if this duty of international police was defined and understood imperially, it was articulated benevolently. Admitting that U.S. interests were in fact being protected by discharging an international police duty, Roosevelt equally defended intervention in the hemisphere as being in the domestic interest—"for their welfare"—of neighboring foreign states. In addition, by ensuring that foreign states are "stable, orderly, and prosperous," "efficient and decent," and able to "keep order and pay [their] obligations," international police could prevent the more general "loosening of the ties of civilized society," which at the turn of the century would have been manifested (for the United States) most notably by the military interventions being launched by European states.

The goal of intervention, then, was said to be promoting domestic order and thereby guarding against barbarism by protecting international "civilization," normative goals that echo what the vocation of police was directed to in ancien regime France (cf. Tomlins 1993, 40–41). Rather than directly regulating relations between sovereign states, international police instead emphasized the domestic securing of order and good administration in foreign countries. In intervening, the United States—as a civilized nation— would thereby spread U.S. enlightenment and democracy abroad (Cleveland 2002, 208), a duty that Roosevelt predicted would be exercised in the future by a permanent international police.

While this apparent benevolence certainly would not have fooled Latin American states (cf. Chayes 1985), invoking the domestic welfare of foreign nations did represent a shift away from Washington support for the private U.S. interests that had been operating in the region. As Veeser's (2002) work *A World Safe for Capitalism* demonstrates, the police power that became the Roosevelt Corollary was also a response to the misdeeds of American capitalists operating in newly independent Latin American countries. The poorly administered and corrupt San Domingo Improvement Company had been running the customs houses of the Dominican Republic. Despite local antagonism, the company, a private U.S. firm, had recently secured a legal victory to ensure its continued payments despite its poor management. The indebtedness of Latin American states being of international concern, international police provided a mechanism for separating U.S. foreign policy from historically powerful private sector interests (Veeser 2002). Under the logic of international police, foreign finances were to be brought into order: the U.S. firm no longer had any privileged status and ceased to exist a few years later (Veeser 2002; Weeks 2004). International police, then, was an echo in international relations of the nineteenth-century restrictions on private capital that marked the domestic cornerstone of *salus populi* in the United States (Novak 1996).

Roosevelt's emphasis on international police as *salus populi* is developed, at some length, in James Holmes's (2003) perceptive analysis of the role that the domestic police power played in animating the policies of U.S. foreign affairs in this period. The "police science" that underwrote Roosevelt's international police has been largely ignored; Holmes thoroughly demonstrates that Roosevelt's emphasis on domestic order, and in particular his emphasis on police, was a police based on "a kind of stewardship" in international relations. In contrast to military aggression, this international police, discharged by the United States, would be "a benign, transitory imperialism" and thereby "superior to the amoral, self-interested brand practiced by the European states" (133). It is precisely this notion of stewardship that is based on Roosevelt's personal inclination toward the nineteenth-century governmentality of police in the United States and an explicit emphasis that steers away from *law* in favor of *police*.

As Holmes describes, a police emphasis on a strong state that would secure the welfare of its citizens was in the air during Roosevelt's public service career, and the states' police power would have been recognized and taught in the brief time he spent at Columbia University's law school (2003, 127–28). Drawing on a reading of Roosevelt's letters and speeches, Holmes concludes that the Corollary to the Monroe Doctrine in fact stemmed from this faith in police—so that the articulation of an international police was not simply Washington's militaristic enforcement of values but was conceived of in terms "necessary for the sake of the welfare of mankind" (2003, 132). As a result, this international police was not even to be exercised solely by the United States, in an exceptionalist role. Although falling to the United States at this geohistorical conjuncture, police, Roosevelt later indicated, should similarly be exercised by Japan over China, a realpolitik interest articulated as "for the interest of all of the world that each part of the world should be prosperous and well policed" (see Holmes 2003, 135).

As evidence for this broad view of international police, Holmes points out that the first reliance on this "quasi-legal international police power" did not produce a repressive U.S. constabulary. While intervening in Santo Domingo in 1904, U.S. intervention sought to achieve orderly civil administration on the island. Taking over the role of customs agents, U.S. forces ensured the payment of foreign creditors and financial administration of the domestic government (Holmes 2003, 126, n. 2, 135). The Marine Corps appears to have included duties of civil administration in its training manuals—issuing travel permits and driving licenses, controlling the prisons, an adjunct role in the policing of local laws, support for the running of local elections, and so on—to establish "peace, order, security, and better government" in the country, and to promote "leading ideas of civilization" (Holmes 2003, 139). Although not noted in Holmes's account, it is important to remember that U.S. intervention was also precipitated by the misdeeds of the San Domingo Improvement Company, so these interventions also sought to bring regulatory control to bear over what was once untrammeled private industry being pursued in foreign states.

However, another significant tension is not developed in this account. Although animating nineteenth-century ideas of police would have been already circumscribed by U.S. postcolonial legal discourse, there appears to be a lack of any *law* guiding the international police Roosevelt proposed. In the way it is articulated, police is instead presented as a freestanding logic, unreliant on law for authority (but see Novak 1996) and which is uncircumscribed domestically or internationally—and police is imagined as continuing in perpetuity, even in more advanced international relations, "under the head of the exercise of a permanent international police."

What one finds in the Roosevelt Corollary, then, is a wholesale replacement of "law" by "police," with Roosevelt overtly suspicious of legal institutions as a promising modality of rule (Dalton 2002, 281; Morris 2001a, xiv). As Jonathan Zasloff argues, even Roosevelt's invocation of the potential of international law, and the work of The Hague conferences, was halfhearted since the President simply "had little interest in international law and institutions" (2003, 285; but see Dalton 2002, 288–89). And so while Roosevelt paid attention to the legal-pacifist movements during the election year of 1904, particularly since there were key individuals investing heavily in such reforms, he soon "lost interest in the matter" (Zasloff 2003, 305) and turned to different logics altogether.

Roots of this disjuncture between "law" and "police" in the international can equally be located in Roosevelt's domestically informed views on law and police as competing modalities and the tension he often drew between legalism and good administration. Prior to assuming the Presidency, Roosevelt had been Police Commissioner for New York (cf. Morris 2001a, 494–533). In reflecting on that time, he describes the institution of police as having as its aim improving the lives of city residents and ensuring their physical health, living conditions, work conditions, and their moral character (including, for instance, the regulation of saloons and liquor sellers, which produced criminogenic spaces that would encourage immorality among the men frequenting them, who were also to be policed). Roosevelt also served on the city's Health Board, seeking to improve the conditions of the city's poor (see Dalton 2002, 152–55). This emphasis on administration comes through in his autobiographical reflections, in which Roosevelt articulates how good police could be achieved in New York and complains of the impediments of legally defined checks and balances for police work, which for him stand in the way of the "good government" that could otherwise be achieved (1913, 175):

> There were two sides to the work: first, the actual handling of the Police Department; second, using my position to help in making the city a better place in which to live and work for those to whom the conditions of life and labor were hardest. The two problems were closely connected. . . . [The police department] represented that device of old-school American political thought, the desire to establish checks and balances. . . . In most positions the "division of powers" theory works unmitigated mischief. The only way to get good service is to give somebody power to render it. . . . If, as we hold, the people are fit for self-government—if, in other words, our talk and our institutions are not shams—we will get good government.

This contrast between good government and the legalism of the "division of powers" reflects Roosevelt's emphasis on a gilded age of progressive reform: though he may have begun his career with a less progressive focus, moral reform and reform in the name of the family soon became some of his central domestic causes, causes that he perceived as often stunted by legal restrictions (see Dalton 2002, 81–84).

This domestic tension between law and police is particularly acute in Roosevelt's account of cigar manufacturing in New York City (Roosevelt 1913, 81–83). As a member of the New York Legislature, Roosevelt found the conditions of tenement houses in which cigars were manufactured to be appalling and supported legislation to regulate its manufacture on public health grounds. As he recounts the unsanitary nature of these homes, one sees the close link he draws between good health and good citizenship: his description of these immigrant-occupied tenements is that the "conditions rendered it impossible for the families of the tenement-house workers to live so that the children might grow up fitted for the exacting duties of American citizenship" and family life (1913, 81; Dalton 2002, 83). Roosevelt was a strong supporter of the legislation, and it passed, but it was later declared unconstitutional by the New York Court of Appeals, in a decision restricting the application of *salus populi suprema lex est* (1913, 82; cf. *In re application of*

Jacobs 1885), leading him to conclude that law is diametrically opposed to social improvement and civilizing practices (Dalton 2002, 153)[4]:

> My experience in the Police Department taught me that not a few of the worst tenement-houses were owned by wealthy individuals, who hired the best and most expensive lawyers to persuade the courts that it was "unconstitutional" to insist on the betterment of conditions. . . . *They made it evident that they valued the Constitution, not as a help to righteousness, but as a means for thwarting movements against unrighteousness.* After my experience with them I became more set than ever in my distrust of those men, whether business men or lawyers, judges, legislators, or executive officers, *who seek to make of the Constitution a fetich for the prevention of the work of social reform, for the prevention of work in the interest of those men, women, and children on whose behalf we should be at liberty to employ freely every governmental agency.* (Emphases added)

Roosevelt's antagonism toward "legalism," the opposition he described between "law" and "justice" (1913, 55), the frustrations that motivated him to leave Columbia University's law school after one year (Holmes 2003, 142, n. 7), and what others regarded as his disregard and disinterest in an expert modality of U.S. constitutionalism (and thereby rejecting any sovereign beyond the people [cf. Tomlins 1993, 95], instead arguing that "the Constitution was made for the people and not the people for the Constitution" [Morris 2001b, 165; see also Morris 2001a, xiv]) is here expressed as a frustration with law's protection of private property over the social improvement that could be produced by a broad vision of the New York City police and legislature.[5]

If the domestic context provides a backdrop for understanding Roosevelt's view of international police as sitting in opposition to law, in the international context the model of police was contemplated as necessary for the development of legal institutions. *If law was unnecessary for the establishment and control of police, police was required to underwrite law.*

Police was not only tied to both order maintenance and militarism through the Roosevelt Corollary but was also the program through which international legal institutions to promote peace could be attained. The importance of police to law is already foreshadowed in his 1904 Message; but in 1910, delivering his Nobel Prize acceptance speech, Roosevelt drew an even closer link between police, law, and peace. Although indicating that he strenuously supported efforts that were under way at The Hague to promote international law and arbitration, he stressed that any such efforts would be stifled by the lack of an international police power to back it up.[6] Ensuring international order required the possibility of sanctions and as a result required an international police force that would guarantee them—so that an international police force was a precondition to both effective law and to any institution seeking to achieve world peace (see also Dalton 2002, 360; Morris 2001a, 595). Until an international police was institutionalized, the duty of police would be discharged by individual nations in the name of civilization:

> The supreme difficulty in connection with developing the peace work of the Hague arises from the lack of any executive power, of any police power to enforce the decrees of the Court. In any community of any size the authority of the courts rests upon actual or potential force: on the existence of a police, or on the knowledge that the able-bodied men of the country are both ready and willing to see that the decrees of judicial and legislative bodies are put into effect. In new and wild communities where there is violence, an honest man must protect himself; and until other means of securing his safety are devised, it is both foolish and wicked to persuade him to surrender his arms while the men who are dangerous to the community retain theirs. He should not renounce the right to protect himself by his own efforts until the community is so organized that it can effectively relieve the individual of the duty of putting down violence. So it is with nations. Each nation must keep well prepared to defend itself until the establishment of some form of international police power, competent and willing to prevent violence as between nations. (Roosevelt 1910)

It is the possibility of police, even without being circumscribed by law, that has the capacity to prevent violence—and this is true whether this police duty is discharged by individuals, nations, or a central authority. And in this model, law is wholly dependent on police, in both the domestic and the international contexts. This is an important point, to which we return toward the end of this chapter: while Roosevelt flagged that the lack of a police power would prevent any successful international law, a regime of law without police is precisely the basis on which international criminal law is presently organized. This divorce of law and police promotes a legal field in which prosecutors are left heavily reliant on the willingness of individual states to cooperate with international tribunals. As a result, this separating out of "law" and "police" has built a structural tension into the development of the permanent International Criminal Court and the field more broadly.

Of course, Roosevelt's interventionist and imperialist policies—and the mechanism of international police—were put to rest three decades later by Franklin D. Roosevelt's "Good Neighbor" diplomacy of 1933, which purported to abrogate military interventionism in Latin America (after a lengthy series of early twentieth-century interventions in the Dominican Republic, Honduras, Cuba, Nicaragua, Haiti, Panama, and Guatemala [cf. Carrasco and Thomas 1996]). Within foreign affairs, this constitutes a rejection of a logic of *police*, in favor of a more *legalist* emphasis on respecting the rights of other states, their sovereignty, the sanctity of international agreements, and the "maintenance of law and the orderly processes of government" (Roosevelt 1933b, 205).[7] In the resurgence of law over police, it is perhaps most significant that Roosevelt's international police was most explicitly laid to rest in the 1934 U.S. ratification of a treaty based on the Declaration of the Rights and Duties of Nations (Sikkink 1997), which enshrined national sovereignties and a principle of nonintervention. As Kathryn Sikkink highlights, this Declaration had been a central project of the American Institute of International Law, connected to the legalist U.S. peace movement, which by that time had engaged for twenty years in a broad project of both codifying and promoting legalism in foreign policy and international affairs (Sikkink 1997, 715–21).[8] These normative commitments were soon institutionalized: by 1944 it was clear that in contrast to his cousin's views at the turn of the century, FDR was staunchly opposed to any permanent institution of international police, preferring judicial resolution through international tribunals and, if necessary, temporary and ad hoc military coordination of the "united nations" (Glennon and Hayward 1994, 1577–78; Hurd 1944).[9]

The Aftermath of War: Technocratic Visions of International Police

We find, then, that an initial separation of law and police motivated the international police that Roosevelt described. Police represented both the capacity to enforce obligations as well as the desire to produce orderly government and civilized society—and it was not bound to any particular legal logic or norms but was instead an independent axis on which to turn international relations and achieve security, both in the absence of law and permanently (even in more "advanced stages of international relations"). Law represented, on the domestic front, an obstacle to police and stood in contrast to justice—but on the international front, where law was not sufficiently institutionalized to pose an obstacle, law would need a regime of police to underwrite it if it were to ever be effective. Either way, in the international context police comes out on top: law is either unnecessary to its functioning or law is dependent on police to underwrite its success. But if Roosevelt's invocation of police created a one-way relationship between "police" and "law" internationally, it is in the interwar period that the idea and plans for an international police force grew into a significant area of attention (on the field of international relations in this period, see, e.g., Wilson 1998).

The evolution of "Good Neighbor" diplomacy had, from President Wilson through FDR, increasingly characterized international police as repressive, extolling instead a more legal paradigm for international relations (culminating in the establishment of the United Nations without a permanent police force). This led proponents of international police to frustration: one recounts how in 1913 President Wilson had expressed the importance of an international police if nations sought to guarantee and secure peace, thereby suggesting a necessary relationship between police and peace. But by 1919, in light of the emerging League of Nations and the conclusion of the Paris Peace Conference, Wilson went on to characterize international police in a more negative and repressive light, concluding that with regard to the League an "armed force is in the background in this programme . . . but that is the last resort, because this is intended as a constitution of peace, not as a League of War" (see discussion in Davies 1930, 106, 131–32).

But if the idea of international police was being tamed within U.S. foreign policy and programs for international governance, there was soon a proliferation of proposals designed to promote it (see Pugh 2002)—and to do so, these proposals sought to develop new relationships between police and law. In the shadow cast by World War I, the idea of international police had resurfaced in programs and proposals: as Sir Derek Bowett's classic text *United Nations Forces* (1964) concludes after reviewing a wide range of these often technical proposals, "During the interval between the World Wars it became fashionable to speak of an 'International Police Force.' The abbreviation 'IPF' was used as if it were as generally known as 'United Nations' is today" (1964, 328).

Yet although these proposals relied on the same language as Roosevelt's "international police," the paradigms they advanced were fundamentally different from those of the turn of the century. Now being contemplated in the aftermath of World War I, international police was no longer imagined as ensuring the orderly domestic administration of foreign states (which would thereby help ensure that international civility was kept), but was instead the device through which humanity itself could become civilized and the devastation of war prevented.

It should be noted that an international police that would act in the service of humanity was alluded to by Roosevelt as well, who after articulating the mandate for U.S. intervention had indicated that, though such cases would have to be rare, in "extreme cases [international police] action may be justifiable and proper" when "strong appeal is made to our sympathies," namely when horrific crimes and atrocities are being committed in other nations (1904). But at the historical conjuncture of the 1920s and 1930s—in the aftermath of a world war and in light of developing U.S. reticence to engage in the policing of foreign states, particularly acute within the U.S. Senate—the idea of international police being advanced was one that contemplated the "international" as a sphere to be governed *as such*, rather than responding to atrocities committed within territories. We suggest, then, that the idea of international police ought not merely to be understood as a tool to deal with international problems; instead, the mechanism of international police was part and parcel of defining the regime of the international itself.

Rather than canvassing a wide array of proposals, we here focus on the most prominent interwar model of international police, which is that advanced by Lord Davies in *The Problem of the Twentieth Century* (1930; cf. Bowett 1964). Lord Davies's text begins in the shadow of World War I, but rather than interrogating the legal questions that had been advanced since the turn-of-the-century Hague conferences, he presents the question of how, in light of the devastation caused by world war, to ensure the welfare of humanity and maintain the tenuous line between civilization and barbarism, particularly given the fear that scientific advances had rendered war ever more lethal and barbaric (1930, 1–2, 39–43). For Davies, the problem of the twentieth century now had little to do with the internal governance of individual states and more to do with a police of the international community to prevent belligerence. As now defined, the problem to be addressed by an international police is the question of how to directly govern international relations between states—to prevent war by "securing justice in the sphere of international relations" (2).

Working within the paradigm of the League of Nations, and well aware of British security needs (Pugh 2002, 99), Davies determines that the capacity to prevent war would require national disarmament; and after citing the pacifist writing of William Penn, Davies argues that the way to achieve this disarmament is to institute a regime of international police. In justifying this position, Davies emphasizes a changing idea of *security* itself: while defining security as "an atmosphere in which the national mind lives, moves and has its being" (24), Davies argues that world war has changed the concept of security away from the achievement of national economic and physical security, so that attaining security is now focused on preventing violations of national borders rather than producing social goods (26–27).

As histories of police demonstrate, achieving security is the core referent of police. And with security now defined as a national experience of the international—as a defense of incursions from the perimeter, rather than as a promotion of the internal order and sense of being of the population from its core—it is not surprising that the logic of police is redefined to match. Though not presenting his analysis as contingent on this redefinition of security, this appears to be what is motivating Davies's otherwise straightforward proposal: if nations focus on the security of their national borders, and if preventing future wars will require disarmament of some sort, nations will simply not disarm unless they are provided with an alternative guarantee. A police—redefined—becomes the answer to this redefined need for security (145–46).

To achieve security, what is needed is a model of international police that can both threaten and enforce sanctions against any rogue aggression (3)—and the existence of "international policemen" would thereby provide the basis for disarmament and the mechanism for abolishing war (6). Davies dismisses more legalist approaches to international relations, which for him are no more than "worshipping at the shrine of ultra-sovereignty" (177). In contrast, he provides copious reference to historical plans for international forces, beginning with ancient Greece and the Amphictyonic League (58–115), credits Roosevelt as being "the chief exponent of the idea of an international police force" (102–5), and goes on to echo a wide range of elite twentieth-century support in the United States, the United Kingdom (including a turn-of-the-century proposal by Sir Charles Watson of a fleet to "police the world's highways" [111–12]), France, and Holland for the use of international forces to back up and enforce international law and arbitration (101–53), including those proposals developed for the 1919 Paris Peace Conference.

The upshot of 1919, however, was a League of Nations without a constabulary through which to exercise a sanctioning power (MacMillan 2002), and this is the foil against which Lord Davies works. From the perspective of police, there simply could be no talk of international "law" without a mechanism of police to enforce sanctions (4). He admits that there was not much law or international agreement to guide and ground this international police—but he suggests that the two modalities of police and law should progress simultaneously, because they are "part and parcel of the same puzzle," so that if they develop concurrently, "they will fall into their proper perspective in the final solution of the problem" (53).

Davies develops this relationship between international police and law by drawing from the domestic context, in which he determines that the police constabularies of the nineteenth century are what provided law with its normative strength, rather than the other way around: it is police that "holds every citizen 'in awe,'" and modern police constabularies are presented as the "visible embodiment" of the equality of all before the law (166–67). Police is thereby at the core of civilization of all and of each: "it inculcates habits of thought and indices a mental outlook consonant with the natural ideas of justice and right" and "reinforces the moral fabric of society" by curbing appetites and allaying passions (168). By itself, law without sanctions would not function, and any conception of the international that valued the legal protections of state sovereignty over a logic of an international police was doomed to produce more victims (177–204). Without police as a corollary, any legal decision made in "the domain of [the] international" would run the risk of being unjust: rather than seeking justice, judges would focus on preventing war (14–15).

In contemplating the "international," then, police and law appear to be of a piece, rather than separate modalities. So while police appears to be at the core of the enterprise—sanctions by police are, for Davies, at the heart of civilization itself—it would work within a regime of international law. Police would serve two functions: it would enforce the judicial rulings of international tribunals, and it would also provide a united force to repel state aggression. Both aspects, though, would operate within a body of law that was itself in the process of being elaborated—and police would thereby be regulated by the Permanent Court of International Justice (360–82).

As Hans Kelsen (1957, 120–25) suggests over twenty years later, this more restricted view of "police"—while perhaps a misnomer within historical uses of the term—would no longer present "police" as a separate modality of rule. Kelsen, of course, saw law as the central organizing principle that could provide collective security but regarded sanctions and force as ontologically necessary to law (6). As a result, an international force would be necessary but would be restricted to the sanctioning of delicts as determined by international law (120–25), rather than enjoying a broad power to police:

> Another terminology, the correctness of which is doubtful, is to designate as an international "police" force only a permanent and separate armed force at the direct disposal of the central organ of an international security community. . . . A police action is any enforcement action performed by an organ of a community for the welfare of its members, their health, morals, prosperity and, especially, their security. However, it is not a sanitary police force or a police force for the purpose of morals or economics, but a security police force with which an international security organization is concerned. The specific functions of a security police force are to prepare and secure by enforcement actions the judicial or quasi-judicial procedure for ascertaining a violation of the law, and to execute the sanction ordered.[10] (Kelsen 1957, 114–15)

The approach that Davies presents, though perhaps the most comprehensive, is not unique. The shift he presents for international police is one that emphasizes an international community to be regulated (one recently cobbled together in the 1919 peace conference), and he proposes a police of that community that rests on a different logic of security and a different imagination of the terrain to be policed. The close relationship he presents between police and law, in which police remains the linchpin of the enterprise but is itself subject to legal control, is part and parcel of the technocratic move that accompanied the problematization of this international sphere where law and police freely commingle, as Davies suggests, as component parts of the same puzzle.

For our purposes we here signal that within these proposals, law and police became intertwined: international law required police to be effective, but police did not present an entirely different modality that could be exercised without legal oversight and control. In the following decades, technocratic questions proliferated: the quota of personnel to be drawn from each state, the weaponry available, financial negotiations, how to ensure uniformity of command and control, and so on, with variants on these proposals reignited following World War II (Beaumont 2001; Bloomfield, Bowman, and Morgenthau 1964; Clark and Sohn 1966; Falk and Mendlovitz 1966; Frye 1957; Mendlovitz and Fousek 1996, 2000; Waskow 1965).[11] Although comparatively little attention was paid to the details of how to ensure this legal oversight of this international police—especially compared to the explicit proposals designed to measure the size, budgets, and command authority of a force—law was neither excluded nor ignored. The stage was set for a closer relationship between police and law in the international.

As these proposals took on different forms, some no longer limited the reach of an international police to the enforcement of jurisdictional and boundary disputes and the enforcement of orders by international tribunals, with police instead brought back into a broader relationship with creating and keeping the peace (Bowett 1964, 313; Pugh 2002). This was designed to keep a logic of "international police" as separate as possible from an aggressive transnational military that would be thought to have little regard for state sovereignty—and, in this way, *international police* could take a position between *law* and *military* force. This was a key component of the 1957 peacekeeping plan advanced by Lester B. Pearson, the Canadian Secretary of State for External Affairs. Written in the shadow of incursions into Egypt, Pearson called for a temporary force that could perform "supervisory police duties" (1957, 402) of peacekeeping within countries:

> Even if governments are unable to give the United Nations a "fighting" force ready and organized . . . they should be willing to earmark smaller forces for the more limited duty of securing a cease-fire already agreed upon

by the belligerents. We might in this way be able to construct a halfway house at the crossroads of war, and utilize an intermediate technique between merely passing Resolutions and actually fighting. (1957, 401)

Although this takes us beyond the scope of the present chapter, with police having been turned to peacekeeping in conflict and postconflict situations, it is important to note that international policing has now reemerged as a central concern for defining the scope of the United Nations (Brahimi 2000). "Police" is invoked for peace building and peacekeeping, with a proliferation of forces: in the Balkans alone, one finds the UN stabilization force (SFOR), the International Police Task Force (IPTF), and the UN Protective Force (UNPROFOR) (e.g., Donais 2003–2004).[12] And in the process of this redefinition of police, it appears to have taken on a logic that may be quite separate from the close ties to law and legal institutions that had been advanced in the interwar and more immediate post–World War II periods (cf. Beaumont 2001; and see chapter 7).

International Law as Values; International Police as Security

If the experience of the world wars had pushed international police toward a policing of borders, peacekeeping, and global security rather than the promotion of domestic order, recent years have witnessed a change back toward securing the domestic good police of foreign states. The reinscribing of good police and administration has brought with it a return to the disentangling of a logic of police from that of law. As we discuss in this section, this echoes, and in fact amplifies, the logic of police within Roosevelt's 1904 speech, in which international security is achieved not by policing international borders and the international as such but instead by ensuring the good domestic governance of foreign states. In the process, law and "legalism" are conspicuously left out of the equation.

A prime example of this new logic of international police found a receptive audience during a speech to Canada's Department of Foreign Affairs and International Trade, in which Michael Ignatieff (2004a) suggested that Canadian foreign policy must change. Presently focused on promoting *values* of human rights, tolerance, multiculturalism, and human security, Ignatieff's proposal is that Canada ought to instead direct its attention toward enabling precarious states to become stable, well governed, and well administered. Enabling stable states, according to Ignatieff, would more closely reflect Canada's interests in global security and stability. Rather than focusing on human rights, then, Canada ought to secure its interests in stable states by promoting models of *peace, order, and good government* internationally. To achieve this goal, a Canadian technocracy should be dispatched to spread good administration to all corners of the globe:

> Just as other nations, like Norway, have concentrated on conflict resolution, secret negotiations to get peace deals, it seems to me our comparative advantage is in good government. . . . We can have a foreign policy based on peace, order and good government that becomes a kind of Canadian imperialism, where we export our successes everywhere. . . . I think we need to be thinking of developing a national civilian capacity to promote peace, order and good government that would rival and complement the capacities of Canadian forces. (2004a)

Further asserting that Canada defines "the purpose of our political union *as* peace, order and good government" (emphasis added), Ignatieff argues that this model could export successful models for rescuing failed or precarious states.

Developing international reform along the lines of peace, order, and good government would, of course, resonate closely with Ignatieff's audience. The Department of Foreign Affairs and International Trade is a federal department—and ensuring peace, order, and good government, commonly referred to as "POGG," is a power constitutionally entrusted to the federal government. Articulated in the British North America Act, "POGG" is the acronym for the federal government's legislative authority "to make laws for the Peace, Order, and good Government of Canada" on issues of national concern.[13] Yet, as Valverde demonstrates, the police logic of peace, order, and good government is not as core to the Canadian national and political identity as Ignatieff suggests and reflects instead a more generic governmentality in British colonial settings (chapter 3). Of course, Ignatieff might have also refrained from drawing stark lines between POGG and the U.S. pursuit of happiness, since even in its heyday the latter was tempered by the logic of *salus populi* (Novak 1996).

What Ignatieff is proposing is an international promotion of police, which relies on a conceptual division between Canada's "values" (human rights) and Canada's "interests" in its own security and welfare (best protected by promoting of global security). Read closely, the speech—and in particular the juxtaposition of "human rights" against "peace, order and good government"—reveals a binary tension presented between "law" and "administration" (cf. Tomlins 1993, 24).

This is developed by presenting law and police as two distinct series. The existing series is presented as values–human rights–law, while the competing series is presented as interests–good administration–security.[14] We have, as a result, two potential sets of international action: a juridical set that commands foreign policy by promoting universal legal values that will be generic and likely ineffectual or a diplomatic set that develops foreign policy based on promoting good governance and state stability, in an effort to capture the possibility of global security. This is further imagined as a Habermasian competition between values (such as human rights) and interests. Promoting POGG worldwide will ensure the domestic political stability of foreign states, in turn serving Canada's own interests in immigration control, population management, and national security, thereby ensuring "a foreign policy for Canadians, not for Scandinavians" (Ignatieff 2004a). In the process, administration, and not law, becomes the lingua franca of international reform.

Ignatieff himself is, of course, quite aware of law and police as potentially competing modalities, having in earlier work drawn the link between the police of the economy and the capacity for distributive justice (Hont and Ignatieff 1983, 13–26). The model of worldwide institution building that he now proposes could have been lifted directly from nineteenth-century *Polizeiwissenschaft* texts:

> The Canadian intuition about development arises from our own experience as a developing nation in the nineteenth century, when the national policy successfully linked government investment in infrastructure, free immigration, protection of basic industries and a vigorous private sector. It is second nature for Canadians to see government regulation not as the enemy of market freedom but as its precondition; second nature for us to see good government as the precondition for development that is equitable between classes, religions and regions. . . . The focus of our foreign policy should be

to consolidate "peace, order and good government" as the sine qua non for stable states, enduring democracy and equitable development . . . we should specialize in a policy framework that brings all our "governance" activity together in a single powerful program of action. (Ignatieff 2004a)

This logic of international reform would mimic domestic governance, to ensure and guarantee strong public authority worldwide (see Tomlins 1993, 45), thereby "cultivating the pastoral" (Gordon 1991, 10) in foreign affairs.

It is important to note, however, that while these two series are presented as conceptually distinct, in Ignatieff's proposal it is precisely *through* good governance that legal values can equally be protected. The two series previously outlined are thereby posited as a pair: the juridical set exists *within* the diplomatic set, since within this formulation legal values are themselves imagined as only possible within a regime of strong state institutions. As a result, although legal values are at first rhetorically displaced in favor of guaranteeing security through police, the logic of *police* and *good administration* is then posited as fundamental to promoting the rule of law worldwide. In response to Eduard Lasker's formulation—that "rule of law and rule of police are two different ways to which history points" (see Tomlins 1993, 45–46)—we instead have law subsumed under police, so that promoting *security* becomes the logic and discourse *through which* to build law and legal institutions. And this will not always be benign: Ignatieff goes on to suggest that achieving "peace, order and good government" will, at times, require military intervention.

Through a logic of police uncircumscribed by law—and with law dependent on police—international police becomes a device through which to secure both Canada's interests and the domestic security of foreign states. This benevolent imperialism, in which law is systematically withdrawn from achieving security and security is given a foundation through the logic of police, promotes a model that stands in the way of legalism, in favor of a benevolent Canadian imperialism to promote civilization through good administration.

International Law without International Police: The Lack of a Police Constabulary in International Criminal Law

To this point, we have focused on the relations between police and law as competing modalities, by emphasizing the lens of police. In this last section, however, we seek to invert the lens, to briefly document the relationship between police and law from the perspective of the legal field, with attention to international criminal law. Although it is the international legal field most closely allied with modern ideas of police, international criminal law has been developed precisely without a regime of police to underwrite it. In the place of a police constabulary, international criminal tribunals instead must rely on often hostile foreign states to voluntarily cooperate: and this international separation of law from police has built in a systematic limit to the field that, we suggest, likely ensures that the most powerful nations will be exempt from its authority.

Over the past decade, the International Criminal Tribunals for Rwanda and the former Yugoslavia (ICTR and ICTY, respectively) have ushered in a new era of international criminal law, with Special Courts in Sierra Leone, East Timor, and Cambodia. These ad hoc tribunals are now complemented by a permanent International Criminal Court (ICC), ratified by over ninety countries. This field of law, however, suffers from what Bassiouni (1974, 426) calls a "split personality": the coercive dimension of criminal law (which presupposes access to a police force) is in tension with its "international" emphasis on the voluntary compliance of sovereign states. This is most evident at the early stages of investigation and arrest: investigations (including exhumations and searches and seizures) are often conducted on the territory of a threatened state, and requests from the tribunal are generally communicated to that state to be carried out (Schabas 2001, 94–117). This lack of a police sits in contrast to the aspirations of the 1940s by the London International Assembly, which in line with the integrative postwar models previously described, sought an international constabulary to "execute the orders of the Court and of the Procurator General" (Sadat 1999, 116).

Yet while not provided with a police constabulary (Mundis 2001, 421, n. 1), international criminal tribunals are charged with UN responsibility for policing an international community (see chapter 7). We have, here, a tension that is created by emphasizing the need to police the international—which includes the need to ensure "the peace, security and well-being of the world," to maintain the "shared heritage" and "delicate mosaic" of all peoples, and to prosecute "the most serious crimes of concern to the international community as a whole." This disjuncture places international criminal law between two poles. Without their own constabulary, tribunals must rely on voluntary state cooperation and national militaries (Wedgwood 2001, 213–14)[15] at the same time they are charged with maintaining and restoring international peace and security (United Nations Secretary General 1993),[16] precisely in the wake of conflict. This is all the more difficult since international criminal law requires the use of coercive police practices of investigations, arrests, and convictions, and these often run against the interests of nation-states and their officials (Wallach 1998; Sadat Wexler 1996, 717). And when states refuse to cooperate, the sanction is itself diplomatic rather than coercive: for instance, at the ICC, the court is to refer noncooperation to either the Assembly of State Parties or the Security Council for sanction (Kittichaisaree 2001, 281), which will result in naming and shaming rather than sanction (Schabas 2001, 106–7).[17]

This split between "law" and "police"—and the reliance on state cooperation—presents challenges that were perhaps less problematic for the international tribunals of the mid-twentieth century:

> It is well known that the Allied Powers that set up the international tribunals at Nürnberg and Tokyo wielded full authority and control over the territory of Germany and Japan respectively and, in addition, had already apprehended the defendants when trials commenced. Consequently, those tribunals did not need the cooperation of the defendants' national authorities or those of other countries for the prosecutors' investigations and collection of evidence. The situation is totally different for the Tribunal. The Security Council, when it established the Tribunal, was aware that it lacked any direct authority over the territories of States Members of the United Nations and, in particular, of the successor republics of the former Yugoslavia. Thus, the Tribunal was not endowed with direct enforcement powers: it has no law enforcement agents at its disposal entitled to carry out investigations, subpoena witnesses, or serve arrest warrants in the territories of States Members of the United Nations. To fulfill all these tasks, the Tribunal must rely upon the domestic legal system and the enforcement machinery of each State. Consequently, all requests from the Tribunal for arrest, search, surrender or transfer of persons are addressed to, and processed by,

the municipal system of the relevant State. In this respect it must, however, be emphasized that all States are under a strict obligation to cooperate with the Tribunal and to comply with its requests and orders. (International Criminal Tribunal for the Former Yugoslavia 1994, ¶ 84)

And perhaps even less optimistically, Antonio Cassese spoke in 1996 of his frustrations as the first President of the ICTY, and the tribunal's dependency on states for investigation and enforcement: "*[It is] like an armless and legless giant which needs artificial limbs to act and move. These limbs are the State authorities* . . . the national prosecutors, judges and police officers. If state authorities fail to carry out their responsibilities, the giant is paralyzed, no matter how determined its efforts" (Pejic 1997; emphasis added). Cassese's frustration was unlikely to surprise anyone. In his presidential report of the same year, he complained of the "general pattern of failure" to cooperate by the Republic of Croatia and the Federation of Bosnia and Herzegovina and reported further noncompliance by the Federal Republic of Yugoslavia and Republika Srpska (Mundis 2001, 424–27). Louise Arbour, as Chief Prosecutor at the ICTY, echoed this concern: the paucity of arrests in the early years of the tribunal was leading to a loss of international credibility (Ames 1996, Hagan and Levi 2004), and she sought to "advance every plausible, credible, legal argument within [her] power to break the unhealthy dependency on State cooperation" (Arbour 1999, 40–41).

But if promoting a model of law without police requires tribunals to rely on state cooperation, it also has the further effect of structuring when international criminal law will be applied. Not having its own police and deferring instead to state cooperation, the permanent ICC has been created as "complementary" to national jurisdictions. The ICC, as a result, has no jurisdiction where "the case is being investigated or prosecuted by a State which has jurisdiction over it, unless the State is unwilling or unable genuinely to carry out the investigation or prosecution" or where "the case has been investigated by a State . . . and the State has decided not to prosecute the person concerned, unless the decision resulted from the unwillingness or inability of the State genuinely to prosecute."

This principle of complementarity was vigorously advocated by the 1998 U.S. negotiating team in Rome. It will likely shield powerful states while subjecting weaker ones to the court's jurisdiction, since it is explicitly linked with state resources: the Rome Statute indicates that, in determining whether a state is *unable* to investigate or prosecute, the court will consider whether, "due to a total or substantial collapse or unavailability of its national judicial system, the State is unable to obtain the accused or the necessary evidence and testimony or otherwise unable to carry out its proceedings." And since powerful states are most likely to have the resources to develop a satisfactory investigatory process, this will likely shield powerful states while subjecting weaker ones to the court's jurisdiction.

Other attempts now under way further indicate that state cooperation with the ICC is in jeopardy: the Bush administration has sought bilateral nonsurrender agreements with over two dozen countries, ensuring that U.S. personnel will not be subject to the court's jurisdiction. From the U.S. position, this displacement of the ICC is claimed to protect its own international police function, in which U.S. citizens undertake peacekeeping and humanitarian missions:

> United States military forces, civilian personnel and private citizens are currently active in peacekeeping and humanitarian missions in more than 100 countries. . . . [These agreements] allow the United States to remain engaged internationally with our friends and allies by providing American citizens with essential protection from the jurisdiction of the International Criminal Court, particularly against politically motivated investigations and prosecutions. (U.S. Department of State, 09/23/2003)

If states do not sign nonsurrender agreements, they may cease to receive military assistance from the United States based on § 2007 of the *American Service Members' Protection Act* (2002), enacted to "prevent the International Criminal court from proceeding against United States personnel."[18]

Conclusion

Where, then, are we left? In earlier and more recent contemplations, we find that international police is often invoked as a modality independent of law and on which law is necessarily parasitic for its own authority. This does not mean, however, that ideas of international police have been stable: whether it is Roosevelt's notion of an international police, the constabularies imagined in the aftermath of world wars, or Ignatieff's model of the global spread of good administration, each has served as a device for imagining the international itself. And the relationship between police and law has, as a result, been variable (Koskenniemi 1996, 488–90): while earlier and later models present police as wholly independent from law, the midcentury models that were designed to police the relations between states accepted a more legalistic frame, and imagined law and police to be more of one piece—although even these rarely articulated this relationship in much detail.

When we invert the lens and turn to the field of international criminal law, we find a similar divorce of law and police. Here, international criminal tribunals have been charged with the mandate of securing world peace, security, and well-being—the very sorts of classic police functions that have often existed in tension with legalist paradigms domestically—while being provided with no police personnel with which to achieve this goal. As a result of this separation between law and police, international criminal law has evolved as a field that is dependent on the voluntary cooperation of states, with further implications for the very design and scope of the emerging ICC. Even exemptions from the reach of international criminal law—such as that promoted in the *American Service Members' Protection Act*—are articulated as the importance of preserving an autonomous police capacity in international peacekeeping operations, beyond the reach of the ICC, so that law and police are separated once more.

Following these circuitous relationships between international police and law provides us with analytic purchase that is otherwise missed. It may be easy enough to determine that, though given the authority to pursue a regime of police, international criminal law lacks much of its authority because of a lack of an independent police constabulary. And as a result, much turns on evaluating the effectiveness of voluntary state cooperation—and though we do not detail it here, this raises the capacity of these tribunals to ally themselves with political tools, influence states, and induce the cooperation they require (Meyer 1987). But when focusing on proposals of international police, we find a very different question emerging, in which law and legality are more often disregarded (cf. Koskenniemi 1995).

What one starts to find, perhaps, is that in the international we have yet to locate the emergence of a paradigmatic discourse that Tomlins documents in the nineteenth-century postcolonial United States. The potential to police becomes problematic precisely when it is attached to a regime of law, since this raises a wide range of concerns regarding the very scope conditions of the "international" and its relationship to state sovereignty. Instead, what we find is a constant alternation of police without law, and law without police. Each of these alternations, of course, allows the international to be contemplated differently: as a zone of international improvement, as the prevention of atrocities, as providing the authority (if not the ability) to prosecute criminal activity, as the promotion of "civilization," and so on. Police provides a defense to law, and law to police. And it is precisely in the alternation that both law and police do their work for those relying on them—police stands for some programs of reform and imperialism (often both), and law for others—resulting in programs, plans, and fantasies that the integration of the two might expose to possible failure.

Notes

We are grateful to Markus Dubber, James Holmes, Christopher Tomlins, and Mariana Valverde for their thoughtful comments and advice while writing this chapter and for the excellent research assistance provided by Vanessa Iafolla, a graduate student at the University of Toronto. Research and writing were supported by the National Science Foundation (SES-0111755), the Social Sciences and Humanities Research Council of Canada (410-2001-1643), the American Bar Foundation, and the Canadian Institute for Advanced Research.

1. In seeking to define this idea of police, Neocleous (2000) draws on Patrick Colquhoun's use of the term to demonstrate that despite criminological emphases on Colquhoun's reforms for the constabulary police, Colquhounian police is closer to what we would now define as social policy. As Foucault (1984, 241) suggests, rather than being limited to the policing of criminal activity, police throughout the seventeenth and eighteenth centuries "signified a programme of government rationality," and a microregulation of nearly everything (Neocleous 1998).

2. At the municipal level, it is in fact often the "police power" that allows U.S. municipalities to legislate in the area of criminal and quasi-criminal law, such as in the context of gang loitering (Levi 2003). Novak's study *The People's Welfare* (1996) demonstrates the continued use of the police power in the nineteenth-century United States to ensure the public welfare even when in conflict with individual rights. This was described as "restraining and regulating the use of liberty and property," developing a well-ordered society through the microregulation of urban space and business activities. Yet while police regulations persisted, by this point they were located within a legal paradigm (see Tomlins 1993, 94).

3. Of course, the whole question of national sovereignty—and, as Foucault (1991, 88–96) points out, the question for Machiavelli of how to govern—is equally tied to international relations.

4. The Tenement House Cigar case (*In the matter of Jacobs* 1885) turned on the conflict between law and police. Jacobs, whose family lived with three other families, was arrested for manufacturing cigars in his home. The New York Court of Appeals, finding no evidence that tobacco was harmful to public health, found the legislation to be an unconstitutional restriction on labor and property (104–5). In relation to public health, the court determined that while the police power "is very broad and comprehensive" and based on *salus populi suprema lex est*, it "is not above the Constitution" and "must be exercised in subordination thereto" (108).

5. Roosevelt further indicates his frustration with law and the courts, complaining that the focus on "legal technicalities" made it nearly impossible to reform the police service by dismissing patrolmen. It is further worth noting Roosevelt's admiration (1913, 55) of James Bradley Thayer at Harvard Law School, best known for the limits he advocated on judicial review in favor of legislative attention to policy decisions (Thayer 1893) and whose work on judicial restraint was later picked up by scholars critical of the U.S. Supreme Court's *Lochner* era (see Flagg 1994, 940–42).

6. In 1902 Roosevelt had noted the importance of "the proper policing of the world" by nations, which rang as imperialist despite that year's U.S. reliance on Hague arbitration in a U.S.-Mexico dispute (Morris 2001b, 176, 193–95).

7. Although not the focus of this chapter, the historical evolution of the "Good Neighbor" policy suggests a lengthier undermining of the logic of *police* by *law*. Prior to FDR's 1933 introduction of the "Good Neighbor" policy in his first inaugural address (1933a), the Roosevelt Corollary had already been undermined in the late 1920s and by the Hoover Administration's public adoption in 1930 of the legalist Clark Memorandum on the Monroe Doctrine (Clark 1930).

8. The institute, which brought together international law societies from across the Americas, was closely aligned with the U.S.-based American Society of International Law, itself drawn from a legalist orientation within the U.S. peace movement of the late nineteenth and early twentieth centuries, the origins of which were focused on the possibilities of a permanent international court and the arbitration of international disputes (cf. Kirgis 1996).

9. The concept of international police is, of course, distinct from international police cooperation (cf. Deflem 2000, 2002; Sheptycki 1998, 2002); the United States became a member of the International Criminal Police Commission in 1938 (Deflem 2000, 754–55).

10. In contrast to Kelsen, Davies does not provide much detail about how this police would be subject to law: instead, he provides a taxonomy of possible avenues for an international police force, all of which would fall under the command of an international authority, but which would either be permanently international or would

instead be mobilized during war (1930, 368). This difference in emphasis is not surprising, given the different projects they each sought to advance.

11. Perhaps the most well-known, presented by Grenville Clark and Louis Sohn (1966), details a proposal for a world police force to gradually replace national forces and that in 1960 would have an estimated budget of nine billion dollars and nearly 1.5 million personnel (314–20). This was merely one of many proposals (Bowett 1964, 313ff.): others, such as Secretary General U Thant (1963), thought a permanent police force was desirable, but politically unfeasible.

12. The lines that are being drawn there—to ensure that such a "police" is working within "law" (e.g., Perritt 1999)—and the relationship of these international police to the local police where they operate, provide additional avenues for investigating the relation of law and police, with the need, as Dean (2004) demonstrates, of understanding the police-military tensions in this process.

13. Since Ignatieff's speech coincides with his recent reflection on his earlier support for the invasion of Iraq (2004b), this valorization of his Canadian diplomatic roots (being the son of a past Canadian Ambassador to the United Nations) and the Canadian POGG power—along with what appears to be a vast staff to promote Canadian administration internationally—is perhaps not surprising.

14. We are indebted to Mariana Valverde for helping us to develop this point in conversation.

15. Aside from detailed, specific requirements on states that they cooperate (see articles 87 through 108), the Rome Statute also has a more general provision requiring state cooperation in the investigation and prosecution of crimes within the jurisdiction of the ICC (at article 86).

16. In the Resolution of the Security Council creating the tribunal, the restoration of "international peace and security" is instead articulated as "peace" alone: "Convinced that in the particular circumstances of the former Yugoslavia the establishment of an international tribunal . . . would contribute to the restoration and maintenance of peace" (United Nations Security Council 1993).

17. Of course, there are other avenues for pursuing investigations and securing arrests, such as complaints to institutions such as the Security Council, the organizing of economic incentives and sanctions, and the sporadic reliance on North Atlantic Treaty Organization (NATO) forces (Scharf 2000; Hagan and Levi 2004).

18. This does not apply to a NATO member country; a major non-NATO ally (including Australia, Egypt, Israel, Japan, Jordan, Argentina, the Republic of Korea, and New Zealand); and Taiwan. There is also a "national interest waiver," allowing a waiver "with respect to a particular country if he determines and reports to the appropriate congressional committees that it is important to the national interest of the United States to waive such prohibition."

References

Agamben, Giorgio. 2005. *State of exception*. Chicago: University of Chicago Press.

American Service Members' Protection Act, 22 U.S.C. 7401 et seq. 2002. Pub. L. No. 107-206, 116 Stat. 820.

Ames, Paul. 1996. Goldstone welcomes Karadzic's departure, says arrests needed. *Associated Press*, July 20, 1996.

Arbour, Louise. 1999. The status of the international criminal tribunals for the former Yugoslavia and Rwanda: Goals and results. *Hofstra Law and Policy Symposium* 3:37–46.

Barnett, Randy. 2004. The proper scope of the police power. *Notre Dame Law Review* 79:429 95.

Bassiouni, M. Cherif. 1974. An appraisal of the growth and developing trends of international criminal law. *Revue Internationale de Droit Pénal* 45:405–33.

Beaumont, Roger. 2001. *Right backed by might: The international air force concept*. Westport, CT: Praeger.

Bentham, Jeremy. 1789. *Plan for an universal and perpetual peace*. Reprinted 1927. London: Sweet.

Black, Henry Campbell. 1990. *Black's law dictionary: definitions of the terms and phrases of American and English jurisprudence, ancient and modern*, 6th ed. St. Paul, Minnesota: West.

Bloomfield, Lincoln Palmer, Edward H. Bowman and Hans J. Morgenthau. 1964. *International military forces: the question of peacekeeping in an armed and disarming world*. Boston: Little, Brown.

Bowett, Derek William. 1964. *United Nations forces: A legal study*. New York: Praeger.

Brahimi, Lakhdar. 2000. *Report of the Panel on United Nations Peace Operations*. United Nations Document A/55/305, S/2000/809, August 21, 2000. New York: United Nations.

Caron, David. 2000. War and international adjudication: Reflections on the 1899 Peace Conference. *American Journal of International Law* 94:4 30.

Carrasco, Enrique, and Randall Thomas. 1996. Encouraging relational investment and controlling portfolio investment in developing countries in the aftermath of the Mexican financial crisis. *Columbia Journal of Transnational Law* 34:539–620.

Chayes, Abram. 1985. Nicaragua, the United States, and the World Court. *Columbia Law Review* 85:1445–82.

Clark, Grenville, and Louis Sohn. 1966. *World peace through world law, two alternative plans*. Cambridge, MA: Harvard University Press.

Clark, Joshua Reuben. 1930. *Memorandum on the Monroe Doctrine*. U.S. Dept. of

State, Publication no. 37. Prepared on December 17, 1928. Washington, DC: U.S. Government Printing Office.

Cleveland, Sarah. 2002. Powers inherent in sovereignty: Indians, aliens, territories, and the nineteenth century origins of plenary power over foreign affairs. *Texas Law Review* 81:1–284.

Dalton, Kathleen. 2002. *Theodore Roosevelt: A strenuous life.* New York: Knopf.

Davies, David. 1930. *The problem of the twentieth century: A study in international relationships.* London: Benn.

Deflem, Mathieu. 2000. Bureaucratization and social control: Historical foundations of international police cooperation. *Law and Society Review* 34:601–40.

———. 2002. *Policing world society: Historical foundations of international police cooperation.* New York: Oxford University Press.

De Zayas, Alfred. 2004. The status of Guantanamo Bay and the status of the detainees. *University of British Columbia Law Review* 37:277–341.

Donais, Timothy. 2003–2004. *Policing human security: The international police task force and peacebuilding in Bosnia.* Canadian Consortium on Human Security (CCHS), Human Security Fellowship Research Paper. Vancouver: Liu Institute for Global Issues, University of British Columbia.

Drago, Luis M. 1902 [reprinted in 2000]. The Drago doctrine. In *Latin America and the United States: A documentary history*, ed. R. Holden and E. Zolov, 88–90. New York: Oxford University Press.

Dubber, Markus Dirk. 2005. *The police power: Patriarchy and the foundations of American government.* New York: Columbia University Press.

Elden, Stuart. 2003. Plague, panopticon, police. *Surveillance and society* 1:240–53.

Falk, Richard, and Saul Mendlovitz, eds. 1966. *The strategy of world order.* Vol. 3. New York: World Law Fund.

Flagg, Barbara. 1994. Enduring principle: On race, process, and constitutional law. *California Law Review* 82:935–80.

Foucault, Michel. 1980. The politics of health in the eighteenth century. In *Power/Knowledge: Selected Interviews and Others Writings, 1972–1977*, ed. C. Gordon, 166–82. New York: Pantheon.

———. 1984. Space, knowledge, power. In *The Foucault Reader*, ed. P. Rabinow, 239–56. New York: Pantheon.

———. 1991. Governmentality. In *The Foucault effect: Studies in governmentality, with two lectures by and an interview with Michel Foucault*, ed. G. Burchell, C. Gordon, and P. Miller, 87–104. Chicago: University of Chicago Press.

Frye, William. 1957. *A United Nations peace force.* New York: Oceana.

Garland, David. 1996. The limits of the sovereign state: Strategies of crime control in contemporary society. *British Journal of Criminology* 36:445–71.

Gathii, James Thuo. 2003. Torture, extraterritoriality, terrorism, and international law. *Albany Law Review* 67:335–70.

Glennon, Michael, and Allison Hayward. 1994. Collective security and the constitution: Can the commander in chief power be delegated to the United Nations? *Georgetown Law Journal* 82:1573–603.

Gordon, Colin. 1991. Governmental rationality: An introduction. In *The Foucault effect: Studies in governmentality, with two lectures by and an interview with Michel Foucault*, eds. G. Burchell, C. Gordon, and P. Miller, 1–52. Chicago: University of Chicago Press.

Hagan, John, and Ron Levi. 2004. Social skill, the Milosevic indictment, and the rebirth of international criminal justice. *European Journal of Criminology* 1:445–75.

Hardt, Michael, and Antonio Negri. 2000. *Empire*. Cambridge, MA: Harvard University Press.

———. 2004. *Multitude: War and democracy in the age of empire*. New York: Penguin.

Holmes, James. 2003. Police power: Theodore Roosevelt, American diplomacy, and world order. *Fletcher Forum of World Affairs* 27:125–42.

———. 2005. *Theodore Roosevelt and world order: Police power in international relations*. Dulles, VA: Potomac Books.

Hont, Istvan, and Michael Ignatieff. 1983. Needs and justice in the *Wealth of Nations*: An introductory essay. In *Wealth and virtue: The shaping of political economy in the Scottish enlightenment*, ed. I. Hont and M. Ignatieff, 1–44. New York: Cambridge University Press.

Horwitz, Morton. 1977. *The transformation of American law, 1780–1860*. Cambridge, MA: Harvard University Press.

Hughes, Joyce. 1999. Flight from Cuba. *California Western Law Review* 36.39–75.

Hurd, Charles. 1944. President outlines U.S. plan for world security union. *New York Times*, June 16.

Ignatieff, Michael. 2004a. Peace, order and good government: A foreign policy for Canada. OD Skelton Lecture, Department of Foreign Affairs and International Trade, Ottawa, March 12.

———. 2004b. The year of living dangerously. *New York Times Magazine*, March 14.

In re Application of Jacobs 1885. 98 N.Y. 98.

International Criminal Tribunal for the Former Yugoslavia. 1994. *Annual report of the international tribunal for the prosecution of persons responsible for serious violations of international humanitarian law committed in the territory of the former Yugoslavia since 1991*. Document A/49/342, August 29.

Janis, Mark. 1984. Jeremy Bentham and the fashioning of "international law." *American Journal of International Law* 78:405–18.

Johnston, Les. 1992. *The rebirth of private policing*. New York: Routledge.

Kelsen, Hans. 1957. *Collective security under international law*. Volume 49 (1954), *International Law Studies*, U.S. Naval War College. Washington, DC: United States Government Printing Office.

Kirgis, Frederic. 1996. The formative years of the American Society of International Law. *American Journal of International Law* 90:559–89.

Kittichaisaree, Kriangsak. 2001. *International criminal law*. New York: Oxford University Press.

Koskenniemi, Martti. 1995. The police in the temple. Order, justice and the UN: A dialectical view. *European Journal of International Law* 6:325–48.

———. 1996. The place of law in collective security. *Michigan Journal of International Law* 17:455–90.

Levi, Ron. 2003. *The constitution of community in legal sites: A study of law, crime and its control*. S.J.D. diss., Faculty of Law, University of Toronto.

MacMillan, Margaret. 2002. *Paris 1919: Six months that changed the world*. New York: Random.

Mendlovitz, Saul, and John Fousek. 1996. The prevention and punishment of the crime of genocide. In *Genocide, war, and human survival*, ed. C. B. Strozier and M. Flynn, 137–52. Lanham, MD: Rowman & Littlefield.

———. 2000. A UN constabulary to enforce the law on genocide and crimes against humanity. In *Protection against genocide: Mission impossible?* ed. N. Reimer, 105–22. Westport, CT: Praeger.

Meyer, John. 1987. The world polity and the authority of the nation state. In *Institutional structure: constituting state, society, and the individual*, ed. G. Thomas et al., 41–70. Newbury Park, CA: Sage.

Mitchener, Kris, and Marc Weidenmier. 2004. Empire, public goods, and the Roosevelt corollary. NBER working paper no. W10729. http://ssrn.com/abstract=587943.

Monroe, James. 1823. *Seventh annual message to congress*. December 2, 1823. http://www.gutenberg.org/etext/5014.

Moore, John Morton. 1986. The secret war in Central America and the future of world order. *American Journal of International Law* 80:43–127.

Morris, Edmund. 2001a. *The rise of Theodore Roosevelt*. Rev. ed. New York: Random.

———. 2001b. *Theodore rex*. New York: Random.

Mundis, Daryl. 2001. Reporting non-compliance: Rule 7bis. In *Essays in ICTY procedure and evidence in honour of Gabrielle Kirk McDonald*, ed. R. May et al., 421–38. The Hague: Kluwer Law International.

Nagan, Winston, and Craig Hammer. 2004. The new Bush national security doctrine and the rule of law. *Berkeley Journal of International Law* 22:375–438.

Nedelsky, Jennifer. 1989. Reconceiving autonomy: Sources, thoughts, and possibilities. *Yale Journal of Law and Feminism* 1:7–36.

Neocleous, Mark. 1998. Policing and pin-making: Adam Smith, police, and the state of prosperity. *Policing and Society* 8:425–49.

———. 2000. Social police and the mechanisms of prevention: Patrick Colquhoun and the condition of poverty. *British Journal of Criminology* 40:710–26.

———. 2004. Theoretical foundations of the new police science. Unpublished paper.

Neuman, Gerald. 2004. Closing the Guantanamo loophole. *Loyola Law Review* 50:1–66.

New York Times. 1904a. "Police constable Roosevelt": London paper so styles the president: Press views of message. *New York Times*, December 7.

———. 1904b. Policeman for the hemisphere. *New York Times*, December 7.

Novak, William. 1996. *The people's welfare: Law and regulation in nineteenth-century America*. Chapel Hill: University of North Carolina Press.

Pasquino, Pasquale. 1991. Theatrum politicum: The genealogy of capital: Police and the state of prosperity. In *The Foucault effect: Studies in governmentality, with two lectures by and an interview with Michel Foucault*, ed. G. Burchell, C. Gordon, and P. Miller, 105–18. Chicago: University of Chicago Press.

Pearson, Lester B. 1957. Force for U.N. *Foreign affairs* 35:395–404.

Pejic, Jelena. 1997. The tribunal and the ICC: Do precedents matter? *Albany Law Review* 60:841–60.

Perritt, Henry H., Jr. 1999. Policing international peace and security: International police forces. *Wisconsin International Law Journal* 17:281–324.

Platt Amendment. Act of Mar. 2, 1901, chap. 803, 31 Stat. 895, 897–98.

Pugh, Michael. 2002. Policing the world: Lord Davies and the quest for order in the 1930s. *International Relations* 16:97–115.

Raeff, Marc. 1983. *The well-ordered police state: Social and institutional change through law in the Germanies and Russia, 1600–1800*. New Haven, CT: Yale University Press.

Ramsey, Michael. 1998. Acts of state and foreign sovereign obligations. *Harvard International Law Journal* 39:1–100.

Roach, Kent. 2002. Did September 11 change everything? Struggling to preserve Canadian values in the face of terrorism. *McGill Law Journal* 47:893–947.

Roosevelt, Franklin Delano. 1933a. Address delivered by President Roosevelt at Washington, December 28, 1933. In *Peace and war: United States foreign policy, 1931–1941*, 204–07. Washington, DC: U.S. Government Printing Office.

———. 1933b. *First inaugural address*. March 4.

Roosevelt, Theodore. 1904. *Fourth annual message to Congress*. December 6.

———. 1910. Nobel lecture. May 5. http://nobelprize.org/peace/laureates/1906/roosevelt-lecture.html.

———. 1913. *Theodore Roosevelt: An autobiography*. Reprinted 1985. New York: Da Capo.

———. 1915. *Why America should join the Allies*. London: Pearson.

Sadat, Leila Nadya. 1999. The establishment of the International Criminal Court: From the Hague to Rome and back again. *Michigan State University—Detroit College of Law* 8:97–118.

Sadat Wexler, Leila. 1996. The proposed permanent International Criminal Court: An appraisal. *Cornell International Law Journal* 29:665–726.

Schabas, William. 2001. *Introduction to the International Criminal Court*. Cambridge, UK: Cambridge University Press.

Scharf, Michael. 2000. The tools for enforcing international criminal justice in the new millennium: Lessons from the Yugoslavia Tribunal. *DePaul Law Review* 49:925–79.

Scheffer, David. 2003. Arresting war criminals: Mission creep or mission impossible? *Case Western Reserve Journal of International Law* 35:319–24.

Shearing, Clifford. 1992. The relation between public and private policing. In *Modern Policing*, ed. M. Tonry and N. Morris, 399–434, Chicago: University of Chicago Press.

Sheptycki, James. 1998. The global cops cometh: Reflections on transnationalization, knowledge work and policing subculture. *British Journal of Sociology* 49:57–74.

———. 2002. *In search of transnational policing: Towards a sociology of global policing*. Aldershot: Ashgate.

Sikkink, Kathryn. 1997. Reconceptualizing sovereignty in the Americas: Historical precursors and current practices. *Houston Journal of International Law* 19: 705–29.

Thant, U. 1963. United Nations peace force: An address to the Harvard Alumni Association, delivered in Cambridge, Massachusetts, June 13, 1964, by the Secretary-General of the United Nations. In *The Strategy of World Order*. Vol. 3, ed. R. Falk and S. Mendlovitz, 526–35. New York: World Law Fund.

Thayer, James Bradley. 1893. The origin and scope of the American doctrine of constitutional law. *Harvard Law Review* 7:129–56.

Tomlins, Christopher. 1990. Law, police and the pursuit of happiness in the new American republic. *Studies in American Political Development* 4:1–34.

———. 1993. *Law, labor and ideology in the early American republic*. New York: Cambridge University Press.

United Nations Secretary General. 1993. *Report of the Secretary-General pursuant to paragraph 2 of Security Council Resolution 808 (1993)*. Document S/25704, May 3.

United Nations Security Council. 1993. *Resolution 808*. Adopted by the Security Council at its 3175th meeting. Document S/RES/808, February 22.

U.S. Department of State. 2003. Article 98 Agreements. Statement by Richard Boucher, spokesman, September 23. Distributed by the Bureau of International Information Programs, U.S. Department of State. http://usinfo.state.gov.

U.S. Treaty Series. 1903a. Treaty Series 418. *Agreement between the United States of America and the Republic of Cuba for the lease (subject to terms to be agreed upon by the two governments) to the United States of lands in Cuba for coaling and naval stations*. 1903 U.S.T. LEXIS 26 (U.S.T., 1903). Signed at Havana February 16, 1903, and at Washington February 23, 1903. Entered into force February 23, 1903.

———. 1903b. Treaty Series 426. *Cuba: Lease of certain areas for naval or coaling stations*. 1903 U.S.T. LEXIS 28 (U.S.T., 1903). Lease signed at Havana July 2, 1903. Entered into force October 6, 1903.

———. 1903c. Treaty Series 437. *Cuba: Relations with Cuba*. 1903 U.S.T. LEXIS 27 (U.S.T., 1903). Signed at Havana May 22, 1903. Entered into force July 1, 1904.

Valverde, Mariana. 2003. Police science, British style: Pub licensing and knowledges of urban disorder. *Economy and Society* 32:234–52.

Veeser, Cyrus. 2002. *A world safe for capitalism: Dollar diplomacy and America's rise to global power*. New York: Columbia University Press.

Wallach, Evan. 1998. The procedural and evidentiary rules of the post–World War II war crimes trials: Did they provide an outline for international legal procedure? *Columbia Journal of Transnational Law* 37:851–83.

Waskow, Arthur. 1965. *Keeping the world disarmed*. Santa Barbara, CA: Center for the Study of Democratic Institutions.

Wedgwood, Ruth. 2001. The United States and the International Criminal Court: The irresolution of Rome. *Law and Contemporary Problems* 64:193–214.

Weeks, Gregory. 2004. Book review of *A world safe for capitalism: Dollar diplomacy and America's rise to global power*, by Cyrus Veeser. *Latin Americanist* 48(1). http://www.cas.ucf.edu/politicalscience/secolas/TLA/issues/fall2004/ index.php.

Wilson, Peter. 1998. The myth of the "first great debate." *Review of International Studies* 24:1–16.

Zasloff, Jonathan. 2003. Law and the shaping of American foreign policy: From the gilded age to the new era. *New York University Law Review* 78:239–373.

Framing the Fragments

Police: Genealogies, Discourses, Locales, Principles

CHRISTOPHER TOMLINS

Prologue

Aron: 'Tis policy and stratagem must do
That you affect; and so must you resolve,
That what you cannot as you would achieve,
You must perforce accomplish as you may.

WILLIAM SHAKESPEARE, *Titus Andronicus*, 2.1.104–7 (ca. 1591)

In chapter 2 of this collection, Pasquale Pasquino, whose "Theatrum Politi-cum" thirty years ago set so many hares running in the quest for a historical epistemology of "police" (Pasquino 1978), draws our attention to an iconic early-modern figuration of the relationship between police and law, the relationship that so many of the essays in this collection have identified as the discursive heartland across which our quest for a "new police science" must move. We encounter, side by side, "two incarnations of the mediator between divine law and worldly order"—a choice, as it were, between the decalogic certainties of the prince (Moses) and the subtleties of the prince's counselor and real-world interpreter (Aaron). This is an encounter with intertwined (indeed fraternal) but nevertheless distinct modalities of rule: one, the application of a received knowledge, invariant, framed in universal statements conveyed from elsewhere; the other, the application of a produced knowledge, attentive to context and desired outcomes, to technique and practicality, a local knowledge that "speak[s] with regard to the concrete cases of life" (chapter 2, 48).[1]

There is no Moses as such in Shakespeare's *Titus Andronicus*, though Titus himself is formed, and betrayed, by his reverence for the certainties of Mosaic rule. There are two Aarons, of a sort, although only one is even partially so identified. That one is Aron the Moor, slave and counselor to the barbarian queen Tamora, whose discourse (as we see in this chapter's epigraph) is one not of conformity to received law but of the invention and production of means to achieve outcomes. The other is Titus's brother Marcus, counselor to Titus and to his son Lucius, as manipulative in his ways as they are brutally direct in theirs. The lessons these Aarons teach are decisive. Blood, dismemberment, and death repeatedly undermine Titus's expectations that by conforming to law he will win justice and redemption. The Andronici achieve their several ends only after they have fully absorbed the ways "of policy and stratagem." They are corrupted by the lesson, but then—appearances notwithstanding—they were corrupt from the beginning. *Titus Andronicus* is a lesson in how the world really works.

I advert here at the outset to *Titus Andronicus* because "this dreadful play," as Francis Barker once called it, contains within itself many of the fragments that we new theorists of police have disinterred in our search for the past and current meaning of this potent and prolific yet curiously evasive concept. Our chapters have discovered "police" existing simultaneously at many levels of social organization—households, states, empires. They have revealed its affinity for discourses of practice and strategy, of anticipation and planning, of fluidity and flexibility. They have noticed how "police" dwells in intimate relation with law—in law's shadows and interstices, but also in the very marrow of the law's self-understanding as an instrumentality of order. It is not, it seems to me, merely pretentious to suggest that Shakespeare's most uncompromising and certainly in its day most popular dissection of the structure of human civility is worth some attention once again for what it can tell us about the civilizing missions we currently pursue and the discursive and material resources we devote to their success. This late-Tudor meditation on modernity's contrapuntal anthropology of *civitas* and barbarism, of sovereignty and invasion, and of violence and "policy" and law, has, our chapters demonstrate, "flashe[d] up" once more in the later twentieth century because this is its "moment of danger." The contemporary world is "the instant when it can be recognized" once again (Barker 1993, 205, 143–206; Benjamin 1969, 255; see generally Tomlins 2005a).

I

The "law" of the police really marks the point at which the state, whether from impotence or because of the immanent connections within any legal system, can no longer guarantee through the legal system the empirical ends that it desires at any price to attain. . . . [A] consideration of the police institution encounters nothing essential at all. Its power is formless, like its nowhere tangible, all-pervasive, ghostly presence in the life of civilized states.

WALTER BENJAMIN, *"Critique of Violence"* (1986 [1921])

I want to begin with two preliminary observations, arising from the objectives that this volume's title declares. First, to fashion a new police science is in at least one sense to replicate an ambition of *Polizeiwissenschaft*, and that is to demonstrate that ostensibly disparate phenomena—fragments of meaning, locales of occurrence, conditions of existence, powers "dispersed and uncoordinated"—actually exist as a unified and coherent object of study, with a knowable point of origin, hence open to the construction of causal statements or at least general narratives. Markus Dubber, for example, holds that "there was once a unified concept of police," which is to suggest both that there is no longer and that there can be once again (chapter 4, 107). To fashion a new police science must therefore in part be a labor founded upon recovery of the objects of attention of the old—to know again what police was and is, by investigating what it did and does.

Second, the new police science nevertheless distinguishes itself from the old in three respects. Titularly, at least, it identifies police as a *power* rather than a condition of existence, and one that is *in* governance and law. It also finds police in the international, which to some is a novelty, rather than simply in the domestic, where we can all agree it is not novel at all. Finally, whereas the old police science was characteristically an affirmative and productive project, its texts as much how-to manuals as treatises (chapter 2), the new intends to be a critical, questioning enterprise.

All three of these attempts at distinction are open to doubt. The first two may be contested empirically, as we shall see. The third is of more immediate interest in that, primarily outside this collection but also to some extent within, one finds in fact an interest in having to resort to forms of new police science precisely to underpin an affirmative (and international) police project. Affirmation appears outside, for example, in Michael Ignatieff's neoliberal agenda for breeding "peace, order and good government" throughout the world through the export of Canadian expertise in administrative technocracy to lesser-developed states; what he calls, without obvious irony, a Canadian kind of imperialism (Ignatieff 2004).[2] Ignatieff's ambition is noted and interrogated here by Mariana Valverde (chapter 3) and by Ron Levi and John Hagan (chapter 8). Affirmation appears within in the course of Mitchell Dean's swipe at a posse of current theorists—Giorgio Agamben, Michael Hardt, and Antonio Negri, behind whom lurks the zombie of Carl Schmitt—whose overheated but empty gestures of opposition ("simple hyperbole . . . theoretical overreach . . . obscurantism") to the contemporary Anglophone project to establish new terms upon which others may enjoy sovereignty[3] undermine, in Dean's estimation, the possibility for granting intellectual recognition to modes of police action in international affairs that could be, Dean argues, specific and contained, and hence morally justifiable according to criteria common to all humanity, rather than simply tools of imperialists (chapter 7).

Dean's advocacy of a pragmatic international police—like Ignatieff's pragmatic imperialism, with which it appears comfortably in harmony—suggests that those engaged in the creation of a new police science will find themselves (whether they like it or not) involved in prescriptive debate over what the rule of police should or should not be, particularly in the international sphere, rather than allowed to confine themselves to critical inquiry into the circumstances of police's creation and reproduction. Here is cause for some care. If there is to be something called a "new police science," it will have to work out quite precisely the historical and theoretical relationship between law and police, between, as it were, Moses and Aaron. Hardt and Negri's view of imperial sovereign right as a combination of claimed "juridical power to rule over the exception" and actual "capacity to deploy police force" (Hardt and Negri 2000, 17) poses the question by treating the relationship as one of mutual reinforcement.[4] Dean responds with what appears to be a classically liberal invocation of law as one of two restraints that will guard his pragmatic policing against degeneration into the unilateralism that Agamben et al. denounce.[5] Dean argues that the rule of law successfully renders the state of exception moot. Agamben's "camp" is "open to scrutiny and due process *like any other prison*" (chapter 7, 203; emphasis added).[6]

In *Global Prescriptions*, Yves Dezalay and Bryant Garth have outlined the perils endemic in this kind of exchange. Social scientists "trying to understand the very important transformations in the state and state institutions that are now taking place" are being drawn at an increasing rate to the study of "law, courts and legal institutions." Unfortunately, few of these scholars "actually inquire into the structural history of the creation and production of national legal practices." Instead of investigating the circumstances in which law's rules are produced or what "the rules for the production of th[os]e rules" might be, scholars embrace a quasi-legal discourse that accepts "the credibility and symbolic value of law" and concentrate on extending law's rules to other social and political phenomena (Dezalay and Garth 2002, 311–12). The particular example before us underscores the inadequacy of any critical inquiry into the production and purposes of *police* that is not at the same time critical inquiry into the production and purposes of *law*.

A last preliminary. The "science" of the new police science promises a systematic order of knowledge. Application will determine what is police and what is not. The claim has epistemological and ideological problems, particularly if not located in a context, in its own mode of production. Almost without exception, the chapters in this collection identify police as a concept and a set of practices that exist in time and circumstance and are subject to change. Nevertheless, the time of police represented here is largely the time of scientized knowledge, flowering in the Enlightenment, professionalized in the full emergence of disciplinarity during the course of the nineteenth century, extended ever since. This police is relatively stable in its fundamentals though ever more varied in its expressions. In determining the genealogy of our (largely Anglophone) knowledge, attention here focuses on the later eighteenth century as a particularly fecund moment of emergence and definition, invoking such as Patrick Colquhoun (Neocleous in chapter 1), Adam Smith (Farmer in chapter 5), and William Blackstone (see, for example, Dean in chapter 7 and Dubber in chapter 4).

But police has a more varied genealogy, a longer history, than can be satisfied by locating its "canonical" moment in the later eighteenth century (see, for example, Dubber 2005, 3–47). Although remarked upon—see, e.g., chapter 1)—that longer history is brought into tangible view here only by Pasquino. We need to understand that the police we identify as the object of the new police science's critical attention is but one strand of a vastly multifaceted phenomenon. Indeed, if we are agreed that *our* practice is one of critical inquiry, it seems to me that part of what is actually for construction here is less a new police science than the phenomenon of police as an object of study.

One way of approaching the phenomenon is to try to encompass it objectively. By drawing upon Pierre Bourdieu's language of "field," we can echo Bourdieu's approach to the juridical in identifying police as an area of "structured, socially patterned activity or 'practice'" centered on "a body of internal protocols and assumptions, characteristic behaviors and self-sustaining values" that produce and reproduce both the concept and its effectivity (Bourdieu 1987, 805, 806). This approach is congenial to ambitions for "science" and, indeed, to the Enlightenment moment of police science. It assists us in producing a bounded object for empirical examination. But one of police's characteristics, we know, is its very unboundedness, its indeterminacy. When, for example, we approach the broad prescientific conceptions of police remarked on by Pasquino, we find them far less amenable to the language of field. Yet their significance to our enterprise is undoubted—their implementation occurs in conjunction with and as an expression of an extensive European history of expansion into and ordering of the unknown, both local and transoceanic. This fluid and indeterminate police, to which division into spheres of "the domestic" and "the international" is not relevant, also requires attention in any critical inquiry into police. Here the possibilities for a distinct (though not incompatible) strategy of investigation suggest themselves, a Foucauldian strategy of "problematization," best exemplified here in the approach taken by Mariana Valverde (chapter 3). Rather than attempt fully to encompass police as a determinable field, we can instead consider police as a diversity of strategies and objectives that emerge at specific conjunctures, and attempt to determine the "problematics"—the modes of "problematization" or relations of power and knowledge—that, at those conjunctures, inspire and produce this or that strategy and objective. In this way, we cast our understanding of police loose to an extent from the "formative" constraints of the Enlightenment's progressive historical temporality. We allow ourselves a means to approach police in terms of the circumstances in which it is produced, the actions that signify its presence, the locales in which it occurs, and the modalities by which it rules.

II

Haunting belongs to the structure of every hegemony.

JACQUES DERRIDA, *Specters of Marx* (1994)

The authors whose work appears in this collection are in general agreement that the last thirty years has seen a radical transformation in our understanding of what *police* entails. This collection's stated ambition to construct a "new" and critical police science, notwithstanding some reservations acknowledges that transformation as a shared point of departure and acknowledges also the need to break epistemologically from the "old" and facilitative police science that continues to hold sway over the heartland of conventional criminology, criminal justice studies, and police studies.

The alteration of perspectives on police as an object of study began in the first instance among European scholars. It is attributable to the new criminology of the 1970s (see, e.g., Taylor, Walton, and Young 1973), to the growing influence of "social control" theory in history and the social sciences developed through institutions like the National Deviancy Conference (see, e.g., Fine et al. 1979), and to the enormous impact of Foucault (Foucault 1979, 1980; Burchell, Gordon, and Miller 1991). These developments were sustained and broadened by new ways of thinking about and writing political theory and the history of ideas (see, e.g., Hont and Ignatieff 1983), by innovations in legal history (Tomlins 1993; Novak 1996), by the confluence of history and the social sciences (McDonald 1996), and doubtless by many other influences. The outcome was a growing scholarly recognition of police as something of a "ghostly" presence in an Anglophone historical world overwhelmingly liberal in self-understanding (Benjamin 1986,

287; forcefully restated by Derrida 2002). Police was as yet unnamed as a coherent phenomenon, yet it existed in real time, in innumerable fragments in innumerable locales, as both a means to action, a philosophy of action, and as the state of being that resulted (Knemeyer 1980, 174, 176).

To begin to recognize the police that is the object of the new police science's attention is to have recourse to an emphatically nonliberal account of the conditions of human existence during the past three hundred years, an account that haunts modernity's hegemonic rule of law—both as an alternative reading of it and as an alternative to it. In fact, a full recovery of police as a distinct historical metanarrative requires writing a new history of the last half millennium. For although, as Dean (chapter 7) and Levi and Hagan (chapter 8) indicate, the contemporary international sphere—the new world order—is a crucial context within which the current critical recovery of police must be situated, that recovery must also recognize the salience of police to the original "new world order" initiated in the fifteenth century, from which the current version is descended, to which police contributed so much—and which in turn contributed so much to it.

We flounder in our efforts to recover the spectral presence of police, in good part because we must struggle with a conceptual history that has concealed it in plain view. Drawing upon American constitutional discourse, Markus Dubber shows how the "police power" has been at one and the same time "constructed as . . . self-evident" and "defined as indefinable" (chapter 4, 109). Liberal legality has had occasion to define police *against* law (to which in Dubber's view it is other—the one regulative, preventive, corrective in the pursuit of a public welfare, the other Kantian, an expression of individual rights and individual autonomy; Dubber 2005). From this follows asserted polarities of hierarchy and equality, of heteronomy and autonomy. In fact, there is less difference here than meets the eye. It is worth noting that classic mid-nineteenth-century American legal discourse described *law*, or *legal science*, in precisely the same fashion as police—infinite, indefinable, variable, and securely in control. To David Dudley Field, speaking at the inauguration of the first University of Chicago Law School in September 1859, legal science was, of all the sciences, "the most comprehensive in its compass, the most varied and minute in its details, the most severe in its discipline, and the most important to the order, peace, and civilization of mankind." Its preeminence in scientific and political discourse lay precisely in its mastery of the infinite complexities of human behavior. "The science which is the subject of our discourse governs the actions of human beings, intelligent and immortal, penetrates into the secrets of their souls, subdues their wills, and adapts itself to the endless variety of their wants, motives and conditions":

> Will you compare it with one of the exact sciences—as, for example, with mathematics . . . the science of calculation is occupied with a single principle. This it may go on to develop more and more, till the mind is almost lost in its immensity; yet the development of that one principle can never reach in extent, comprehensiveness, and variety the development of all the principles by which the actions of men toward each other are governed in all their relations. The law, it will be remembered, is the rule of all property and all conduct. (Field 1884, 517, 528, 532)

Notice that Dubber moved us from "police" to "police power," which is placed, as already noted, in (within) governance and law. The law that most justifies this move, the law that the police *power* is most patently "within," is U.S. constitutional law. In the mandarin texts of U.S. constitutional discourse, the language of "police power" suggests an impulse to fold the discourse of police into that of law. Though not enumerated or defined, like other powers, and hence put in its place, police nevertheless appears put in *a* place, one *within* law. Hence William Novak can refer to the police power as a legal technology, a turn to *law* "as a formative and forceful technology of public action" (Novak 2004).[7]

During our discussions in Buffalo in 2004, Mariana Valverde stressed that in constructing a theory of police it was of considerable importance to recognize the immanence of police discourse in legal texts. Immanence need not be understood as containment. Outside the mandarin realm of ultimate, exceedingly rare, and invariably post hoc statements of would-be (but always plausibly deniable) constitutionalized finality[8]—the species of legal restraint upon which Mitchell Dean relies—law is a strategic collaborator in police, whether by presence or absence of mind. Here this is demonstrated quite cogently in Dubber's revealing deconstruction of the quotidian realities of U.S. criminal law and procedure, which culminates in the searing observation that "traditional rules of criminal law . . . survive mainly as the object of theoretical investigation and the subject of university instruction, in a parallel universe largely untouched by the reality of the criminal process" (chapter 4, 130). Nor, in any case, even in the realm of mandarin discourse, does law really contain police.[9] From early in the history of the Republic, U.S. constitutional discourse very deliberately excised significant realms of action from juridical purview. The notion that Congress and its agents could assert "plenary" (exclusive) powers of governance beyond courts' capacity to review, developed in the Marshall Court's Indian cases, was enriched and extended during the course of the later nineteenth century in a series of Supreme Court cases addressing the government, transfer and dispersal of Indian tribes, the regulation and restriction of immigration, and the administration of new territories (continental and transoceanic).[10] Those made subject to Congress's plenary powers were outsiders—usually non-European and "uncivilized," denizens of another, parallel universe to whom traditional rules were made unavailable by a process of jurisdictional accommodation among the juridical, executive, and legislative echelons of the state. The combination of the Court's acknowledgment of the ascendancy of plenary over juridical authority with its development of "political question" doctrine—in which it refused to exercise the jurisdiction it did possess in matters considered "inherently political" and hence the business of the executive and legislative branches of government[11]—erects a constitutional law that constrains not police but rather the effectivity of liberalism's constitutionalist panacea itself.

The parallels in U.S. discourse with the British imperial genealogy of "peace, order and good government" powers outlined by Valverde (chapter 3) are striking. We should not be too surprised, however, for they share a common root. Ambition to spread "settled and quiet Government" (and subject indigenous inhabitants to it) was embedded in the discourse of Anglo American colonizing from the moment of its first formal-legal expression in the first Virginia charter (1606). After independence it was embedded in the successor state constitutions as authority over the state's internal police. Clear echoes can also be found in the preamble to the U.S. Constitution: "to form a more perfect Union, establish Justice, insure domestic Tranquility, provide for the common defence, promote the general Welfare."[12]

Lindsay Farmer proposes that we address the space of disjunction between discourses of police and law by turning to jurisprudence, notably to the pre-disciplinary jurisprudence of Adam Smith wherein, Farmer argues, theorists of the new police will discover the means to construct a "jurisprudence of security" that can encompass the terrain of police. "Modern jurisprudence," he argues, "has been almost exclusively focused on the question of sovereignty. This leads to a viewing of issues in terms of control or juridical power, with certain fields (security, police) being seen as executive powers that are beyond control" (chapter 5, 161). The key structuring concepts of U.S. constitutionalism—checks and balances, federalism, judicial review—are all instances of the jurisprudence of sovereignty. In directing our attention to Smith's *Lectures on Jurisprudence* (Meek, Raphael, and Stein 1978), Farmer identifies a key historical moment outside the temporality of liberalism, in which police, law, and economy can be observed as elements in the same discourse, and in which the central question for determination is not how individual liberty is to be maximized *against* government, but rather what rules should direct civil governments in the pursuit of their main objectives—"the maintenance of justice, the provision of police [sanitation, security, plenitude], the raising of revenue and the establishment of arms" (chapter 5, 145). Jurisprudence, in other words, becomes the *ur*-discourse of law *and* government, and security—economic and social, local and translocal—one of its most important objects of attention. Indeed one can argue that by addressing security in the context of this predisciplinary conjunction of police, law, and economy, we can resolve a tension between "matter[s] of private right" and matters of collective interest through exploration (as indeed would occur in *Wealth of Nations*) of the political economy of transactions. As Smith points out there, security in market transactions is self-actuating, hence "invisible," because the work of transacting is governed by the impulse of self-interest. But the sentiment of self-interest does not stand alone from "sympathy, or feeling for one's fellow man," which Smith's earlier work suggests as "an antecedent principle and overall conditioner of the moral, legal and social environment in which the price system operates" (McNulty 1980, 38; see also Coase 1994, 75–116; Phillipson 1983). In other words, the Smithian formulation of jurisprudence's province—contract and interpersonal relations (which I have in turn labeled transactions)—allows us to produce a jurisprudence of security that does not sequester police in the realm of threats but renders the concept expansively, the means of producing what Smith's "rude" American counterpart William Manning identified as the proper object of governance, the "safety and happiness" of the whole population (Merrill and Wilentz 1993, 130; see generally Tomlins 1993, 1–8).

But if Farmer's objective here is to reveal police in broad aspect through resort to a predisciplinary mode of jurisprudential inquiry that can evade the limitations of a modern, disciplinary concentration upon sovereignty, other essayists argue police is fully revealed in sovereignty. As Dubber puts it, "To govern is always also to police. Sovereignty without the power to police is no power at all" (chapter 4, 109). The power to police is the very essence of sovereignty. It is the power to exercise power.[13]

Dubber's magnificent, sweeping synthesis is in many ways a sampler for his recent book, *The Police Power: Patriarchy and the Foundations of American Government* (2005), which in its turn corrects Agamben's view that "the concept of sovereignty has been . . . introduced into the figure of the police" only relatively recently (2000, 102). Dubber identifies the power to police as *patria potestas*, patriarchal power, founded in the ancient household, the Aristotelian *oikos*. The *oikos* is an autarkic world, a closed space, whose internal economy (*oeconomy*) is designed specifically to support the household master in a life of *ta kala*, or noble and free action (Booth 1993, 27, and, generally, 1–93; see also Tomlins 1995, 71–73). In Dubber's perception, the *oikos* is a ruled hierarchy, its master a sovereign within its bounds, a sovereignty replicated in the larger and all-encompassing sovereignty of the macro householder, the monarch (or equivalent regime), within which the micro household of each familial patriarch is enfolded and to whose government they are ultimately subject. Thus, governance is a ruled patriarchal hierarchy, sovereignty its expression, and the patriarchal household its model and point of replication—"a basic mode of governance that can be traced throughout the history of Western politics." Criminal law is the most palpable representation of sovereign governance in action (chapter 4, 109).

On its own terms, Dubber's analysis is very convincing. Farmer (chapter 5) tells us that Dubber's is a theory of the police power that is "historical and contextual," but this is not really so. Dubber's argument mobilizes materials we may call historical, but it is not particularly sensitive to their context. There is no particular reason it should be, for Dubber's goal is not a historical narrative as such but the construction of a model to support an argument that will compel us to see police (and sovereignty, and contemporary criminal law) in a new and original light. If approached as if it were indeed an exercise in "historical and contextual" analysis, however, the argument becomes vulnerable to qualification.

First, it seems to me that in late-medieval and early-modern English social practice, the familial authority of the micro householder is not absolute within its bounds but provisional because subject to a cacophony of intervening claims—of *ligeance*, of the locality, of the church (see, e.g., Brewer 2005; Wrightson 1980; Hindle 2002). In early-modern English political theory there is no specifically "patriarchal" theorization of the foundation of the political obligation of householders to the macro household of the king prior to Filmer, in whose work it emerges in contest with contractual theories, which have their own history. Both Sir Thomas Smith and Richard Hooker, for example, mix contractual foundations with patriarchal practices; Hooker for states, Smith for states *and* households. One can certainly recognize that patriarchy was a habit of rule, but one should not assume that it must always have been rule's theorization (Smith 1906, 22–26; Schochet 1975, 50–63; see also Underdown 1985).

Second, Dubber's reading of the state—facsimile of the ruled hierarchy of the patriarchal household enfolding micro households—as a basic mode of governance traceable in the history of Western politics ignores aspects of the Aristotelian representation of *oikoi* that would put their purpose and relationship to "the state" in a somewhat different light. In Aristotelian discourse the purpose of the "contained" household economy was to make possible the household master's uncontained realization of *ta kala* in the *polis*, a space not of hierarchy but of equality, freedom, and virtuous civic participation (Booth 1993). I do not question that the *oikos* is a ruled hierarchy, or that it is patriarchal, or that it is quite feasible to model the state as a facsimile of that structure. But the latter is not a necessary consequence of the former: *oikoi* are not necessarily component elements of a macro household that reproduces their micro hierarchies on a societal scale. Indeed, in the Aristotelian *polis*—an example of a unity constituted in a "multiplicity of voluntary acts" (Heller, quoted in chapter 2, 42)—one finds inspiration for a distinct and potent theory of late-medieval and early-modern Western politics. Take, for example, Nicolai Rubinstein's observations on William of Moerbeke's thirteenth-century translation of Aristotle's *Politics*, the source of much of Europe's political vocabulary over the next four centuries. "In the *Politics*," says Rubinstein, "the adjective *politikos* shares with the other derivatives from *polis* a variety of meanings. The word could relate to the *polis*—the city or state—to its constitution, and to one of the three 'true' constitutions, that is the constitution in which the many rule with a view to the common interest. . . . Another derivative of *polis* is *politeia*, which can signify the constitution in general, or the constitution under which the many rule with a view to the common good." When regard is given to the latter sense, Aristotle's definition of *politeia* becomes "when the masses govern the state for the common interest, the government is called by the generic name common to all constitutions—a politeia" (Rubinstein 1987, 42–43).[14]

Translation of the *Politics* assisted an appropriation of *politicus* and its derivatives for republican and constitutional discourse. "By the beginning of the fourteenth century, the word *politicus*, and its Latin and Italian equivalents *civilis* and *civile*, had been squarely pre-empted for the republican regime. As a constitutional term, its principal features were the institutional restraints to which the government was subjected, and the popular source of its authority" (Rubinstein 1987, 45). In England, for example, Sir John Fortescue (ca. 1394–1476) adopted the republican distinction between *regimen regale* (monarchy) and *regimen politicum* (republic), arguing that the latter might also describe that form of monarchy—*dominium regale et politicum*—that was based on the people's constituting itself a "body politic" and electing a king to rule "by suche lawes as thai all wolde assent unto." As Rubinstein puts it in discussing Fortescue, "The king who rules *politice* may not, like the one ruling *principatu regali*, change laws without the assent of the people, nor burden it against its will with taxes" (Rubinstein 1987, 50–51). England, Fortescue held, was *dominium regale et politicum*.

Fortescue employed the classical vocabulary of Aristotelian political science without translating it into a constitutionalist idiom. The meaning of *politeia*—fundamental settlement of public authority—entered contemporary political discourse by means other than a language of constitutions (Stourzh 1988, 35). In sixteenth-century France the operative discourse was one of *police*, not as a representation of the power of the macro householder, the absolute sovereign, but as an assertion of proper purpose that imposed restraint upon that power. In England, *politeia* gained entry through the discourse of commonwealth or "the common weal," an idiom that by Fortescue's time had already proven itself of immense significance, both in "encircling" kingship and as a challenge to it (Rollison 2003). Thus the earliest (1598) English-language translation of Aristotle's *Politics* translates "politeia" as "policy" and defines it as "the order and description . . . of that which hath the greatest and most soveraine authority: for the rule and administration of a Commonweale, hath evermore power and authority joined with it: which administration is called policie in Greek, and in English a Commonweale" (Stourzh 1988, 35).

Police, in short, has more than one political meaning, more than one embodiment, and certainly more than one relationship with sovereignty. One may work through a few of these alternatives in short succession, as they clustered to mark paths rejected and taken in the opening phases of the American Revolution, just by reading Thomas Paine's *Common Sense*. As Dubber notes, the principal rejection upon which all revolutionaries could agree was of allegiance to the macro householder, *in personam*, embodied in the patriarchking, "the Royal Brute of Britain." Where, though, to turn? To impersonal sovereigns, Dubber suggests—to god, the flag, law. And of course *Common Sense* recognizes both god and law, and for that matter the idea of a constitution too, as candidates in the pantheon of potential sovereigns[15]:

> Where says some is the King of America? I'll tell you Friend, he reigns
> above and doth not make havoc of mankind like the Royal Brute of Britain.
> Yet that we may not appear to be defective even in earthly honours, let a
> day be solemnly set apart for proclaiming the charter; let it be brought forth
> placed on the divine law, the law of God; let a crown be placed thereon,
> by which the world may know, that so far as we approve of monarchy, that
> in America THE LAW IS KING. For as in absolute governments the King is
> law, so in free countries the law *ought* to be King; and there ought to be no
> other.

But Paine does not stop with these sovereignties, nor, indeed, fully endorse them. In 1776, at least, god's sovereignty is "above," not earthly. And on the revolutionary earth, though law is the modality of rule appropriate to a free country, it does not make freedom. The free country already exists before it crowns law king. And in fact to call law king is to suggest only a qualified endorsement "so far as we approve of monarchy," which in 1776 was not very far at all. What then is left? What creates the free country and is its ultimate guarantor? The answer lies in the words that follow, but are never quoted: "But lest any ill use should afterwards arise, let the crown at the conclusion of the ceremony be demolished, and scattered among the people whose right it is" (Paine 1776, part 3 ¶ 49). Royal prerogative is overthrown in favor of law, but freedom is secured only by in turn subjecting law to a dispersed sovereignty residing in the people—an Aristotelian police exercised by a "murmuring commons" (Rollison 2003).

In the U.S. case, the possibility of a democratized police encountered the "long-standing American distrust of democratic legislatures" (Nedelsky 1981, 310) within a few years of the revolution (Tomlins 1993, 63–73). Police was removed to the constraining ambit of law (common and constitutional) in good part from elite fears of the antinomian politics of the commons (Tomlins 1993, 89–94). This was a process replicated at both local and national levels. Thus in 1805, when the language of police as well-ordered, energetic government was invoked in Boston by Peter Oxenbridge Thacher (soon to be public prosecutor and later Chief Judge of Boston's most important criminal court), it was in the service of repudiating governance by town meeting—"baseless, unbalanced, inefficient, and liable to be moved about by every afflation of the popular breath"—in favor of governance by elites, "the gravest and wisest of citizens." Such would better reflect "the spirit of our republican constitutions." It would protect "the ark of our political safety" from "bold and lawless innovation" (Thacher 1805, 5–21).[16]

According to work by William Novak, the "science" of well-ordered government, the creation of a "well-regulated society," was elaborated largely in local legislative initiatives, as an extrapolation upon common-law rules, becoming by midcentury the "police power" (Novak 1996). The relationship of "internal police" to the federal constitution was explored by the U.S. Supreme Court, more or less for the first time, in *New York v. Miln* (1837), where it was acknowledged that "a state has the same undeniable and unlimited jurisdiction over all persons and things, within its territorial limits, as any foreign nation; where that jurisdiction is not surrendered or restrained by the constitution of the United States." It was a state's "solemn duty," the Court continued, "to advance the safety, happiness and prosperity of its people, and to provide for its general welfare, by any and every act of legislation, which it may deem to be conducive to these ends," and "all those powers which relate to merely municipal legislation, or what may, perhaps, more properly be called internal police, are not thus surrendered or restrained" leaving the authority of the state in those regards "complete, unqualified, and exclusive."[17] Some years later, in *Commonwealth v. Alger* (1851), to which several authors in this collection advert, Massachusetts Chief Justice Lemuel Shaw offered an elaborated commentary upon the police power that dwelt upon its continuity with regimes of governance dating to the earliest moment of colonizing. Shaw built the police power (defined as "the power vested in the legislature by the constitution to make, ordain and establish all manner of wholesome and reasonable laws . . . as they shall judge to be for the good and welfare of the commonwealth, and of the subjects of the same"[18]) on a string of conveyances of *sovereignty* (his term): the Charter of New England (1620) that had clothed government with so much of the royal prerogative as was necessary to maintain and regulate public right in the colony; the Declaration of Independence and the Treaty of Paris (1783) that had dispelled whatever royal prerogative capacity remained; and the Massachusetts constitution that had secured the entirety of sovereign power—dominion and regulation of the public right—to the new postcolonial government. Shaw excluded, or at least did not mention, politics. Texts conveyed sovereignty and created the means to establish *Alger*'s well-ordered society rather than any explicit act of sovereign popular consent or active involvement.[19]

Considered historically, then, what we encounter in the Anglophone tradition through, say, the mid-eighteenth century is a lively discourse of police with a diversity of implications echoed in political thought and practice: the police of *patria potestas* exhibited in Dubber's micro familial and macro state households and generalized in Blackstonian common law; the police of the enlightened cameralist state that mobilized people and commodities as resources for the collective welfare; and also the police of the murmuring commons, exhibited in the distinctively popular language and meanings of commonwealth. What we can observe thereafter is a forestalling of certain of these possibilities; a narrowing and institutionalizing of police discourse, its removal from democratic or popular politics, and its redeployment in an increasing variety of locales in the service of an increasingly technologized and instrumentalized agenda of control and discipline. Each of these newly visible ambitions for the mobilization of police has its own history: the periodization I suggest is not intended to be more than an approximation and, in any case, describes the onset of a moment when ambition could be married to institutional-administrative capacity and thus actually realized, rather than the moment of ambition's own birth. Nevertheless, this is the end of predisciplinary police. From this moment on, police "science"—whether in high administrative or low coercive idiom—takes on its own disciplinary existence and increasingly crowds out the field.

III

The purpose of traffic laws is to protect all those who share our streets and highways. It is important to remember that everyone must obey the orders of a police officer, firefighter or uniformed adult school crossing guard who is directing traffic.

Illinois Rules of the Road, chapter 3 (www.CyberDriveIllinois.com)

To tell the history of some major strands of political theory is to locate a substantial fragment of police. But other fragments abound, most obviously the uniformed (and plainclothes) police, whose practices, Alan Hunt (chapter 6) and Markus Dubber (chapter 4) remind us, we must not forget in our zeal for a new police science that will escape the disciplinary grasp of criminal justice.[20] Hunt, in particular, well acknowledges the attraction of recovering the broad meaning of police through acts of historical reconstruction yet wants to complicate the alternative linearity suggested by the "new" police discourse by showing how, in connections between local action and wider focus, modern uniformed police practices replicate and even amplify the diversity of police's regulatory impulse. To this end, Hunt has us examine the uniformed police's most banal yet also most pervasive regulatory activity—traffic policing. Traffic policing exemplifies the purposefulness of the "civilizing process." It comprises a widely dispersed and technologically sophisticated disciplining of the driver, the passenger, the pedestrian—in fact of all users of public space—who are enjoined to behave predictably in accord with an established infrastructure of social relations and instincts while engaging in activities embraced in twentieth-century popular culture as the absolute epitome of empowerment—autonomy, individuality, unimpaired mobility.

Noticeably, the infrastructure of control is constructed in a language that offers manifold opportunities for slippage from the specificities of the traffic function to the wider discourse of police that these chapters seek to explore. Traffic *management*, for example, applies strategies of risk management, responsibilization, and prevention and discourses of discipline, efficiency, security, and surveillance to human behavior that is, socially and politically, completely uncontroversial. Two examples suffice. First, as Hunt shows (chapter 6), the routine involvement of police in verification of automobile insurance and the clerical management of accident records for insurance purposes merges two modalities of risk management: "real-time" authority over movement in and through public space and remote management of movement through the imposition of actuarial disciplines upon human affairs. Second, note how the London Congestion Charge adopted in 2003 to manage access by vehicle to central London requires and facilitates the accumulation of a vast bank of security-related information through a dedicated supervisory infrastructure. The charge is implemented through en masse monitoring of vehicle registration numbers to track the flow of vehicles into, through, and out of central London. A total of 230 video cameras, 180 installed around the edge of the zone and 50 within it, monitor vehicle access. Additional mobile camera units are available for deployment anywhere within the zone. Virtually all vehicles (98 percent) moving within the zone are tracked. "The video streams are transmitted to a data centre in Central London where a computer system equipped with Automatic number plate recognition software detects the registration plate of the vehicle. A second data centre provides a backup location for image data."[21] Such data would no doubt go far to meet the need to "know who is in London" articulated by the Commissioner of Metropolitan Police in London as justification for the far more controversial proposal to introduce national identity cards in the United Kingdom (chapter 1, 37). Neocleous comments, "Just imagine a system that allowed the state, police, and security services to know exactly who was in London at any one time." In fact, as the congestion scheme suggests, significant components of such a system are already in place.[22] The example is used not to suggest that traffic policing is simply camouflage for security policing, but rather to underscore how porous the line between the two is when "safety" and its offshoots become hegemonic in the discourses that describe and routinize policing.[23]

Notwithstanding that, as we have now seen, the genealogy of politics and *oeconomy*, of safety and "settled government," contribute substantial fragments to a common discourse of police, police as a unified field remains elusive. The elements of police are unstable: they are unstable in translation from one political-legal culture to the next (the police of absolutist European states and of Revolutionary American state constitutions, for example, was quite distinct); they are unstable in institutional expression, in extent, and in effectivity; unstable in their relationship to each other; unstable across time. In the chapters presented in this collection, authors have stressed the dispersed and heterogeneous character of the subjects of police, the diversity of the institutional formations through which policing is conducted, and in general the need for historical and conceptual specificity if police is to become an idea with critical bite. The instability of police when considered as a phenomenon may simply serve to underline the conclusion that, conceptually, police as such is indefinable. So let us consider an alternative course of action. Let us seek police not in definitions but rather in activities in its dispersed locales. Let us examine these for commonalities.

Of those identified in these essays, I want to focus briefly on four: work, the household, the city, and the colony.

WORK

Mark Neocleous calls work the first principle of police (chapter 1). Taking his cue from police's historical (early-modern) commission as the promotion of general welfare, the achievement of plenitude, and the maximization of resources and of social order, Neocleous attempts to lend specificity to the implementation of that commission by reference to the fabrication of work regimes. The particular regime to which Neocleous draws our attention is wage labor, and indeed his illustration of the process of fabrication through the work of Patrick Colquhoun is well merited. No one who has read Colquhoun's treatises *The Police of the Metropolis* (1796), *The Commerce and Police of the River Thames* (1800), and *Indigence* (1806) could disagree that what he contemplated was a systematic consolidation of the terms of all transactions involving labor power around the money wage, complemented by "a free circulation of labour." At the same time, one can fairly observe that the fabrication of work regimes had long been an object of attention and by all kinds of authorities. Household labor, as Dubber shows us, was produced by the coercive capacities of the micro householder, craft labor by guilds (which exercised rigorous corporate policing powers over the regimes of craft work), and indentured servitude and plantation slavery by mercantile companies and colonial authorities (see generally chapter 4; Leeson 1979; Steinfeld 1991, 2001; Tomlins 2004). In the Anglo American case, systematic state attempts to mobilize population as workforce date at least from the mid-sixteenth century: the Tudor Statute of Artificers (1563), for example, consolidated many hitherto distinct regimes of ordering, putting people to work in service of a general prosperity and a general discipline.[24] Vagrancy laws policed labor mobility on both sides of the Atlantic (Dubber 2005; see also Stanley 1998, 98–137, 248–62). Colquhoun's police of the Thames waterfront was itself the culmination of an intensification of work discipline, an assault on leisure preference, and a persistent criminalization of perquisites that had begun nearly a century before (Tomlins 1993, 114–24; 1995, 56–65).

Population of course becomes subject to police in a wide variety of regulatory regimes, but Neocleous is quite correct to emphasize that work appears early in the piece as a significant locale of regulation. Nevertheless, if one is looking for the shared components of a generalized discourse of police it may be a mistake to concentrate on work as the first principle and instead examine work as a major instance of the more general principle of control over the deployment of resources. For a work regime is only as secure as the means to prevent departure from it. Indeed, mobility—or as the Argus-eyed Blackstone has it, "loco-motion" (Blackstone 1979a, 130)—is the major point of overlap of the four locales of police under examination here. Neocleous notes that Blackstone thought vagrancy "the ultimate police problem" (chapter 1, 24), but in that Blackstone was merely reflecting the preoccupations of half a millennium's concentration upon achieving the most productive disposition of population in motion.

THE HOUSEHOLD

Both in his contribution to this collection and more extensively in his recent book, Markus Dubber has emphasized the household as the point of origin of the concept of police.[25] Two modalities of governance exist in Western political theory and practice, he argues: autonomy, or self-government, and heteronomy, or government of the self by others. Governance rarely exists in any polity in one or other pure form, but this does not preclude an idealization of these modalities as distinct in essence. "From the perspective of law, the state is the institutional manifestation of a political community of free and equal persons. The function of the law state is to manifest and protect the autonomy of its constituents in all of its aspects, private and public. From the perspective of police, the state is the manifestation of a household. The police state, as *paterfamilias*, seeks to maximize the welfare of his—or rather its—household" (Dubber 2005, 3).

Seen in Aristotelian terms, the law state could exist only on the basis of the police state. The political community of free and equal persons was precisely the community of household masters, or (in Roman law) *paterfamiliae*, each rendered free from the necessities and obligations of self-support by a household of subordinates—"wife, servant, slave"—organized to undertake the "necessitous struggle for livelihood" that sustained the master in his enjoyment of a life of virtuous civic action (Booth 1993, 27). The fundamental legal-political distinction that emerged from the household polity was, then, that between householder and household. The exterior of the household— the polity itself, and politics—became identified with the condition of the tiny minority of household masters, such that masters became the prototype of free men. But for the vast majority who lived on the interior of the household and participated in its economy, household governance (police) "defined daily life" (Dubber 2005, 10). Household governance diminished distinctions among subjects in the face of the fundamental distinction between subject and master, from which emerged the classic exchange that defined the household model of rule—loyalty in exchange for protection (Dubber 2005, 11–14, 49–50). The pattern was repeated on the grand scale of the king's household, effectively coextensive with the realm and point of origin of the state, into which all micro householders were incorporated as subjects of the king's authority as macro householder.[26]

Dubber focuses primarily on the transmission of patriarchy from household to state form and only secondarily on household relationships as a locale for the detailed exercise of police. Recent U.S. research has provided a new chronology for what remains otherwise an old representation of the flow of authority within households (and one of modernity's favorite clichés), movement "from status to contract" (Shammas 2002). In fact, as the patriarchal role was assumed by the state, the household stands out as a crucial point of disciplinary intersection (see, e.g., Grossberg 1985). Court-administered heteronomy is manifest in the law of service and of employment, the law of conjugal and familial relations, and the law of slavery. These are strands that later twentieth-century legal discourse has tried to pick apart,[27] but earlier writers treated their interrelationship as both obvious and natural, a discursive homology—"the domestic relations"—that defined normative social life.[28]

THE CITY

Court-administered heteronomy intensified in the early twentieth-century United States, particularly in urban areas. Urban court systems were reconstructed as municipal managers of metropolitan populations through the discretionary application of "socialized" law to families and their members (Willrich 2003, 98, and see generally xxxi–xxxii, 96–115). Socialized law meant the establishment of centralized criminal justice bureaucracies and of specialized branches focused (in Chicago's case) on discrete populations and "problems"—domestic relations, morals, and juveniles (Willrich 2003, xxxii, 114–15). Municipal court systems acquired a therapeutic role. The socialization of law brought the installation of "staffs of disciplinary personnel" or "social experts" as strategic players in the court bureaucracies. "Psychologists, psychiatrists, physicians, social workers, and probation officers . . . examined offenders and advised judges on the best 'individual treatment' given the offenders' mental makeup, family background, and social history" (Willrich 2003, xxxii). As Progressive Era innovations spread, "treatments" proliferated:

> To the conventional punitive measures of fines and incarceration, state legislatures added the far more discretionary techniques of indeterminate sentences, probation, parole, compulsory medical treatment, routine commitment to state institutions for the insane or feebleminded, and eugenical sterilization. In socialized criminal justice, the case was only the starting point for a much broader set of investigations and interventions that aimed not so much to punish crime but to reform criminals and the larger social world that had produced them. (Willrich 2003, xxxii–xxxiii)

The elaboration of municipal-disciplinary complexes in U.S. cities during the early twentieth century offers a telling example of the city as a locale of police. Indeed, the city, I think it goes without saying, is a prime locale for police in virtually every regulatory capacity one could imagine. Such reference to the city is manifest in many of the chapters gathered here—Pasquino, Neocleous, Valverde, and Farmer all touch upon it. Farmer in particular demonstrates how Adam Smith in effect simply assumed without more ado the conjunction of police and city. The physical conditions of the city (concentration of population) demanded a police of sanitation; its economic conditions (demand for food far in excess of immediate sources of supply) demanded a police of markets, provisioning, and transportation to ensure plenty; its built environment (streets, alleys) required police in the sense of surveillance to ensure security from crime or civil disturbance. The examples Smith drew on to make his points were, naturally, cities: London and Paris; Glasgow and Edinburgh; his purpose, to underline the difference between an effective and an ineffective police (chapter 5).

Contemporary with the emergence of police in its productive phase—that is to say from the late sixteenth century on—one finds the high point of what Engin Isin has recently termed "eutopolis": the dream of the rational city made a reality, where population is organized as subjects arrayed in ranked order, simultaneously spatial and political, an order that could single out the ideal citizen, the freeman, and separate him from the rest—"vagrants, poor, vagabonds, beggars" (Isin 2002, 160).[29] The city, in other words, joins with work and the household and family as a site for the exercise of jurisdiction over mobility, both social and physical.

THE COLONY

A particularly interesting aspect of the eutopolitan city is that in English discourse it is simultaneously the quintessential cultural expression of the process of transatlantic colonization. Nowhere is the conjunction of eutopolis with colonizing better expressed than in the late sixteenth-century writings of Richard Hakluyt the elder, where the city stands as the perfected representation of civil association and civilization, the seat of sovereignty, the center of commerce and the citadel of evangelism. Creating the city in the transatlantic wilderness was *the* essential condition for success in colonizing. It meant the creation of actual "cities"—physical emplacements of Englishness, of brick and stone, houses and roofs and walls—but also of all those other "thinges without which no Citie may bee made nor people in civill sorte be kept together"—legalities, revenues, arms, authority, relations of power and acquiescence (Hakluyt 1578; Tomlins 2001, 327).

Unsurprisingly, from the Virginia Colony to New England to Carolina to Pennsylvania to Georgia, the creation of cities and townships—ordered mobility—stood at the center of colonizers' strategies for securing terri- tory, governing locomotion, and planning inhabitation. Concentration of population, not dispersed settlement, was the key. The first settlement in the Chesapeake Bay was named James City (colloquially, Jamestown), the second Charles City. The projectors of the so-called particular plantations, such as Berkeley Plantation, planned settlement on the basis of the establishment of towns (Canny 1998, 10). In New England, famously, John Winthrop's Arbella sermon on "Christian Charity" denominated the Massachusetts Bay colonizing project an exemplary eutopolis, "a city upon a hill" (Win- throp 1630, 47). The proprietary colonies of the Restoration further elab- orated the model. The creation of a city was prominent in the Carolina proprietors' plans for their colonizing project. Their fundamental constitu- tions framed local government in a meticulously detailed spatial structure of signiories, baronies, colonies, and manors. The objective was the foundation in landed property of an elaborately hierarchical culture of governance that invested authoritative oversight in a local hereditary nobility fused insti- tutionally with the proprietors (see generally Weir 1998). William Penn followed a similar course in Pennsylvania, planning a city, contiguous con- centrated settlement patterns, and an elaborated political order all well in advance of actual settlement. What was being pursued in all these cases was not simply a formal allocation of space but a political or civic order with corresponding spatial embodiment, all created in advance of settlement to receive and organize the migrating population: a further locale, in other words, for the exercise of jurisdiction over mobility (see generally Tomlins 2001, 315–47).

And who was that population to be but the "excess" of England, mo- bilized for colonizing for the general good. Propagandists of colonization argued that overseas settlement would "draw off the excess population and put to some productive use the swarms of sturdy vagrants who roamed the countryside and infested the city slums" (Bailyn 1986, 52). The refrain in the works of the Hakluyts was constant. "Yea, if we woulde beholde with the eye of pitie how al our prisons are pestered and filled with able men to serve their Countrie," wrote the younger Hakluyt in 1582, "wee would hasten and further every man to his power the deducting of some colonies of our superfluous people into those temperate and fertile parts of America" (Hakluyt 1582, 175–76). In his *Discourse of Western Planting*, published two years later, the revival of decayed English trades and the employment of the idle was made second only to the advancement of Christianity in the colonial project. "Wee for all the Statutes that hitherto can be devised, and the sharpe execution of the same in poonishing idle and lazye persons for want of sufficient occasion of honest employmente cannot deliver our common wealthe from multitudes of loiterers and idle vagabondes" (Hakluyt 1584, 234, and, generally, 218–34). Hakluyt the elder likewise emphasized how, through settlement overseas, "the poore and Idle persons wch nowe are ether burdensome or hurtefull to this Realme at home" might be made "profytable members," particularly the young, with whom "the Realme shall abound too too much" (Hakluyt 1585, 330; Hakluyt n.d. [1585?], 340).

The colony—the city in the wilderness with its novel work regimes—also stands for what Neocleous and Farmer among others here have identified as perhaps the supreme concept in discussion of police—security.[30] For the city is a secured sovereignty. It stands both for sovereignty's plenitude and order and for the chaos that lies beyond secured terrain. The polarities of order and chaos, of civility and barbarity, of policed plenitude and unpoliced wilderness are absolutely central to early-modern European discursive comprehension of the world—geographic, cartographic, literary, legal—and add up to a set of statements precisely about securing and improving places and peoples (Tomlins 2005a; Barker 1993, 143–206).[31]

Considered as a central component in the production in real time of modernity's anthropology of us and them, as a technology of colonizing employed during the first great outward thrust from Europe, police in this most general aspect has been of global significance for half a millennium.[32] We can see this best in the intimate relationship between early-modern international law—the law of war and peace—and colonizing's ideology of improvement. We find that police as an expression of "due regulation and . . . order" is not at all a phenomenon restricted to a "domestic" sphere of operations. The international is not a newly discovered realm for police. Police has been international since the sixteenth century.

IV

Some loving friends convey the emperor hence,

And give him burial in his father's grave.

My father and Lavinia shall forthwith

Be closed in our household's monument

As for that ravenous tiger, Tamora,

No funeral rite, nor man in mourning weed,

No mournful bell shall ring her burial,

But throw her forth to beasts and birds to prey.

Her life was beastly and devoid of pity,

And being dead, let birds on her take pity.

WILLIAM SHAKESPEARE, *Titus Andronicus*, 5.3.191 (ca. 1591)

To frame the inquiry, let us return to chapter 7, and in particular to Mitchell Dean's observations on Carl Schmitt. As Dean describes it,

> In Carl Schmitt's analysis of the system of international law that governed military combat between the seventeenth and early twentieth centuries, the *jus publicum Europaeum*, war is regarded as being conducted among equal European sovereign states, in which combatants recognized each other as *justi hostes* (just enemies) and in which what Schmitt calls a "non-discriminatory" war was possible. "Both belligerents had the same political character and the same rights; both recognized each other as states" (Schmitt 1950, 142). This system achieved a "bracketing" of war in that formally conducted war between legitimate sovereigns was not subject to moral-theological evaluation of just causes. . . . Schmitt was hostile to what he perceived as the degeneration of war into a police action. (chapter 7, 197)

The sign of degeneration was the transformation of just enemies into "trouble-makers, criminals, and pests" (chapter 7, 190).

Schmitt's characterization of the law of war is couched within the contours of a particular, carefully contained, state system—the so-called Westphalian system of sovereign state interactions, dating from the mid-seventeenth century, concentrated at the western end of what Mackinder called the Eurasian "world island" (Mackinder 1904), subsequently extended to the peripheral states of European settlement in North America and Australasia. This is the system around which much of the substance and conceptualization of international law has been built. It furnishes the backdrop for current controversies over preemption, conditional sovereignty, and representations of military action as police action.

But suppose one is not interacting with "states" at all but acting beyond any such system. Suppose one is not engaging another *justus hostis* but, rather, engaged in processes of intrusion upon the lands of "brutes," the rules of which European states (succeeding the papacy) constructed as among themselves. This is the earlier, formative era of international law developed in the late sixteenth and early seventeenth centuries, international law that addresses not interstate relations but the rights of the community of the civil in their interactions with those outside that community, beyond civility. European expeditions of expansion into South and North America, culminating in the devastation of indigenous societies by massacre, mass execution, disease, and the enslavement and deportation of survivors, invoked—indeed depended for their sense of legitimacy upon—a discourse of "just war." The *nomos* of English colonizing in Virginia and New England, for example, obtained its philosophical coherence from the contrapuntal anthropology of Christian, European civility and New World barbarism that had informed the whole project of New World contact since Columbus. Thus in his *De Iure Belli* published in 1588, Alberico Gentili, Regius Professor of Civil Law at Oxford, held—rather like Tony Blair—that "nature has established among men kinship, love, kindliness, and a bond of fellowship." Those who violated nature—"who practiced abominable lewdness . . . who ate human flesh"— were outside humanity, brutes, upon whom war might justly be made "since we may also be injured as individuals by those violators of nature" (Gentili 1933, 67, 123–24). So also, in humanist discourse, might brutes' vacant lands be appropriated; so also might they be enslaved. In his better-known *De Iure Belli Ac Pacis*, first published in 1625, Hugo Grotius followed Gentili's text, declaring that kings had a right to exact punishments "not only for injuries committed against themselves, or their Subjects, but likewise, for those which do not peculiarly concern them, but which are in any Persons whatsoever, grievous Violations of the Law of Nature or Nations. . . . War is lawful against those who offend against Nature" (Grotius 1738, bk. 2, chap 20 ¶ 40).[33]

Alongside the gestures of courtesy, as it were, that autonomous self-governing sovereign Westphalian states paid each other lies another realm of action—yet another parallel universe[34]—that I would argue is far more characteristic of world historical experience, at least until the decolonizing window of the second half of the twentieth century (which may now be closing), a realm reflected in a humanist international law that invokes the judgments of "nature" and the community of the humane as necessary and sufficient basis for making war to improve (bring order and civility to) barbarism. This was the discourse that sustained European colonialism for half a millennium as it expanded into the "state of exception" that it had created for itself beyond the boundaries of the old European map. This was, as Levi and Hagan demonstrate, the discourse that underlay Theodore Roosevelt's early twentieth-century restatement of the Monroe Doctrine as license to engage in civilizing missions abroad (chapter 8).[35] Let us not forget in this current world order one of the most interesting signifiers of the first new world order—the seal of the Massachusetts Bay Company on which appears an indigenous inhabitant of that region and a script pleading (in suitably Pauline terms, for a collection on police) "come over and help us" (Chaplin 2001, 26).[36]

Colonizing, one may argue, is the permanence of exception. It occurs in the barbaric regions of exception and as an unending condition of emergency—the unending necessity that order and civility be visited upon the disordered. Colonizing, then, is one of the most potent instances of police discourse in practice.[37] But colonizing is as potent a metaphor for the state's attempts to create "due regulation and order" in locales of exception within the physical boundaries of the realm as in the world, and in fact connects the two. I referred earlier to the eighteenth century in England as a century characterized by an intensification of police. Here I am thinking primarily of the disciplining of labor through the successive master and servant acts passed at regular intervals throughout the century (Tomlins 1995, 56–61). But the intensification of labor discipline was located within the pattern of what Michael Brogden, writing of the nineteenth century, has called the "internal colonization of the island," a description given added bite in Robert Storch's telling description of police as "domestic missionaries" (Brogden 1987; Storch 1976).[38] The two ideas—disciplining labor, colonizing the island—come together early in the eighteenth century in the political economy of Daniel

Defoe, who wrote vehemently in 1724 of the absolute necessity to quash the leisure preference of the poor and to discipline work (Defoe 1724) and over the next two years in his closely related *Tour Throughout the Whole Island* of the disorder of Britain's extra metropolitan extremities (Defoe 1971).[39]

Defoe's *Tour* manufactured (fabricated?) nation, from the metropolis outward. Consistently fascinating in its capacity to express the island's regional variation, Defoe's chorography always suggested that variation was in fact alterity to a metropolitan norm. Take, for example, his well-known account of the "Peakrills"—the cave-dwelling lead miners of the Derbyshire peak district, whom Defoe described as "subterranean wretches," creatures from "the dark regions below" whose speech required the services of an interpreter before it could be comprehended in "the world of light." So great was their remove from the nucleated villages and country estates of the south, for which Defoe earlier in the *Tour* had displayed an amiable fondness, that the Peakrills seemed a different race of beings, "rude boorish" and "uncouth" in manner, collectively "strange, turbulent, quarrelsome." Or in other words foreign, disordered, uncivilized. Describing his descent into the West Riding of Yorkshire from Blackstone Edge in the Pennines, Defoe employed a trope at once familiar and unmistakable that put the region's alterity beyond doubt: *"We thought now we were come into a Christian country again*, and that our difficulties were over; *but we soon found our selves mistaken in the matter"* (1971, 460–68, 490; emphases added).[40]

To locate police in the pursuit of colonizing is to relativize the domesticity of police. We have all seen, and none would disagree, that police has major domestic expression. But it is a fundamental error, I think, to treat Blackstone as a canonical data point, or definition. The trajectory of police, rather, is cumulative (one might even say it gathers speed)—from the civic humanists and the city; through the propagandists of voyaging and the colony; to the theorists of empire, domestic order, a "whole" island, disciplined labor, and political economy such as Defoe and later Colquhoun and much later Theodore Roosevelt. To return to Defoe as exemplar, his travel narratives and his writings on economics constantly stressed (as did the Hakluyts) the intimate relationship between English domestic prosperity, labor mobilization, and transoceanic colonizing. Thus, in his *Plan of the English Commerce*: "An Encrease of Colonies encreases People, People encrease the Consumption of Manufactures, Manufactures Trade, Trade Navigation, Navigation

Seamen, and altogether encrease the Wealth, Strength and Prosperity of *England*" (Defoe 1728, 367). Similarly, Colquhoun's own *Police of the Metropolis* (1796) needs to be read alongside his later *Wealth, Power and Resources of the British Empire* (1814).

To light on the relationship of police to colonizing is to identify Mariana Valverde's contribution to this collection (chapter 3), specifically, its refusal "to take the distinction between the domestic and the international as given," as of the first importance in indicating the synthesis toward which "the new police science" might most productively be directed. It is, as she demonstrates, precisely the police of colonizing that is expressed in the "peace, order and good government" hailed by Michael Ignatieff as Canada's indigenous invention and potential imperialist export. POGG powers, we have seen, are in fact an imperial British invention—a police power of immense latitude and flexibility. Wherever some form of decolonization has occurred they become the practical expression of colonial police's continuity, representing a colonial governmentality "infolded" into the postcolonial successor state, to be used as tools of "internal colonialism" for such domestic purposes as seem fit and, as Ignatieff would have it, as tools of the successor state's own foreign or imperial policy too. Meanwhile, they remain available to serve where necessary as the justification for a traditional imperialism—as in the case of Diego Garcia—retailored as the geopolitics of security. Valverde does not ask us to choose between domestic and international expressions of police—her point rather is to notice that the foundations, the flow, and the extensibility of police make the distinction theoretically meaningless.

Valverde's insights are relevant far beyond her immediate Canadian point of reference. First, the infolding she describes is a phenomenon identifiable in all the states of succession in Anglophone settler societies—in Canada, obviously, in Australia and New Zealand, and also, of course, in the United States.[41] In the U.S. case we have already seen infolding expressed in *Alger*, through Shaw's legitimating trajectory of textual transmission. The same can, of course, be found expressed more extensively in the Marshall Court's Indian lands jurisprudence and its later transpacific cognates.[42] As important, Valverde's refusal—flowing from her analysis of infolding—to accord meaningful theoretical distinction to the tendency to separate domestic and international, to explore instead their productive reciprocities, comports with what a reader will conclude from the collection as a whole (even if most chapters read individually will lend themselves in orientation to one or the other side of that distinction).

V

Every image of the past that is not recognized by the present as one of its own concerns threatens to disappear irretrievably.

WALTER BENJAMIN, *Theses on the Philosophy of History* (1940)

This collection's cornucopia of conceptual and theoretical viewpoints on, narratives and histories of, and arguments about police will, I hope, generate many reactions, set many more hares running. The recovery of police and the hard work of rendering it recognizable to the present in all its historical richness and eclecticism is a major achievement. Are there any overall recommendations that emerge, more than already reflected in my own observations in this concluding chapter? Well, to summarize: first, law and police are distinguishable as ideational complexes, but both are strategies for ruling and are intertwined. The history of both can be written according to attempts made to draw hard and fast distinctions between rule of police and rule of law, but actually to assert the reality of hard and fast distinction is a species of normative rather than critical argument. Second, police seems to me less easily apprehended as a science per se than as something else—a field, a problematic, a strategy of governance operative in identifiable locales. Third, taking locales as the point of departure, we should note that police, though dispersed, is not unconnected. As we have seen, population, territory, work, household, city, and colony constitute an institutional-organizational complex throughout which the technology and assumptions of police are prominent. As the elder Richard Hakluyt observed more than four centuries ago, processes of manning and planting, and keeping are intimately related (Hakluyt 1585, 333).

It may be helpful to add a final observation that perhaps may assist our attempt to study police as a coherent phenomenon, suggested by my own work in the history of English colonizing. The creation of colonies can be seen as a cameralist process, which is to say a conscious process of planning—

assembling resources, bringing definition to territory, creating institutions, transporting and managing population. The charters that founded English colonies in North America prescribed in detail the order of things to be undertaken to transform the wilderness. They were of course occupied by the concrete—harbors to be established, buildings to be built, fortifications erected, productive tasks undertaken—but also with the elaboration of an architecture of license, power, and authority in colonial societies, from land tenures to the establishment of markets, manors, churches, assemblies, and courts to the levying of customs and the distributions of arms, to the control of entry and exit. Thus the charters gave expression not merely to the institutional practicalities of state formation but to a discourse of civic organization and above all of *jurisdiction* (Tomlins 2001, 315–47).

If one of the tasks of this collection is to assemble the organizing principles of a new knowledge of police, the principles from which an interrogation of the concept can begin, it is worth advancing "jurisdiction" as a useful category of analysis. Jurisdiction offers a means by which police's irregularities—its dispersal, lack of coordination, institutional particularities and complexities, radically different appearance in different locales, in short its apparent lack of a common likeness—may be rendered less significant. By jurisdiction I mean "the unity of decision on a territory" (see chapter 2, 42) and the processes whereby unity is formed and maintained in a multiplicity of transactions. "Unity of decision" is not a synonym for centralization: it does not mean concentration of all decision making on all subjects at one point. Considered over the long term, jurisdiction is layered and fragmented. Distinct "unities" of decision with distinct objects of attention have had distinct institutional embodiments in the same locale—familial, ecclesiastical, municipal, corporate-economic, and so forth. Their objects of attention may be the same phenomenon, differently observed.[43] Historically, however, state formation has tended to operate as a process that produces new supervening embodiments of "unity of decision" by creating new institutions and new discourses of authority that seek to rearrange (or eliminate) existing claims to accommodate new hierarchies of relative authority. This "subsumption of singularities in the totality" (Hardt and Negri 2000, 87) is often a process of aggrandizement and conflict. The point is, however, that the process is not bound to any particular limits. Hence, we may think of police both as an emblematic unity of decision and as a strategy for aggrandizing.

But even if no first principles can be abstracted from the materials presented here, these chapters abound in points of entry for critical inquiry into the general phenomenon of police, whether its organizing rubric be science or field or problematic or strategy. Neocleous's deliberate embrace of "anachronism" identifies, like Pasquino, police's long sub rosa conceptual history; his nomination of work as an essential arena of definition and application is of major importance. Dubber's *patria potestas* unearths another, overlapping, institutional locale—the patriarchal household—as a concrete setting in which police powers develop. Farmer recovers the eighteenth century's distinctive predisciplinary province of jurisprudence, which encompasses police no less than law, and then argues for a reincarnation of the predisciplinary standpoint in a new "jurisprudence of security" that, better than police, can provide a unified perspective to interrogate contemporary criminal law and administrative penalty. Hunt's conceptualization of police in the discourse of civilizing process helps us understand the routines and extensions and implications of "real" (domestic) police work. Dean and Levi and Hagan give us crucial points of entry to international policing, while also providing contrasting assessments of the novelty and implications of "policing" claims made there. Finally, Valverde's colonial governmentality offers a careful and original argumentative synthesis of police in its several locales that helps draw into fruitful conjunction many of the distinct analyses of operation and conceptualization presented by other authors.

Differences will continue to abound over how best to pursue the project of a new police science, a new way of knowing police. But this collection has established the broad contours of the territory to be explored and, while mapping the variety of routes that might be taken, has identified those likely to prove most fruitful. The continuation of difference will be productive and stimulating, therefore, because difference exists within what is now established as a community of argument. The creation of that community means that the project of establishing police as a new object of study is now fully under way.

Notes

1. On the legend of the foreign founder as lawgiver in Western political culture, see Honig 2001, notably (in the matter of Moses) 15–32. Honig's account of law's

"alienness" gives us much to explore in considering the relationship between police and law, given police's intimate involvements in daily life. The potential to which I advert here became clear in conversations with Ron Levi, to whom I am indebted.

2. As Levi and Hagan point out (chapter 8), Ignatieff's comments were directed to an audience of Canadian foreign affairs professionals. More recently, addressing a U.S. audience, Ignatieff recolored his neoliberalism in shades of the messianic Jeffersonianism fashionable among south-of-the-border intelligentsia. See Ignatieff 2005.

3. For journalistic accounts and commentary, see McSmith and Dillon 2003; Deliso 2003; Wolfe 2005.

4. But this is hardly new, as Levi and Hagan show us in chapter 8. This point is developed further later.

5. The other restraint is self-restraint—witness Dean's invocation (chapter 7, 194) of the U.S. Army *Field Manual on Stability Operations and Support Operations* as surety.

6. Empirically, this claim of "likeness" is not particularly convincing (see chapter 4). Even if it were, Dubber's analysis of U.S. prisons in general suggests that likeness is hardly the product of rule-of-law "scrutiny and due process."

7. Ernst Freund noted in 1904 that the language of police power was "in constant use and indispensable in the vocabulary of American constitutional law." He also noted in the same breath that "police power . . . remained without authoritative or generally accepted definition" (Freund 1904, iii). For explicit adoption of police provisions in the first state constitutions, see Adams 1980; Palmer 1987. Policelike discourse can also be found in the preamble to the U.S. Constitution (see text accompanying note 12). In England, Blackstone positions police fully within "The Laws of England" (Blackstone 1979b).

8. Such statements have tended to arise from circumstances of emergency but usually appear only after the emergency is over. See, e.g., *Ex Parte Milligan*, 71 U.S. 2 (1866), and compare *Ex Parte Vallandigham* 68 U.S. 243 (1864); *Abrams v. United States*, 250 U.S. 616 (1919); *Schenck v. United States*, 249 U.S. 47 (1919; dissents of Justices Holmes and Brandeis); *Ex Parte Endo*, 323 U.S. 283 (1944); *Hirabayashi v. United States*, 320 U.S. 81 (1943); *Korematsu v. United States* 323 U.S. 214 (1944).

9. Although occasionally the attempt has been made. See, for example, *Wabash, St. Louis, and Pacific Railway Co. v. Illinois*, 118 U.S. 557 (1886); *Chicago, Milwaukee, and St. Paul Railway Co. v. Minnesota*, 134 U.S. 418 (1890); *Allgeyer v. Louisiana*, 165 U.S. 578 (1897); *Lochner v. New York*, 198 U.S. 45 (1905). On the significance of the *Lochner* decision, see Dubber 2005, 190–210.

10. See, for example, *Johnson v. McIntosh*, 21 U.S. 543 (1823); *Cherokee Nation v. Georgia*, 30 U.S. 1 (1831); *United States v. Rogers*, 45 U.S. 467 (1846); *United States v. Kagama*, 118 U.S. 375 (1886); *Chae Chan Ping v. United States*, 130 U.S. 581 (1889); *Nishimura Ekiu v. United States*, 142 U.S. 651 (1892); *Fong Yue Ting v. United States*, 149 US 698 (1893); *DeLima v. Bidwell*, 182 U.S. 1 (1901); *Downes v. Bidwell*, 182 U.S. 244 (1901); *Dorr v. United States*, 195 U.S. 138 (1904).

11. "Political question" doctrine originated in *United States v. Rogers*, 45 U.S. 467 (1846).

12. For the first charter of Virginia, see Thorpe 1909, 3783. See also, for example, the charters of Maryland and Pennsylvania (both granting all necessary powers for "good and happy government") in Thorpe 1909, 1669 and 3035. For the first state constitutions, see Adams 1980.

13. It is important here both to note and to endorse Mariana Valverde's comments refusing to reduce the concepts of sovereignty and discipline to "binary opposition" (chapter 3, 103, note 3). In my view, Valverde's comments contribute very productively to the law-police debate that I have argued the new police science must have.

14. This paragraph and the next two are heavily dependent upon Tomlins 1993, 44–45.

15. The flag would, of course, have to wait for the War of 1812, at which point it is endowed with a sovereign mystique conveyed, in the United States, quite uniquely, in the language of sacrality.

16. We should of course note that there is no given outcome in the triangular relationships among law, police, and politics. Indeed, tension abounds. Law and police intrude upon each other, and both intrude upon politics, for both visit displacement, juridical in the one case, administrative-regulative in the other, upon political struggles (Honig 1993, 14).

17. *New York v. Miln*, 36 U.S. 102, 139 (1837).

18. *Commonwealth v. Alger*, 61 Mass. 53, 85 (1851).

19. Ibid., 65–83.

20. Markus Dubber's chapter is particularly ingenious in first positing the broad conception of police as the desired objective to be recovered and then, once recovery has been effected, using that broad conception as a standpoint from which to interrogate critically, and thus reintegrate, the genealogy of criminal law and procedure.

21. For details, go to http://en.wikipedia.org/wiki/London_Congestion_Charge.

22. The actual monitoring of vehicle movement upon which the congestion scheme depends appears publicly uncontroversial. "At least a hundred cities in the United Kingdom and around the world have watched with interest the successful introduction of the charge in London and many are likely to follow London's example, though not necessarily using the same technology." In London "discussions are under way about extending the zone to cover more of the boroughs of Westminster and Kensington and Chelsea. There has been some talk of a separate zone for the area of acute traffic congestion and pollution around Heathrow [London's international airport] and for some suburban London town centres." In the longer term, "the most important long-term impact of the congestion charge will probably be the boost it has given to the principle of traffic demand management. Emboldened by London's success, the Government has now set up a working group to investigate the

possibility of introducing a national road user charging scheme." For details go to http://www.transport2000.org.uk/activistbriefings/CongestionCharging.htm.

23. Indeed, as Hunt (chapter 6) notes, the use of video and closed-circuit TV (CCTV) cameras in public places is widely accepted. This is particularly the case in the United Kingdom, where in the immediate aftermath of the July 7, 2005, bombings of London transportation sites, it was reported, "there are at least 500,000 cameras in the city, and one study showed that in a single day a person could expect to be filmed 300 times." Throughout the United Kingdom there are approximately seven million CCTV cameras. (*Wall Street Journal* 2005).

24. Such mobilizations began in the fourteenth century, although the legislation passed at that time was not enforced for long. For details, see Palmer 1993, 14–23.

25. This section relies largely on Tomlins 2005b and Tomlins 1995.

26. All households manifested variety in contents—persons of different status, animals, material goods. But all differences "paled in comparison to the one defining distinction, that between every constituent of the household and the householder" (Dubber 2005, 16–18). Dubber's succinct but necessarily condensed summary of a long and complex historical process leaves him acknowledging but not investigating the contours of potent jurisdictional conflicts between the claims of the king and of "inferior" householders outside the arena of criminal law. On the structures and ideologies of governance that claimed and distributed jurisdiction to rule in early-modern England, see, e.g., Lachmann 1987, Brewer 2005.

27. For examples of work attempting (from rather different perspectives) to bring employment and family law back together, see Glendon (1981) and Stanley (1988, 1998).

28. See, e.g., Reeve (1816); Kent (1826–1830, vol. 2, part 4); Schouler (1870). Not until the early twentieth century did master and servant become clearly distinct, its earlier placement among the domestic relations treated in American treatises as a matter of antiquarian interest. See, e.g., Labatt (1913, vol. 1, 14). On the "jurisdictional war" among treatise writers in the half century following the Civil War over the appropriate categorization of master and servant law, see Glendon (1981, 147–48). We should note that Timothy Walker distinguished the law of employment from the law of the household some sixty years earlier, though he seems to have been motivated primarily by concern to underline that master-servant law was relevant to all forms of employment and not just employment of domestic servants (Walker 1837, 250).

29. Isin shows how the city expands and elaborates its policed civic persona in succeeding incarnations as the nineteenth century's "metropolis" and the later twentieth century's "cosmopolis" (2002, 191–274).

30. See also chapter 8, 225. The redefinition of security as "defense of incursions from the perimeter" to which Levi and Hagan advert, if more than simply tactical, actually suggests an end to the cartography of modernity, established in the early sixteenth century as "a shift from a dominant spatial model in which the dominant Mediterranean centre of the world was poised against a liminal, uncivilized and pos-

sibly non-human periphery, to a model which translated the earthly globe into a vast pictorial frame circumscribing a space ready for European inscription" (Klein 2001, 6). In fact, as we shall see, the contemporary Western cartographic *imaginaire* is more akin to a combination of the medieval and the modern: a savage and threatening periphery from which the center recoils and simultaneously, for its own security, *re*inscribes.

31. Note the following passage from Nathan Fiske's sermon "Remarkable Providences," preached at Brookfield, Massachusetts, and later published (see Fiske 1776, 25–26; Lepore 1998, 186): "'Tis with pleasing wonder that we look back upon this country in general, and this town in particular, and compare the present condition and appearance with what they were a century ago, yea but little more than half a century ago. Instead of a desolate uncultivated wilderness—instead of mountains and plains covered with thick untraversed woods—and swamps hideous and impassable, the face of the earth is trimmed, and adorned with a beautiful variety of fields, meadows, orchards and pastures. *The desert blossoms as the rose: the little hills rejoice on every side; the pastures are clothed with flocks, the valleys also are covered over with corn; they shout for joy, they also sing.* Instead of the dreary haunts of savage beasts, and more savage men, wounding the ear and terrifying the heart with their dismal yells, we find now only harmless retreats, *where the fowls of heaven have their habitation which sing among the branches.* Instead of the smoaky huts and wigwams of naked swarthy barbarians, we now behold thick settlements of a civilized people and convenient and elegant buildings . . . improvements in arts, agriculture and all the elegances of life" (emphases in original).

32. The terms of debate, as Levi and Hagan show, have been remarkably consistent for a remarkably long time.

33. The references to Gentili 1933 and Grotius 1738 are taken from Tuck 1999, 34–5, 102–03. Tuck notes (at 103) that among the crimes against nature punishable by war adverted to by Grotius in 1625 was that of resistance to European settlement.

34. See p. 258.

35. Nineteenth-century Marshallian ideology of "domestic" dependent nations becomes in the early twentieth century a progressive ideology of efficient international stewardship—of the hemisphere and the transoceanic world—just as (as we have already seen) police is applied in new forms to efficient domestic stewardship—of the environment (Hays 1959), of the population at large (Willrich 2003), and so forth.

36. "And a vision appeared to Paul in the night: a man of Macedo'nia was standing beseeching him and saying, 'Come over to Macedo'nia and help us'" Acts 16:9 (KJV).

37. It is worth exploring the parallel between the Roosevelt Corollary's declaration of the "duty of civilized nations to secure the welfare of foreign states by ensuring they are orderly and well-administered in their domestic affairs" (chapter 8, 214) and Ignatieff's desire to see order exported to the disorderly. Ignatieff wants to export

order because the disorderliness of others threatens "us" domestically. Other states are to be taught to become our assistants in managing our domestic order. We export order to them so that they will not export disorder to us. Police, then, becomes a condition of existence within the occidentally defined world community, a damper of risk. Risk to whom? It is interesting to speculate which society is seen to be at risk by the activities held to require a visitation of policing. Theirs or ours? In whose social security are we interested when we confront "failed states?"

38. See also Carson 1984, 1985. The ultimate target in processes of internal colonization is, of course, the disciplined self. See Barker 1984; Tomlins 1993, 352–63.

39. We have already seen in the work of the Hakluyts how colonization and labor interact as strategies of "improvement," although their terms were somewhat different: a disorderly population that threatens social order within the realm is improved by sending it to plantations overseas where it can become a productive labor force and hence "improve" the colonized wilderness, transactions that redound in every aspect to metropolitan benefit. In Defoe's version, disorderly labor is not exported but disciplined at home, part of a larger process of improving the realm. Some years ago, we should note, Marc Raeff (1983, 23) drew scholars' attention to the intimate "feedback" relationship between colonial rule and metropolitan outcome. "What lessons colonial rule could have for the administration of the homeland, how the feedback mechanism worked . . . are topics that deserve more attention than they have received." I am grateful to Mariana Valverde for drawing Raeff's thoughts on this matter to my attention.

40. Defoe's *Tour* pointedly contrasts barrenness and plenitude, wilderness and cultivation, arbitrariness and authority. See, for example, his palpable relief upon arrival at the Duke of Devonshire's estate at Chatsworth in Derbyshire, the civility and social-spatial order imparted by aristocracy, amid the deep foreignness and desolation of the peaks. To the northeast of Chatsworth lay "a vast extended moor or waste, which, for fifteen or sixteen miles together due north, presents you with neither hedge, house or tree, but a waste and howling wilderness, over which, when strangers travel, they are obliged to take guides. . . . Nothing can be more surprising of its kind, than for a stranger . . . wandering or laboring to pass this difficult desert country, and seeing no end of it, and almost discouraged and beaten out with the fatigue of it . . . on a sudden the guide brings him to this precipice, where he looks down from a frightful height, and a comfortless, barren, and, as he thought, endless moor, into the most delightful valley, with the most pleasant garden, and most beautiful palace in the world" (1971, 476–77, and, generally, 475–77). As we have seen (and see also the passage from Fiske 1776 in n. 31), the discursive tropes of savagery and civility, waste and garden, barbarity and *civitas* are deeply embedded in English colonizing discourse, and, more generally yet, in the cultural negotiations of early modernity.

41. POGG powers turn up virtually wherever the British have been, in one form or another. On Australia, see, for example, the Commonwealth of Australia Act (63

and 64 Vic. C. 12, 1900), at 1.V.51; the New South Wales Act (1823), 37 ("peace, welfare and good government"), also in the New South Wales Constitution Act (1842), 19 and the Australian Constitutions Act (1850), 9, all available at http://www .foundingdocs.gov.au/default.asp. On New Zealand, see the preamble to the Treaty of Waitangi (1840), the founding document of nonindigenous government in Aotearoa, where it is stated, "Her Majesty, Victoria, Queen of the United Kingdom of Great Britain and Ireland, regarding with Her Royal Favour the Native Chiefs and Tribes of New Zealand, and anxious to protect their just Rights and Property, and to secure to them the enjoyment of Peace and Good Order . . . therefore being desirous to establish a settled form of Civil Government . . . invite[s] the confederated and independent Chiefs of New Zealand to concur in the following Articles and Conditions." Available at http://www.treatyofwaitangi.govt.nz/treaty/index.php. In the matter of India, see, for example, the Indian Councils Act (1861), paragraphs 23, 42, 44 and 48 ("peace and good government"), available at http://projectsouthasia .sdstate.edu/Docs/history/primarydocs/Political_History/ABKeithDoco31.htm. See also, generally, Hussain 2003. Also see the Anguilla Act, 1971, passed in response to the protracted Anguilla crisis and resulting police action of 1967–1972, which states, "Her Majesty may by Order in Council make such provision as Her Majesty thinks fit for securing Peace, Order and Good Government in Anguilla" (Westlake 1972, 259). In 1967 Anguilla made a unilateral declaration of independence from the postcolonial federated state of the Leeward Islands constructed by the United Kingdom. After two years of desultory negotiation, in 1969 British paratroopers invaded the island and installed a Commissioner. A unit of the London Metropolitan Police was dispatched with the paratroopers and assumed sole paramilitary police authority until 1972. Anguilla became a British Dependent Territory in 1980, with a Governor representing the Crown. See generally Westlake 1972. It is worth noting that the Anguilla Squad of the Metropolitan Police remained intact after its return from the Caribbean and was used for crowd control policing in London.

42. See note 35.

43. See, for example, Farmer's description (chapter 5) of the multiple "authorities" enabled to obtain Anti-Social Behaviour Orders (ASBOs).

References

Adams, Willi Paul. 1980. *The first American constitutions: Republican ideology and the making of the state constitutions in the revolutionary era*, trans. R. and R. Kimber. Chapel Hill: University of North Carolina Press, for the Institute of Early American History and Culture.
Agamben, Giorgio. 2000. *Means without ends: Notes on politics*, trans. Vincenzo Binetti and Cesare Casarino. Minneapolis: University of Minnesota Press.

Bailyn, Bernard. 1986. *Voyagers to the west: A passage in the peopling of America on the eve of the revolution.* New York: Knopf.

Barker, Francis. 1984. *The tremulous private body: Essays on subjection.* London: Methuen.

———. 1993. *The culture of violence: Essays on tragedy and history.* Chicago: University of Chicago Press.

Benjamin, Walter. 1940 [1969]. Theses on the philosophy of history. In *Walter Benjamin, Illuminations: Essays and reflections,* ed. H. Arendt, trans. H. Zohn, 253–64. New York: Schocken Books.

———. 1986. Critique of violence. In *Walter Benjamin, Reflections: Essays, aphorisms, autobiographical writings,* ed. P. Demetz, trans. E. Jephcott, 277–300. New York: Schocken Books.

Blackstone, William. 1979a. *Commentaries on the laws of England.* Vol. 1. Chicago: University of Chicago Press.

———. 1979b. *Commentaries on the laws of England.* Vol. 4. Chicago: University of Chicago Press.

Booth, William James. 1993. *Households: On the moral architecture of the economy.* Ithaca: Cornell University Press.

Bourdieu, Pierre. 1987. The force of law: Toward a sociology of the juridical field, trans. R. Terdiman. *Hastings Law Journal* 38:805–53.

Brewer, Holly. 2005. *By birth or consent: Children, law and the Anglo-American revolution in authority.* Chapel Hill: University of North Carolina Press, for the Omohundro Institute of Early American History and Culture.

Brogden, Michael. 1987. An act to colonise the internal lands of the island: Empire and the origins of the professional police. *International Journal of the Sociology of Law* 15(2): 179–208.

Burchell, Graham, Colin Gordon, and Peter Miller. 1991. *The Foucault effect: Studies in governmentality.* Chicago: University of Chicago Press.

Canny, Nicholas. 1998. The origins of Empire: An introduction. In *The origins of Empire: British overseas enterprise to the close of the seventeenth century,* ed. N. Canny, 1–33. Oxford: Oxford University Press.

Carson, W. G. 1984. Policing the periphery: The development of Scottish policing, 1795–1900, part 1. *Australian and New Zealand Journal of Criminology* 17(4): 207–32.

———. 1985. Policing the periphery: The development of Scottish policing, 1795–1900, part 2. *Australian and New Zealand Journal of Criminology* 18(1): 3–16.

Chaplin, Joyce E. 2001. *Subject matter: Technology, the body, and science on the Anglo-American frontier, 1500–1676.* Cambridge, MA: Harvard University Press.

Coase, Ronald H. 1994. *Essays on economics and economists.* Chicago: University of Chicago Press.

Colquhoun, Patrick. 1796. *A Treatise on the police of the metropolis, explaining the various crimes and misdemeanors which at present are felt as a pressure upon the com-*

munity; and suggesting remedies for their prevention. By a magistrate. London: H. Fry, for C. Dilly.

———. 1800. *A treatise on the commerce and police of the River Thames: Containing an historical view of the trade of the Port of London and suggesting means for preventing the depredations thereon by a legislative system of river police: With an account of the functions of the various magistrates and corporations exercising jurisdiction on the river and a general view of the penal and remedial statutes connected with the subject.* London: J. Mawman.

———. 1806. *A treatise on indigence; exhibiting a general view of the national resources for productive labour; with propositions for ameliorating the condition of the poor, and improving the moral habits and increasing the comforts of the labouring people.* London: Printed for J. Hatchard.

———. 1814. *A treatise on the wealth, power, and resources of the British Empire, in every quarter of the world, including the East Indies; the rise and progress of the funding system explained.* London: J. Mawman.

Defoe, Daniel. 1724. *The great law of subordination consider'd; or, the insolence and unsufferable behaviour of servants in England duly enquir'd into.* London: S. Harding et al.

———. 1728. *A plan of the English commerce. Being a compleat prospect of the trade of this nation, as well the home trade as the foreign.* London: printed for Charles Rivington.

———. 1971. [1724–1726] *A tour through the whole island of Great Britain.* London: Penguin Books.

Deliso, Christopher. 2003. Globalization and the future of western intervention (July 17), http://antiwar.com/deliso/?articleid=677.

Derrida, Jacques. 1994. *Specters of Marx: The state of the debt, the work of mourning, and the new international,* trans. P. Kamuf. New York: Routledge.

———. 2002. Force of law: The mystical foundation of authority. In *Acts of religion/Jacques Derrida,* ed. G. Anidjar, 230–98. New York: Routledge.

Dezalay, Yves, and Bryant G. Garth. 2002. Legitimating the new legal orthodoxy. In *Global prescriptions: The production, exportation and importation of a new legal orthodoxy,* ed. Y. Dezalay and B. G. Garth, 306–34. Ann Arbor: University of Michigan Press.

Dubber, Markus Dirk. 2005. *The police power: Patriarchy and the foundations of American government.* New York: Columbia University Press.

Field, David Dudley. 1884. Magnitude and importance of legal science. In *Speeches, arguments, and miscellaneous papers of David Dudley Field.* Vol. 1, ed. A. P. Sprague, 517–33. New York: D. Appleton.

Fine, Bob, et al., eds. 1979. *Capitalism and the rule of law: From deviancy theory to Marxism.* London: Hutchinson, for the National Deviancy Conference.

Fiske, Nathan. 1776. *Remarkable providences to be gratefully recollected, religiously improved, and carefully transmitted to posterity. A sermon preached at Brookfield on the last day of the year 1775.* Boston, New-England: Printed by Thomas and John Fleet.

Foucault, Michel. 1979. *Discipline and punish: The birth of the prison.* New York: Vintage.

———. 1980. *Power/knowledge: Selected interviews and other writings, 1972–1977,* ed. C. Gordon. New York: Pantheon.

Freund, Ernst. 1904. *The Police power: Public policy and constitutional rights.* Chicago: Callaghan.

Gentili, Alberico. 1933. *De iure belli,* ed. C. Phillipson, trans. J. C. Rolfe. 2 vols. Oxford: Oxford University Press.

Glendon, Mary Ann. 1981. *The new family and the new property.* Toronto: Butterworths.

Grossberg, Michael. 1985. *Governing the hearth: Law and the family in nineteenth-century America.* Chapel Hill: University of North Carolina Press.

Grotius, Hugo. 1738. *The rights of war and peace, in three books.* London: Printed for W. Innys.

Hakluyt, Richard (the elder). 1578. Notes on colonization. In *The original writings and correspondence of the two Richard Hakluyts,* ed. E. G. R. Taylor (1935), 116–22. London: The Hakluyt Society.

———. 1585. Pamphlet for the Virginia enterprise. In *The original writings and correspondence of the two Richard Hakluyts,* ed. E. G. R. Taylor (1935), 327–38. London: The Hakluyt Society.

———. n.d. [1585?]. Pamphlet for the Virginia enterprise. In *The original writings and correspondence of the two Richard Hakluyts,* ed. E. G. R. Taylor (1935), 339–43. London: The Hakluyt Society.

Hakluyt, Richard (the younger). 1582. Preface to divers voyages. In *The original writings and correspondence of the two Richard Hakluyts,* ed. E. G. R. Taylor (1935), 175–81. London: The Hakluyt Society.

———. 1584. Discourse of western planting. In *The original writings and correspondence of the two Richard Hakluyts,* ed. E. G. R. Taylor (1935), 211–326. London: The Hakluyt Society.

Hardt, Michael, and Antonio Negri. 2000. *Empire.* Cambridge, MA: Harvard University Press.

Hays, Samuel P. 1959. *Conservation and the gospel of efficiency: The progressive conservation movement, 1890–1920.* Cambridge, MA: Harvard University Press.

Hindle, Steve. 2002. *The state and social change in early modern England, c. 1550–1640.* New York: Palgrave.

Honig, Bonnie. 1993. *Political theory and the displacement of politics.* Ithaca, NY: Cornell University Press.

———. 2001. *Democracy and the foreigner.* Princeton, NJ: Princeton University Press.

Hont, Istvan, and Michael Ignatieff, eds. 1983. *Wealth and virtue: The shaping of political economy in the Scottish enlightenment.* Cambridge, UK: Cambridge University Press.

Ignatieff, Michael. 2004. Peace, order and good government: A foreign policy agenda for Canada. *O. D. Skelton Memorial Lecture,* Ottawa, March 12, 2004. http://www.dfait-maeci.gc.ca/skelton/menu-en.asp.

———. 2005. Who are Americans to think that freedom is theirs to spread? *New York Times Magazine,* June 26.

Isin, Engin. 2002. *Being political: Genealogies of citizenship.* Minneapolis: University of Minnesota Press.

Kent, James (Chancellor). 1826–1830. *Commentaries on American law,* in 4 vols. New York: O. Halsted.

Klein, Bernhard. 2001. *Maps and the writing of space in early modern England and Ireland.* New York: Palgrave.

Knemeyer, Franz-Ludwig. 1980. Polizei, trans. K. Tribe. *Economy and Society* 9(2): 168–96.

Labatt, Charles Bagot. 1913. *Commentaries on the law of master and servant,* in 8 vols. Rochester, NY: Lawyers Cooperative.

Lachmann, Richard. 1987. *From manor to market: Structural change in England, 1536–1640.* Madison: University of Wisconsin Press.

Leeson, Robert A. 1979. *Travelling brothers: The six centuries' road from craft fellowship to trade unionism.* London: Allen & Unwin.

Lepore, Jill. 1998. *The Name of war: King Philip's war and the origins of American identity.* New York: Knopf.

Mackinder, Halford J. 1904. The geographical pivot of history. *The Geographical Journal* 23 (1904): 421–37.

McDonald, Terrence J., ed. 1996. *The historic turn in the human sciences.* Ann Arbor: University of Michigan Press.

McNulty, Paul J. 1980. *The origins and development of labor economics: A chapter in the history of social thought.* Cambridge, MA: MIT Press.

McSmith, Andy, and Jo Dillon. 2003. Blair seeks new powers to attack rogue states. *Independent,* July 13, 2003. http://www.globalpolicy.org/security/issues/iraq/justify/2003/0713humanitarian.htm.

Meek, R. L., D. D. Raphael, and P. G. Stein, eds. 1978. *Adam Smith: Lectures on jurisprudence.* Oxford: Clarendon Press.

Merrill, Michael, and Sean Wilentz, eds. 1993. *The key of liberty: The life and democratic writings of William Manning, "A laborer," 1747–1814.* Cambridge, MA: Harvard University Press.

Nedelsky, Jennifer. 1981. Judicial conservatism in an age of innovation: Comparative perspectives on Canadian nuisance law, 1880–1930. In *Essays in the history of Canadian law.* Vol. 1, ed. David Flaherty, 281–322. Toronto: University of Toronto Press, for the Osgoode Society.

Novak, William J. 1996. *The people's welfare: Law and regulation in nineteenth-century America*. Chapel Hill: University of North Carolina Press.

———. 2004. Law and the state control of American capitalism. [Unpublished paper in my files.]

Paine, Thomas. 1776. *Common sense*. Philadelphia: printed and sold by W. and T. Bradford. www.bartleby.com/133/.

Palmer, Robert C. 1987. Liberties as constitutional provisions, 1776–1791. In *Liberty and community: Constitution and rights in the early American republic*, by W. E. Nelson and R. C. Palmer, 55–148. New York: Oceana Publications.

———. 1993. *English law in the age of the black death, 1348–1381: A transformation of governance and law*. Chapel Hill: University of North Carolina Press.

Pasquino, Pasquale. 1978. Theatrum politicum: The genealogy of capital—police and the state of prosperity. *Ideology and Consciousness* 4:41–54.

Phillipson, Nicholas. 1983. Adam Smith as civic moralist. In *Wealth and virtue: The shaping of political economy in the Scottish enlightenment*, ed. I. Hont and M. Ignatieff, 179–202. Cambridge, UK: Cambridge University Press.

Raeff, Marc. 1983. *The well-ordered police state: Social and institutional change through law in the Germanies and Russia, 1600–1800*. New Haven: Yale University Press.

Reeve, Tapping. 1816. *The law of baron and femme, of parent and child, guardian and ward, master and servant*. New Haven, CT: Printed by Oliver Steele.

Rollison, David. 2003. The spectre of the commonalty: Class struggle and the common weal before 'The Atlantic world'. Paper presented at the conference *Class and Class Struggle in North America and the Atlantic World*, Big Sky, MT.

Rubinstein, Nicolai. 1987. The history of the word politicus in early-modern Europe. In *The languages of political theory in early-modern Europe*, ed. A. Pagden, 41–56. Cambridge, UK: Cambridge University Press.

Schmitt, Carl. 2003. [1950]. *The nomos of the earth in the international law of the jus publicum europæum*, trans. G. Ulmen. New York: Telos Press.

Schochet, Gordon J. 1975. *Patriarchalism in political thought: The authoritarian family and political speculation and attitudes especially in seventeenth-century England*. Oxford: Blackwell.

Schouler, James. 1870. *A Treatise on the law of the domestic relations; embracing husband and wife, parent and child, guardian and ward, infancy, and master and servant*. Boston: Little, Brown.

Shakespeare, William. 2000. *Titus Andronicus*, ed. R. McDonald. New York: Penguin Putnam.

Shammas, Carole. 2002. *A history of household government in America*. Charlottesville: University of Virginia Press.

Smith, Sir Thomas. 1906. *De republica anglorum: A discourse on the commonwealth of England* (1583), ed. L. Alston. Cambridge, UK: Cambridge University Press.

Stanley, Amy Dru. 1988. Conjugal bonds and wage labor: Rights of contract in the age of emancipation. *Journal of American History* 75(2): 471–500.

———. 1998. *From bondage to contract: Wage labor, marriage, and the market in the age of slave emancipation*. Cambridge, UK: Cambridge University Press.

Steinfeld, Robert J. 1991. *The invention of free labor: The employment relation in English and American law and culture, 1350–1870*. Chapel Hill: University of North Carolina Press.

———. 2001. *Coercion, contract, and free labor in the nineteenth century*. Cambridge, UK: Cambridge University Press.

Storch, Robert D. 1976. The policeman as domestic missionary: Urban discipline and popular culture in northern England, 1850–1880. *Journal of Social History* 9(4): 481–509.

Stourzh, Gerald. 1988. Constitution: Changing meanings of the term from the early seventeenth to the late eighteenth century. In *Conceptual change and the constitution*, ed. T. Ball and J. G. A. Pocock, 35–54. Lawrence: University Press of Kansas.

Taylor, Ian, Paul Walton, and Jock Young. 1973. *The new criminology: For a social theory of deviance*. London: Routledge & Kegan Paul.

Thacher, Peter Oxenbridge. 1805. *An address to the members of the Massachusetts charitable fire society, at their annual meeting, in Boston, May 31, 1805*. Boston.

Thorpe, Francis Newton. 1909. *The federal and state constitutions, colonial charters and other organic laws of the states, territories and colonies now or heretofore forming the United States of America, compiled and edited under the act of congress of June 30, 1906*. Washington: Government Printing Office.

Tomlins, Christopher L. 1993. *Law, labor and ideology in the early American republic*. Cambridge, UK: Cambridge University Press.

———. 1995. Subordination, authority, law: Subjects in labor history. *International Labor and Working-Class History* 47 (Spring 1995): 56–90.

———. 2001. The legal cartography of colonization, the legal polyphony of settlement: English intrusions on the American mainland in the seventeenth century. *Law and Social Inquiry* 26(2): 315–72.

———. 2004. Early British America, 1585–1830: Freedom bound. In *Masters, servants, and magistrates in Britain and the empire, 1562–1955*, ed. D. Hay and P. Craven, 117–52. Chapel Hill: University of North Carolina Press.

———. 2005a. Law's wilderness: The discourse of English colonizing, the violence of intrusion, and the failures of American history. In *New world orders*, ed. J. Smolenski and T. Humphrey, 21–46. Philadelphia: University of Pennsylvania Press.

———. 2005b. To improve the state and condition of man: The power to police and the history of American governance. *Buffalo Law Review* 53(4): 1215–71.

Tuck, Richard. 1999. *The rights of war and peace: Political thought and the international order from Grotius to Kant*. Oxford: Oxford University Press.

Underdown, David. 1985. The taming of the scold: The enforcement of patriarchal authority in early modern England. In *Order and disorder in early modern*

England, ed. A. Fletcher and J. Stevenson, 116–36. Cambridge, UK: Cambridge University Press.

Walker, Timothy. 1837. *Introduction to American law: Designed as a first book for students*. Philadelphia: P. H. Nicklin & T. Johnson.

Wall Street Journal. 2005. Watch on the Thames. *Wall Street Journal, Marketplace*, July 8, 2005.

Weir, Robert M. 1998. "Shaftesbury's Darling": British settlement in the Carolinas at the close of the seventeenth century. In *The origins of Empire: British overseas enterprise to the close of the seventeenth century*, ed. N. Canny, 375–97. Oxford: Oxford University Press.

Westlake, Donald E. 1972. *Under an English heaven*. New York: Simon & Schuster.

Willrich, Michael. 2003. *City of courts: Socializing justice in progressive era Chicago*. Cambridge, UK: Cambridge University Press.

Winthrop, John. 1630. A modell of Christian charity. http://history.hanover.edu/texts/winthmod.html.

Wolfe, Tom. 2005. The doctrine that never died. *New York Times*, January 30, 2005. http://www.globalpolicy.org/empire/intervention/2005 /0130 doctrine .htm.

Wrightson, Keith. 1980. Two concepts of order: Justices, constables and jurymen in seventeenth century England. In *An ungovernable people: The English and their law in the seventeenth and eighteenth centuries*, ed. J. Brewer and J. Styles, 21–46. New Brunswick, NJ: Rutgers University Press.

Index

aboriginal people, 6; in Canada, 10, 74, 82, 87, 89, 95–96, 98, 104*n*12

absolutism, 60–61, 66*n*7, 267

Abu Ghraib, 187, 202

Actor Network Theory, 102*n*1

actus reus, 132–34, 136

Afghanistan, 195, 199

Agamben, Giorgio, 3, 13, 251, 252; on camps, 3, 116, 187, 252; on military, 185–87, 193, 199, 201, 204*n*3; on sovereignty, 259

Albright, Madeleine, 192, 196

Alger, Commonwealth v., 27, 264, 278

American Institute of International Law, 222, 239*n*8

American Revolution, 119–21, 125, 262

American Service Members' Protection Act (U.S.), 236, 237

ancient entitlements, 32

Anti-Social Behaviour Order (ASBO) (U.K.), 15, 136, 148, 156–60, 164*n*12, 287*n*43

Anti-Terrorism, Crime and Security Act (U.K.), 38

Arbella, John Winthrop, 272

Arbour, Louise, 235

Arditi, Jorge, 173

Aristo-democratic Monarchy (Turquet), 186–87

Aristotle, 5, 53, 64, 260–62, 269

Arnisaeus, Henning, 53

ASBO. *See* Anti-Social Behaviour Order

Ashworth, Andrew, 158

Australia, 79, 88, 89, 90–91, 96, 191, 278

autonomy: in Canada, 75, 89–96, 100, 104*n*10; legitimacy and, 11, 138; police power model of criminal process vs., 11, 138–39; self and, 37, 268

Balkans, 13, 192, 229

Bancoult decision (*The Queen [Bancoult] v. Foreign and Commonwealth Office*), 82–86, 103*n*4

Banton, Michael, 180

Barker, Francis, 249

Bassiouni, M. Cherif, 233

Benjamin, Walter, 176, 250, 279

Bentham, Jeremy, 90, 169, 208

Biblische Policey (Biblical Police) (Reinkingk), 8–9, 52–56, 64–68; axioms and *exempla* in, 54–56; cameralism and, 55; Moses and Aaron in, 46–48, 55; order in, 53–56, political iconography in, 44–48; three estates in, 53–55, 57

Big Stick policy, regarding Panama, 215

biopolitical power, 80, 187

BIOT. *See* British Indian Ocean Territory

Blackstone, William, 253; on common law, 264; on game laws, 113; on paternalism, 79, 100; on police, 5, 7, 11, 12, 169, 188, 282*n*7; on vagrancy, 24, 268

Blair, Tony, 189, 200

Bluntschli, Johann, Kaspar, 61

BNA Act. *See* British North America Act

Bornitz, Jakob, 52

Bottmässigkeit, 63

Bourdieu, Pierre, 253

295